GLOBAL TRADE IN SERVICES

Fear, Facts, and Offshoring

MIX
From responsible sources
FSC® C010236
FSC
www.fsc.org

GLOBAL TRADE IN SERVICES

Fear, Facts, and Offshoring

J. Bradford Jensen

PETERSON INSTITUTE FOR INTERNATIONAL ECONOMICS
WASHINGTON, DC

AUGUST 2011

J. Bradford Jensen, senior fellow, is professor of economics and international business at the McDonough School of Business at Georgetown University. He is also a senior policy scholar at the Georgetown Center for Business and Public Policy and a research associate of the National Bureau of Economic Research. He has been affiliated with the Peterson Institute for International Economics since 2003, serving as deputy director from 2003 to August 2007. Before joining the Institute, he served as director of the Center for Economic Studies at the US Census Bureau and on the faculty of the Heinz School of Public Policy and Management at Carnegie Mellon University.

**PETER G. PETERSON INSTITUTE
FOR INTERNATIONAL ECONOMICS**
1750 Massachusetts Avenue, NW
Washington, DC 20036-1903
(202) 328-9000 FAX: (202) 659-3225
www.piie.com

C. Fred Bergsten, *Director*
Edward A. Tureen, *Director of Publications,
Marketing, and Web Development*

Typesetting by Susann Luetjen
Printing by United Book Press, Inc.
Cover design by Peggy Archambault
Cover photo: © Andrey Prokhorov—iStockphoto

Printed in the United States of America
13 12 11   5 4 3 2 1

**Library of Congress Cataloging-in-
Publication Data**
Jensen, J. Bradford.
 Global trade in services : fear, facts, and offshoring / J. Bradford Jensen.
   p. cm.
 Includes bibliographical references and index.
 ISBN 978-0-88132-601-7
 1. Service industries. 2. Service industries—United States. 3. International trade. I. Title.
 HD9980.5.J46 2011
 382.'45000973—dc23

                               2011027280

Contents

9 Conclusions and Policy Implications 181

Appendices

References 233

Index 237

Tables

Figures

Maps

Preface

The service sector is large and growing. International trade in services is also growing rapidly. Yet there is a dearth of empirical research on the size, scope and potential impact of services trade. The underlying source of this gap is well-known—official statistics on the service sector in general, and trade in services in particular, lack the level of detail available for the manufacturing sector in many dimensions. There is limited industry and product detail; there is limited geographical detail. The time series available are also limited.

Because services are such a large and important component of the US economy, understanding the implications of increased trade in services is crucial to the trade liberalization agenda going forward. We at the Peterson Institute for International Economics have long been frustrated by the lack of existing research on trade in services to draw upon. The purpose of this book is to start to fill that gap.

This study represents basic research and, as such, is somewhat of an unusual undertaking for the Peterson Institute. The Institute typically conducts studies that draw upon existing research, refining and tailoring it to specific policy questions and specific contexts. Yet, because of the importance of understanding the service sector combined with the absence of existing research, the Institute initiated this unusual project.

This is thus a path-breaking study, in which J. Bradford Jensen conducts primary research using a range of data sources to produce the most detailed and robust portrait available on the size, scope, and potential impact of trade in services on the US economy. Jensen opens the book by characterizing the importance of the service sector. He notes that business services, a sector containing software, financial services, engineering and architectural services and a primary focus of the book, is *twice* the size of the manufacturing sector and accounts for 25 percent of total US employment. In addition to being more numerous than manufacturing jobs, business service jobs pay better. Workers in business services have significantly higher earnings than manufacturing workers.

Jensen then presents the fundamental contribution of the project: a new methodology to identify, at a very detailed level, which service activities—both service industries and service occupations—are tradable. Jensen's methodology is intuitively appealing. He uses the mismatch in the geographic location of production and consumption of services within the United States to identify which service activities are provided at a distance. He persuasively argues that if it is technologically possible to deliver the service at a distance within the United States, it is also possible, at least in principle, to trade these service activities internationally. Using the detailed identification the methodology delivers, Jensen estimates that a significant share of employment in the United States is employed in tradable service industries—more, in fact, than in the entire manufacturing sector.

In the third chapter, Jensen uses the detailed identification of tradable service industries and occupations to present a comprehensive picture of the characteristics of workers employed in tradable services. The results are striking. Workers in tradable services are qualitatively different from workers in nontradable services and the manufacturing sector. Workers in tradable services have considerably higher levels of educational attainment and significantly higher earnings. Even controlling for educational attainment and other individual characteristics associated with higher wages, workers in tradable business services have almost 20 percent higher earnings than similar workers in nontradable business services (and recall that business services pay significantly higher wages than the manufacturing sector).

Other economists and commentators have observed that high-skill, high-wage service activities are tradable and argued that the United States is at risk of losing a significant share of these jobs to low-wage, labor-abundant countries like India. In the fourth and fifth chapters of the book, Jensen addresses these concerns. He presents evidence from a range of sources—including pioneering work he has done on the impact of trade on the manufacturing sector using microdata—to show that comparative advantage is a useful guide to understanding how increased trade in services is likely to play out. He notes that, tradable services are indeed high-skill, high-wage. Yet, it is precisely because tradable services are high-wage and high-skill that the United States is likely to retain and even expand these tradable service activities. The United States is thus poised to benefit from increased trade in services.

Jensen presents new evidence on the prevalence of service firm participation in international trade. He finds that, in spite of US comparative advantage in service activities, service firms' export participation lags manufacturing firms. Jensen evaluates the impediments to services trade and finds evidence that there is considerable room for liberalization—especially among the large, fast-growing developing economies.

The policy recommendations coming out of this path-breaking study are quite clear. The United States should not fear trade in services. It should be pushing aggressively for services trade liberalization. Because other advanced economies have similar comparative advantage in service, the United States should make common cause with the European Union and other advanced economies to encourage the large, fast-growing developing economies to liberalize their service sectors through multilateral negotiations in the General Agreement on Trade in Services and the Government Procurement Agreement. Jensen notes that the coming global infrastructure building boom is of historic proportions and provides an enormous opportunity for US service firms if the proper policies are in place. Increased trade in services might help rebalance the global economy, and both developed and developing economies would benefit from the productivity-enhancing reallocation increased trade in services would bring.

The Peter G. Peterson Institute for International Economics is a private, nonprofit institution for the study and discussion of international economic policy. Its purpose is to analyze important issues in that area and to develop and communicate practical new approaches for dealing with them. The Institute is completely nonpartisan.

The Institute is funded by a highly diversified group of philanthropic foundations, private corporations, and interested individuals. About 35 percent of the Institute's resources in our latest fiscal year was provided by contributors outside the United States. Generous support for this study was provided by the Alfred P. Sloan Foundation, the John D. and Catherine T. MacArthur Foundation, and the National Science Foundation.

The Institute's Board of Directors bears overall responsibilities for the Institute and gives general guidance and approval to its research program, including the identification of topics that are likely to become important over the medium run (one to three years) and that should be addressed by the Institute. The director, working closely with the staff and outside Advisory Committee, is responsible for the development of particular projects and makes the final decision to publish an individual study.

The Institute hopes that its studies and other activities will contribute to building a stronger foundation for international economic policy around the world. We invite readers of these publications to let us know how they think we can best accomplish this objective.

C. Fred Bergsten
Director
August 2011

Author's Note

Some of the research presented in chapter 5 was conducted at the International Investment Division, US Bureau of Economic Analysis, under arrangements that maintain legal confidentiality requirements. Views expressed are mine and do not necessarily reflect those of the Bureau of Economic Analysis.

Some of the research presented in chapters 2, 4, 5, and 6 was conducted while I was a Special Sworn Status researcher at the Center for Economic Studies at the US Census Bureau. Any opinions and conclusions expressed herein are mine and do not necessarily represent the views of the US Census Bureau. All results have been reviewed to ensure that no confidential information is disclosed.

J. BRADFORD JENSEN
July 2011

Acknowledgments

This project benefited from the comments, suggestions, encouragement, and support of many people. I thank my colleagues at the Peterson Institute for their support of this effort, particularly Lori Kletzer and Catherine Mann. I owe a special debt of gratitude to J. David Richardson for encouraging me to pursue this study and for serving as an invaluable resource throughout the process. I appreciate the comments, suggestions, and encouragement Andrew Bernard, Antoine Gervais, Stephen Redding, and Peter Schott provided at various points throughout the study.

I thank Pietra Rivoli for comments on an earlier draft, Evan Gill for research assistance, Jennifer Nurmi for initial editorial assistance, and Carole Sargent and the writers' workshop at Georgetown University for support. I acknowledge and appreciate Frank Levy, Sean Randolph, Tim Sturgeon, Aaditya Mattoo, and Ingo Borchert for allowing me to use material from their studies.

I am grateful to C. Fred Bergsten for letting me begin this project while I served as his deputy director. I also thank the Sloan Foundation, the MacArthur Foundation, and the National Science Foundation (SES-0552029) for generous financial support. Ed Tureen, Madona Devasahayam, Michael Treadway, and Susann Luetjen of the publications team at the Institute provided editorial assistance and guidance throughout the publication process.

Overview

Should the United States fear increased trade in services?

Several years ago the answer to this question might have entailed a simple "No, services are nontradable" or a dismissive "Why worry about trade in services? The service sector isn't that important—manufacturing is what matters." More recently, however, one is more likely to hear, "Yes, of course, the United States will lose millions of service jobs to India, just like it lost millions of manufacturing jobs to China."[1]

Much of this concern is driven by the unknown. Which services are tradable? Which services will become tradable tomorrow? How many jobs are in tradable services? Which service jobs are likely to face competition from low-wage, labor-abundant countries such as India? Answers to these and other questions about services are hard to come by. One reason is the lack of detailed official statistical data on services in general and trade in services in particular.

This book tries to draw a more detailed picture of US services in the national and global economies. It attempts to provide the most comprehensive fact base on services to date, a framework for interpreting the facts, and a set of factual answers to the many questions that trade in the service sector raises. This task is well worth undertaking, because services are a large and vital part of the US economy and because trade in services is growing rapidly, potentially affecting millions of US workers. Understanding the impact of international trade as a whole on the US economy and the US labor market thus requires a better understanding of service trade.

It is also an ambitious task, and I must acknowledge at the outset that it is not completely fulfilled. The book does not establish once and for all every

---

1. This concern is perhaps best exemplified by the *Foreign Affairs* article "Offshoring: The Next Industrial Revolution?" by Alan Blinder (2006), discussed in chapter 4.

relevant fact that one would like to know about service trade, nor are all the facts that it does establish integrated into a seamless explanation. Available data simply do not support this more satisfying type of analysis.

Instead, the book presents a mosaic of results from a variety of data sources and perspectives, taking what it can from what each has to offer. This mosaic also draws on a large and growing literature examining the impact of trade on the US manufacturing sector, using the very detailed, plant-level data that do exist for that sector. The hope is that the framework presented here, developed from theory and research on the manufacturing sector, combined with the most detailed picture of the service sector possible, will produce a set of analytical results that prove helpful in informing the public debate on services and service trade. As a natural by-product, I hope that this book will dispel some common misconceptions about the service sector, trade in services, and the risk of losing high-skill service jobs to low-wage countries.

The book provides detailed "how and why" answers to several key questions, both about the service sector itself and about how it compares with the manufacturing sector:

- Is the service sector important?
- Is trade in services important today? Is it potentially important in the future? Which services are "tradable"?
- What is likely to happen as global trade in services increases?
- In particular, is the United States likely to lose service jobs to lower-wage countries?
- Is there evidence of these predicted trends?
- What should the United States do to maximize the opportunities from the service sector?

To anticipate the main results, the mosaic reveals the following broad picture regarding trade in services:

- The service sector is a large and growing contributor to the US economy, employing a majority of American workers. Some important subsectors within services pay high wages, in some cases higher than the average manufacturing wage.
- Trade in services, both imports and exports, is growing and the share of employment in tradable services activities is large, potentially exposing a large share of the US workforce to foreign competition. In that large share of tradable service jobs are many high-skill, high-wage jobs.
- Even though these jobs pay high wages, they are not likely to be lost to low-wage countries. Indeed, precisely because they are high-skill, high-wage jobs, they are jobs that the United States is likely to retain and that can support exports. The United States has comparative advantage in high-skill, high-wage activities.

- Despite rising total imports and a widening trade gap over the past few decades, the United States still imports little high-wage, high-productivity manufacturing output from low-wage countries and continues to export high-wage, high-skill products. There is every reason to think that US service trade will play out similarly, with trade in services that provide high-wage job opportunities growing at the expense of services that pay lower wages.

- The United States has comparative advantage in services and has been successful in exporting services. Indeed, the nation consistently runs a trade *surplus* in services. But US service firms' participation in the international economy lags that of US manufacturing firms: A far smaller share of service output than of manufacturing output is traded. Thus, there seems to be considerable opportunity for US firms and workers from increased service trade.

- But increased service trade does pose some risks. It will undoubtedly cause some dislocation of production and jobs, just as happened in manufacturing. Yet a relatively small share of US employment in tradable services is in the low-wage, low-skill activities likely to face competition from low-wage, labor-abundant countries. The majority of employment in tradable services is in activities where the United States is likely to export *more*. Recent trends offer little evidence of greater job loss in tradable services than in nontradable services.

The analysis yields the following conclusion: The United States should *not* fear increased trade in services. To the contrary, the United States should be aggressively seeking to liberalize the policy impediments to service trade, to take advantage of the many opportunities that expanded service trade offers.

One outstanding opportunity is presented by the enormous infrastructure boom that the developing world will undergo over the next 20 years. Building that infrastructure will require inputs from a wide array of engineering, technical, and other business services in which US firms are highly competitive. Therefore, as an organizing principle and motivating focus for service trade liberalization, the United States should set a goal of ensuring the ability of US service firms and workers to compete fairly for participation in this historic undertaking.

The following more specific findings buttress the above conclusions:

- The business service sector (which includes, among many others, information, financial, scientific, and managerial services) alone accounts for 25 percent of employment in the United States—more than *twice* as many jobs as the manufacturing sector (figure O.1). (It employed only half as many as manufacturing 50 years ago.) Employment in the business service sector *increased* almost 30 percent over the decade 1997–2007, while manufacturing employment *decreased* by over 20 percent.

Figure O.1   Sectoral composition of US employment, 2007

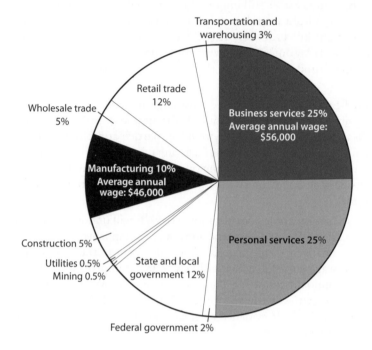

Sources: 2007 Economic Census; 2007 Census of Governments.

- The popular perception that most service jobs are "bad jobs with low wages" is wrong. In fact, the business service sector pays significantly higher wages and salaries on average than the manufacturing sector. Average annual wages in the manufacturing sector in 2007 were about $46,000. The figure for business services that year was about $56,000—more than 22 percent higher (figure O.1).

- Service exports, as measured in official data, have expanded dramatically over the past decade, doubling between 1997 and 2007 (see figure 1.9 in chapter 1). And although service imports have also increased significantly over the same period, the United States consistently runs a trade surplus in services—in contrast to its sizable trade deficit in goods (figure 5.1 in chapter 5).

- Many service activities—movie and music recording production, software production, research and development services, and engineering services, to cite a few examples—appear to be "traded" (that is, transacted across distances) within the United States and thus are at least potentially tradable internationally. Approximately 14 percent of the US workforce is in business service industries that this book classifies as tradable. By comparison, about 10 percent of the workforce is in the entire manufacturing

Figure O.2 Average differences in earnings between US workers in tradable and nontradable industries and occupations

percent

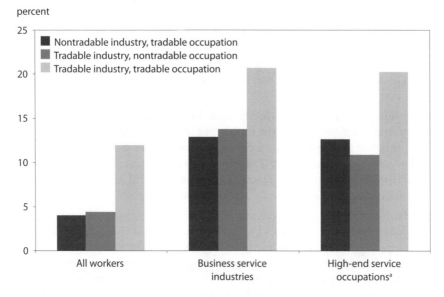

- Nontradable industry, tradable occupation
- Tradable industry, nontradable occupation
- Tradable industry, tradable occupation

a. Occupations in the following Standard Occupational Classification (SOC) groups: management (SOC 11), business and financial operations (SOC 13), computer and mathematical (SOC 15), architecture and engineering (SOC 17), life, physical, and social sciences (SOC 19), legal (SOC 23), health care practitioner and technical (SOC 29), and health care support (SOC 31).

Note: The figure shows the percentage by which the wages of the average worker employed in either a tradable industry or a tradable occupation, or both, exceed the wages of the average worker in a nontradable occupation within a nontradable industry, as estimated in a regression that controls for workers' demographic characteristics.

Source: Author's calculations using the 2007 American Community Survey.

sector. When workers in tradable occupations (such as computer programmers in the banking industry, or medical transcriptionists in the health care industry) within nontradable industries are included, the share of the workforce in tradable service activities is even higher.

- Tradable service jobs, such as those at engineering or research and development firms, are good jobs, paying higher than average earnings. Part of this premium is due to workers in these activities having higher educational attainment on average than other workers, but even when one controls for educational and other personal differences, workers in tradable service activities have 10 percent higher earnings. Within business service industries, a worker in a tradable industry and a tradable occupation has almost 20 percent higher earnings than a similar business service worker in a nontradable industry and occupation (figure O.2).

- The fact that earnings in tradable service activities are high does not mean that these jobs will be lost to low-wage countries. High-wage, high-skill activities are consistent with US comparative advantage. In the manufacturing sector, it is low-wage, labor-intensive industries like apparel that have been most vulnerable to low-wage import competition. Just as the United States continues to have strong export performance in high-wage, skill-intensive manufacturing industries, so it should continue to perform well—and retain and even create jobs—in high-wage, skill-intensive service industries.

- Although it is common to discuss jobs "lost" and jobs "created," in the long run trade does not affect the number of jobs in the economy. As evidence of this, large trade deficits are typically associated with periods of relatively low unemployment. What trade does affect is the *composition* of activities in the economy: Jobs are created in some sectors and lost in other sectors, reallocating economic activity across industries.

- Many commentators on service trade focus on the US jobs that are threatened by foreign competitors but neglect the fact that the United States has comparative advantage in many service activities. For example, the United States is currently a net exporter of high-wage, high-skill services like computer software and satellite telecommunications services. Increased trade in services is likely to lead to increased US exports of services (and to more "inshoring" than "offshoring"), to the benefit of many US firms and workers.

- In contrast to the general impression that the United States imports services primarily from low-wage, labor-abundant countries like India, most US service imports come from other high-wage, high-skill countries. This supports the notion that it is skill-abundant (and high-wage) countries that have comparative advantage in high-wage, high-skill services.

- As many as two-thirds of jobs in tradable business service industries require a high enough level of skill to be consistent with US comparative advantage. US workers and firms in these industries are likely to be beneficiaries of increased trade in services through increased export opportunities. Only about one-third of jobs in tradable service activities will face meaningful competition from low-wage countries (or risk being offshored) in the medium term.

- To date, there is little evidence of trade in services influencing US labor market outcomes. Net employment growth in the average tradable service activity is roughly the same as net employment growth in nontradable service activities. Median wage growth in tradable service occupations is nearly equal to wage growth in the average nontradable occupation. Rates of job displacement in tradable service activities are no greater than in nontradable service activities—and much lower than displacement rates in the manufacturing sector.

- Although traditional trade barriers such as tariffs and quotas seldom apply to services, many other impediments to trade in services do exist, ranging from language and cultural differences to regulation and technological barriers. These impediments are likely to provide some protection for some US service firms and workers from import competition but also likely to restrain exporting by these firms and workers and others. These impediments reduce the gains to the United States (and the rest of the world) from trade in services, thus slowing the rise in living standards that such trade promotes.

- Despite US comparative advantage in the high-skill, high-wage business services that are tradable, the sector still lags behind manufacturing in terms of participation in exporting. In the manufacturing sector, about 25 percent of plants export; in business services, only about 5 percent do. Exports-to-sales ratios for service exporters are slightly lower than those in manufacturing. These statistics suggest that the impediments to trade in services, whether they are culture and language differences, technological barriers, or policy impediments, remain significant.

- Exporters within the business service sector show the same desirable characteristics as exporters in manufacturing: They tend to be larger and more productive and pay higher wages than nonexporting business service firms. In fact, exporter wage premiums in business services are double what they are in manufacturing. When one compares exporters and nonexporters within services without taking into account which specific industry they are in, one finds that exporters pay 40 percent higher wages. When exporters and nonexporters within an industry are compared, exporters pay 20 percent higher wages.

What do these findings imply for US trade policy? Although the United States has comparative advantage in services, turning that advantage into real economic benefits for US firms and workers is not automatic. A number of large and fast-growing economies around the world are less open to service trade than the United States. Liberalizing service trade with these countries is sure to be difficult, because it means not just reducing tariffs and other border controls as was the case with trade in manufactures, but also fighting through a tangle of regulations, licensing requirements, and other barriers well within countries' borders. But the historic opportunity that increased service trade represents, in particular because of the coming infrastructure boom—over $20 trillion by some estimates—in the developing world, well justifies the effort required. Other developed economies also have comparative advantage in services and would be natural partners with the United States in persuading the large, fast-growing countries with high service barriers to liberalize. This leads to the first key policy implication:

The United States, working through the General Agreement on Trade in Services (GATS), should join with other developed countries in pushing for further liberalization of business services, to ensure that US service firms and workers have the opportunity to compete in the coming infrastructure boom.

Much of the spending for infrastructure in the coming boom is likely to be controlled or financed, at least in part, by governments—national, regional, and local. Those governments are sure to be subject to domestic political pressure to favor domestic producers in granting contracts for this work. This makes guaranteeing equal treatment in government procurement a crucial issue for foreign service providers.

The World Trade Organization's (WTO) Agreement on Government Procurement was negotiated during the Tokyo Round of the General Agreement on Tariffs and Trade (GATT) negotiations in the early 1980s with the intention of reducing preferences to domestic firms in public procurement and opening public works spending to international trade. Its coverage was extended tenfold in the subsequent Uruguay Round and now extends to government purchases totaling several hundred billion dollars annually. However, this large sum obscures the fact that to date only a relative handful of countries have signed the agreement, virtually all of them in the developed world. In particular, none of the large developing countries expected to account for the bulk of infrastructure spending in coming decades—Brazil, China, India, and Russia—are participants in the agreement. From this stems a second key policy implication:

The United States, again in cooperation with other developed countries, should strongly encourage large and fast-growing countries to sign on to the WTO government procurement agreement.

Although liberalizing policy toward services abroad will benefit the United States and the rest of the world, there is also work to be done within the United States to strengthen and maintain the nation's comparative advantage in high-skill, high-wage services. Here the most important task involves education.

Some observers contend that service offshoring negates the benefits of education, claiming that having an education does not prevent one's job from being outsourced. But this is far from true. What *is* true is that having an education does not prevent one's job from being *tradable*. Indeed, tradability and education are positively correlated: workers in tradable jobs, in both manufacturing and services, tend to have more skills and more education than workers in nontradable jobs. But to argue that because a job is tradable it will therefore be traded away, and that therefore education confers no protection, is a counsel of despair—and unwarranted. In fact, high-skill, high-wage service jobs are precisely the types of jobs that are likely to stay in the United States. That is the lesson of comparative advantage—and of the US experience in manufacturing. Also, better-educated workers have lower displacement rates and higher reemployment rates.

Education remains a good investment for individual workers. The United States has historically been well out in front of the rest of the world in the share of its workforce that is college educated. However, this is less true today than it has been in the past, and from that unfortunate fact flows the third policy implication:

The United States should make access to a good primary, secondary, and postsecondary education a high national priority.

So, should the United States fear increased trade in services? No. Indeed, quite the contrary: The United States should embrace trade in services and pursue liberalization in the service sector aggressively. Both the United States and the world have much to gain and little to lose.

1

Some Basic Facts about the Service Sector and Service Trade

Services are widely recognized as making up the majority of the US economy and indeed of the economies of most developed countries. There is also widespread recognition that services' share of the nation's output and employment is growing. Yet there seems to be little understanding of the service sector beyond the fact that it is large and growing—and little appreciation for the sector's role in the economy.

One reason that impressions of the service sector are fuzzy is that the sector is as diverse as it is large. Indeed, its diversity makes even defining the service sector a challenge. Some people consider everything outside of goods production—agriculture, mining, and manufacturing—to be "services." In this expansive view, the service sector would include construction, utilities, retail and wholesale trade, finance and insurance, real estate, business services, personal services, accommodations and restaurants, and public administration. A more standard, somewhat narrower classification is presented below and is used in most of this book.

Another reason for the service sector's relative obscurity is that for decades manufacturing has been regarded by many as the most important sector. Recall that it was the president of General Motors, not of General Services, who in the 1950s famously identified the good of his company with the good of the nation.[1] Why this preoccupation with manufacturing? There seem to be several possible reasons.

First, when economists in the early 20th century began studying the relationship between economic structure and economic growth, the share of employment in manufacturing was observed to be positively correlated with

---

1. For a more recent example see Cohen and Zysman (1987).

income per capita across countries. The notion of a close relationship between manufacturing and development became ingrained, to the point where policymakers and official statisticians routinely used the terms "industrialized countries" and "developed economies" interchangeably.[2] Manufacturing, in this view, was "good," that is, associated with higher living standards. A related notion is that manufacturing jobs are "good jobs" whereas service jobs are low-skill, low-paying, "burger-flipper" jobs. Because service jobs are widely considered not to be good jobs, some policymakers and some in the media have tended to emphasize growth in manufacturing jobs at the expense of growth in good jobs in the service sector. A key focus of this book is to challenge these long-held views and shed some light on the true nature of service employment.

Another reason for the lack of attention to the service sector is that service firms (and establishments) have long been thought of as small relative to manufacturing firms (and plants). Somewhere along the way, the size of a firm or establishment came to be regarded as a measure of the importance of the sector to which it belongs. Not only is this the wrong measure of importance, but the notion that the overwhelming majority of service firms are small is also wrong, or at least misleading. This chapter presents detailed information on the size of service establishments to show that the averages hide the real picture.

Yet another reason, and perhaps the most important of all, why services get so little respect is the lack of data on the service sector. Although the official statistics on services are improving, the level of detail and the richness of the data collected for the service sector still lag far behind what is available for agriculture and manufacturing. (Of course, the data inadequacies could be both cause and effect of the relative disregard of services—perhaps fewer service data were collected *because* services were deemed unimportant.) The problem is particularly acute for information on trade in services (see box 1.1).

This chapter presents some basic facts about the service sector using official statistics; the next few chapters develop new ways of classifying the data aimed at improving one's ability to analyze the impact of trade in services. A key feature of this analysis is that it makes use of a variety of data sources, trying to capitalize on the strengths of each and using the data in a way that minimizes potential weaknesses. At times this creates dissonance, as the numbers are not exactly the same. This is due to a variety of data issues: sampling and scope differences, minor differences in classification, differences in measurement concepts, sampling error, classification error, response and reporting errors, and so forth. The same story, however, emerges from the various datasets.

The rest of this chapter provides an overview of the role of services in the US economy. The objective is to provide a more complete and updated picture of the economic importance of the service sector and to dispel some of the misconceptions regarding the role of services.

---

2. Recently, however, the International Monetary Fund, in its Global Data Source data series, renamed the "industrial countries" group the "advanced economies" group.

Box 1.1 Official sources of data on trade in services

The Bureau of Economic Analysis (BEA) collects information on trade in services and presents aggregate data on international service transactions through three publication programs: cross-border trade in services data in the international transactions accounts; sales of services through affiliates of multinationals, some portion of which represent cross-border trade; and benchmark input-output tables.

The program on cross-border trade in services provides the basis for all of BEA's service trade data. As a result, this publication program provides the best sense of what trade data BEA collects:

> The estimates of cross-border transactions cover both affiliated and unaffiliated transactions between U.S. residents and foreign residents. Affiliated transactions consist of intra-firm trade within multinational companies—specifically, the trade between U.S. parent companies and their foreign affiliates and between U.S. affiliates and their foreign parent groups. Unaffiliated transactions are with foreigners that neither own, nor are owned by, the U.S. party to the transaction.
>
> Cross-border trade in private services is classified into the same five, broad categories that are used in the U.S. international transactions accounts—travel, passenger fares, "other transportation," royalties and license fees, and "other private services." (*Survey of Current Business,* November 2001)

Data on affiliated transactions are collected through BEA's US Direct Investment Abroad and Foreign Direct Investment in the US programs. Comprehensive benchmark surveys are collected every 5 years, and less comprehensive collections are conducted annually.

BEA collects data on US international transactions in private services with unaffiliated foreigners through 11 surveys. These surveys fall into three broad categories: surveys of "selected" services, which cover mainly business, professional, and technical services; specialized surveys of services, which cover construction, engineering, architectural, and mining services as well as insurance services, financial services, and royalties and license fees; and surveys of transportation services. These collection programs are the principal source of BEA's estimates of trade in services, but the estimates for some services are based on data from a variety of other sources, including US Customs and Border Protection and surveys conducted by other federal government agencies, private sources, and partner countries. Detailed data on international services transactions are currently available from 1986 through 2006, for cross-border trade. Service imports and exports are reported for approximately 30 (1986–91) to 35 (1992–2006) service types; for some categories additional detail is available on whether the transactions are between affiliated or unaffiliated parties. These data are available by country for approximately 35 countries and country groupings for 1986–2006.

(continued on next page)

Size and Growth of the Service Sector

The growing importance of the service sector is by no means a recent phenomenon. The principal facts—that services account for a majority of US economic
activity and that their share of employment is growing—have been recognized,
if not widely known, for decades. Allan Fisher (1935), Colin Clark (1940), and
Victor Fuchs (1965) all identified the long-run trends early on.

These trends continue today. Figure 1.1 shows the shares of private
employment in goods (excluding agriculture but including construction) and
services in the United States for the period from 1960 to 2007.[3] It shows that
services, broadly defined, now account for the vast majority—about 85 percent—
of nonagricultural employment in the United States, having risen from about
65 percent (already a substantial majority) 50 years ago. Meanwhile the share
of nonagricultural employment in the goods-producing sector has exhibited a
steady decline.

The definition of the service sector used in figure 1.1 is so broad, however,
as to be of little analytical value. It also obscures some important trends within
the sector. For example, business services (that is, services typically provided
by one business to another—see the next section) increased from 15 percent of
total nonagricultural employment in 1960 to 21 percent in 2007 (figure 1.2).
Thus, whereas in 1960 the business service sector employed only half as many
workers as the manufacturing sector, by 2007 business services employed just
over twice as many.

"Other services" (a category made up mainly of personal services, that is,
services typically provided to individual consumers) also saw its share of total

---

3. These data are from the *Economic Report of the President* (ERP) and use a slightly different set of
categories from that used later in this chapter. In the ERP the utilities sector is included in services,
as part of the trade, transportation, and utilities category, whereas below it is included in the
goods production category.

Figure 1.1 Shares of nonagricultural employment in the United States, by major sector, 1960–2007

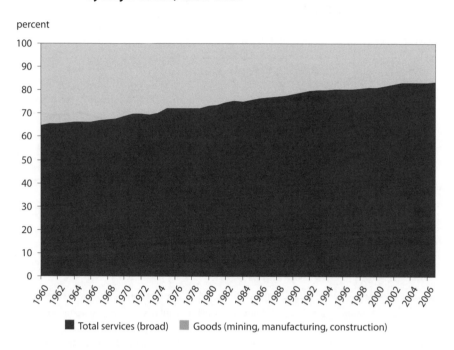

percent

Legend: ■ Total services (broad) ■ Goods (mining, manufacturing, construction)

Source: Economic Report of the President, 2009.

nonagricultural employment increase, from 14 percent in 1960 to 27 percent in 2007 (figure 1.2). Like business services, this sector started the period with employment about half that in the manufacturing sector, but its employment grew to more than two-and-a-half times manufacturing employment. Thus, taken together, professional services and "other services" went from having about the same number of workers as the manufacturing sector in 1960 to having about five times as many in 2007. Employment in the other categories— natural resources and construction; trade, transportation, and utilities; and government—remained roughly constant over the period.

Services in More Detail

The set of activities included in services in figure 1.1 is too diverse to meaning-fully analyze in the aggregate. Any statement one could make along almost any dimension of such a broad range of economic activity would be subject to so many exceptions and would obscure so much important detail as to be misleading. Therefore, to make the analysis more tractable, this chapter focuses on two important subcategories, business services and personal services (thus omitting government services and trade, transportation, and utilities).

Figure 1.2   Shares of nonagricultural employment in principal service subsectors and manufacturing in the United States, 1960–2007

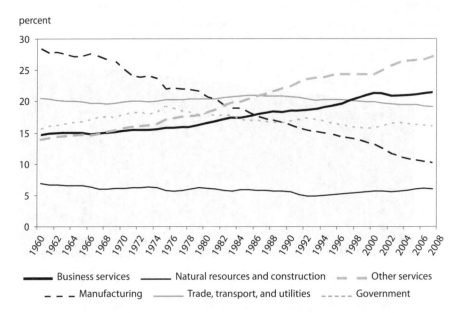

Note: The definition of "business services" used here may differ slightly from that used elsewhere in the book.
Source: Economic Report of the President, 2009.

Table 1.1 lists the major sectors of the economy using the North American Industry Classification System's (NAICS) categories and two-digit codes. (See appendix C for a brief description of each sector.) Using this standard classification, all economic activity can be grouped into five broad categories:

- Goods production: agriculture, mining, construction, utilities, and manufacturing (NAICS sectors 11, 21 through 23, and 31 through 33).

- Trade activities: wholesale trade, retail trade, and transportation and warehousing (NAICS sectors 42, 44, 48 and 49).

- Business services: information; finance and insurance; real estate; professional, scientific, and technical services; management of companies and enterprises; and administrative and waste remediation services (NAICS sectors 51 through 56).

- Personal services: educational services; health care and social assistance; arts, entertainment, and recreation services; and accommodation and food services (NAICS sectors 61, 62, 71, 72, and 81).

- Public services: public administration (NAICS sector 92).

Table 1.1 Economic sectors and their two-digit NAICS codes

NAICS code	Sector
11	Agriculture, forestry, fishing, and hunting
21	Mining
22	Utilities
23	Construction
31–33	Manufacturing
42	Wholesale trade
44–45	Retail trade
48–49	Transportation and warehousing
51	Information
52	Finance and insurance
53	Real estate and rental and leasing
54	Professional, scientific, and technical services
55	Management of companies and enterprises
56	Administrative and support and waste management and remediation services
61	Educational services
62	Health care and social assistance
71	Arts, entertainment, and recreation
72	Accommodation and food services
81	Other services (except public administration)
92	Public administration

NAICS = North American Industry Classification System

Source: US Census Bureau, www.census.gov.

Table 1.2 provides a more detailed picture of the composition of employment and its growth by sector, including that within business services and personal services, using data from the 1997 and 2007 Economic Census.[4] The table reveals that manufacturing employment fell from 1997 to 2007 not only as a share of total employment but also in terms of the absolute number of workers employed. Indeed, the reduction was significant: Manufacturing employment decreased by just over 20 percent over that period. In stark contrast, business and personal service jobs grew at a relatively rapid pace: by almost 30 percent and over 20 percent, respectively, over the same period. Each of these two broad service categories now accounts for about 25 percent of total employment.

---

4. The Census provides more detailed information on employment by sector than is available from the *Economic Report of the President,* which, however, provides a long time series—an example of how this book's mosaic has to be assembled from multiple sources.

Table 1.2   Employment and wages by two-digit NAICS sector, 2007

| NAICS code | Sector | Employment | | | Average annual wage, 2007 (dollars) |
		Thousands of workers	Share of total employment (percent)	Growth, 1997–2007 (percent)	
21	Mining	703	0.5	38	53,060
22	Utilities	632	0.5	–10	80,473
23	Construction	7,399	5.5	31	47,052
31–33	Manufacturing	13,333	9.9	–21	45,935
42	Wholesale trade	6,295	4.7	9	53,395
44–45	Retail trade	15,611	11.5	12	23,381
48–49	Transportation and warehousing	4,436	3.3	52	38,813
51–56	Business services	33,431	24.7	29	56,086
51	Information	3,428	2.5	12	65,157
52	Finance and insurance	6,563	4.9	12	75,350
53	Real estate and rental and leasing	2,249	1.7	32	37,899
54	Professional, scientific, and technical services	8,121	6.0	51	63,424
55	Management of companies and enterprises	2,916	2.2	11	91,324
56	Administrative and support and waste remediation services	10,154	7.5	38	28,614

61–81	Personal services	34,596	25.6	23	29,125
61	Educational services	562	0.4	75	25,941
62	Health care and social assistance	16,860	12.5	24	39,493
71	Arts, entertainment, and recreation	2,071	1.5	30	27,793
72	Accommodation and food services	11,588	8.6	23	14,657
81	Other services (except public administration)	3,516	2.6	8	28,389
	Federal government	2,462	1.8	—	—
	State and local government	16,400	12.1	—	—

NAICS = North American Industry Classification System

Sources: 2007 Economic Census; Census of Governments.

Wages in the Service Sector

To summarize the preceding section: Whereas in the 1960s manufacturing was the sector with the largest share of employment, today business services and personal services each employ more than twice as many workers as manufacturing, and altogether, services account for more than half of total employment in the United States. But what about the widespread perception that, yes, there are a lot of service jobs, but they are not "good jobs with good wages" like most manufacturing jobs?

This perception is wrong.

Table 1.2 also reports average annual salaries and wages by sector, and by subsector within business services and personal services, using data from the 2007 Economic Census. The table shows that the business service sector—which, again, alone employs more than twice as many Americans as manufacturing—pays significantly higher wages and salaries, on average, than manufacturing: The average annual wage in the business service sector was about $56,000 a year in 2007, or over 22 percent more than in manufacturing, where the average was about $46,000 a year. Some other sectors also often classified within services, such as utilities, construction, and wholesale trade, also pay more on average than manufacturing. On the other hand, some service sector jobs, notably in personal services and the retail sector (often considered part of services) do pay lower average wages than the manufacturing sector.

The Service Sector and the Broader Economy

Besides contributing a huge share of total output and many good jobs, the service sector provides key intermediate inputs to other sectors—including manufacturing. Banking, legal services, marketing, R&D, design, engineering, project management, software, and telecommunications all provide crucial inputs to other activities throughout the economy. These business services have the capacity to improve the quality, efficiency, and competitiveness of other firms in the economy. In addition, these services establish key linkages to the global economy—and, as a result, are key drivers of export growth (even of manufactured goods).

Joseph Francois and Bernard Hoekman (2010) review a range of studies covering a number of countries that demonstrate the broad-based impact of a competitive service sector. They cite studies showing that service sector productivity is a key driver of aggregate productivity growth differences across developed economies. They also cite a range of studies showing that increased levels of competition in the service sector—and the higher levels of service provision that such competition encourages—have a positive impact on manufacturing productivity and lead to increases in manufacturing exports.

Characteristics of Service Producers: A Closer Look

The aggregate data presented thus far give a sense of the economic importance of the service sector but reveal little about the nature of today's individual service firms. When most Americans, including even many who work in the service sector, think about the productive side of the economy, they probably think first of large manufacturing corporations. And indeed, many of the iconic American corporations—General Motors, General Electric, and Boeing, for example—are manufacturers. In some ways the sheer scale of these large manufacturers (and perhaps the political presence they derive from their size) tends to make manufacturing seem more important than other sectors, where the typical firm and the typical operation are—in the public mind, at least—much smaller. But here, too, the picture is changing.

The first column of table 1.3 reports the average sales, employment, and wages of producers in manufacturing (NAICS 30s), business services (NAICS 50s), and personal services (NAICS 60s, 70s, 80s). These measures broadly confirm the standard preconceptions about the service sector. For example, the average manufacturing plant employs about 70 workers, about five times as many as the average business service or the average personal service establishment (15 workers for both). Sales of the average manufacturing plant's output are more than seven times that of the average business service establishment, and close to twenty times that of the average personal service establishment.

However, merely comparing averages does not fully capture the differences (or the similarities) across sectors. For one thing, the standard deviations associated with all the above averages (second column of the table) are many times the averages themselves, indicating that all these measures vary across a wide range. The final column in table 1.3 presents another measure, called the coworker mean. This measure (described in Davis, Haltiwanger, and Schuh 1996) is constructed by weighting a given establishment characteristic by employment and then taking the average; it thus represents the size of the establishment where the average worker is employed.[5] By this measure, the average worker in the business service sector works in an establishment that is actually significantly larger (over 1,200 employees) than the plant where the average manufacturing worker works (about 1,000 employees). The large difference between the simple establishment mean and the coworker mean results from the presence of a large number of very small establishments in the service sector. Although the service sector has many more of these very small establishments than does manufacturing, the bulk of service workers work in relatively large establishments, and this raises the coworker mean.

---

5. For example, imagine that there are three plants in an industry, two of which employ 1 person each whereas the third employs 10 people. The simple average of employment across plants in this industry is thus $(1 + 1 + 10)/3 = 4$. However, the employment-weighted average (the coworker mean) is $[(1 \times 1) + (1 \times 1) + (10 \times 10)]/12 = 8.5$. This number gives a better sense of the size of the plant in which most workers work.

Table 1.3 Sales, employment, and average wage per establishment in manufacturing and services, 2002

Sector	Mean	Standard deviation	Coworker mean
Manufacturing (NAICS 30s)			
Sales (thousands of dollars)	19,378	151,147	380,329
Employment	72	264	1,042
Average annual wage (dollars)	34,604	13,723	39,346
Business services (NAICS 50s)			
Sales (thousands of dollars)	2,632	58,343	180,429
Employment	15	135	1,238
Average annual wage (dollars)	35,870	56,505	44,677
Personal services (NAICS 60s, 70s, 80s)			
Sales (thousands of dollars)	1,073	9,905	54,177
Employment	15	101	700
Average annual wage (dollars)	29,566	109,801	30,188

Source: Author's calculations using data from the 2002 Economic Census.

Table 1.4 confirms this by providing more detail on the full distribution of producers by number of employees in manufacturing, business services, and personal services. The top panel shows that establishments with five or fewer workers make up over half of establishments in both the business service and the personal service sectors, but only about 11 percent of manufacturing establishments. The large number of very small service sector establishments pulls down the sector's average establishment size.

The bottom panel of the table reports shares of workers by establishment size class. Here the two service subsectors look much more similar to the manufacturing sector. Although the share of employment in very small service establishments is still larger than in the manufacturing sector, the difference is much smaller. In both service subsectors, only about 9 percent of workers are employed in the more than 50 percent of establishments with five or fewer employees. In the manufacturing sector, the 7 percent of plants in this size range account for less than 1 percent of employment. At the other end of the distribution, the largest establishments (those with more than 1,000 employees) account for a similarly large share of employment (roughly 20 percent) in both business and personal services and in manufacturing. Thus, although the number of large service producers is small relative to the total population of service producers, they account for a larger share of employment in the sector than their number might suggest. This is consistent with the finding in table 1.3 that, measured by the coworker mean, the average business service worker works in an establishment that is larger than that of the average manufacturing worker.

Table 1.4 Size distribution of establishments in manufacturing and services (percent)

Establishment employment	Manufacturing	Business services	Personal services
	Share of all establishments in sector		
1 to 5 workers	11.41	62.63	56.65
6 to 10	15.78	15.29	19.58
11 to 25	27.34	12.37	14.54
26 to 50	17.48	4.62	4.66
51 to 100	12.50	2.60	2.35
101 to 250	10.07	1.63	1.57
251 to 500	3.41	0.52	0.34
501 to 1,000	1.36	0.22	0.15
1,001 to 2,500	0.52	0.10	0.12
2,501 and above	0.12	0.03	0.04
	Share of total sectoral employment		
1 to 5 workers	0.55	8.52	8.83
6 to 10	1.74	6.91	9.15
11 to 25	6.43	11.72	14.14
26 to 50	8.78	9.72	10.04
51 to 100	12.42	10.90	10.19
101 to 250	21.76	14.88	14.54
251 to 500	16.42	10.58	7.08
501 to 1,000	12.85	9.11	6.54
1,001 to 2,500	10.56	8.42	10.96
2,501 and above	8.49	9.24	8.54

Source: Author's calculations using data from the 2002 Economic Census.

Regarding wages, one sees in the less aggregated data the same patterns as in the aggregates. Although some service industries clearly do pay lower wages than manufacturing, table 1.3 shows that the average establishment in the business service sector actually pays higher average wages than the average manufacturing plant, $35,870 per year versus $34,604. The difference in co-worker means is somewhat larger.[6]

In short, while the average service establishment is small, most service workers work at large producers that pay relatively high wages.

---

6. These numbers on wages for the average establishment differ substantially from the average worker wages reported in the Overview because large establishments tend to pay higher wages, so taking the average across establishments results in a lower number.

International Comparisons

As already mentioned, early studies of the process of economic development likely contributed to the widespread perception of manufacturing's greater economic importance. For example Simon Kuznets (1957), reported that the share of output in the manufacturing sector was positively correlated with income per capita across countries, but that the share of output in the service sector was not.

Fifty years after Kuznets's work, a reevaluation of the relationship between the size of a country's manufacturing sector and its standard of living seems in order. Figure 1.3 shows the shares of employment in services, agriculture, and manufacturing for eight large economies. In most, the service sector accounts for more than half of employment. In the more advanced economies such as the United States, the United Kingdom, and the European Union, the figure is two-thirds or more. But even in some economies with lower income per capita, such as Russia and Brazil, the service sector accounts for more than 60 percent of employment, and the figure for Mexico is almost 60 percent. Meanwhile in China and India, countries with still lower income per capita, the service sector accounts for only about a third of employment, but even this is larger than manufacturing's share. Thus, even this simple figure shows that large service sectors are not the exclusive domain of advanced economies, and there appears to be a positive relationship between the service sector's share of economic activity and living standards.

Figure 1.4, which covers a much larger group of countries, shows the same positive relationship. Here each point represents a single country, and although there is considerable variation, most countries lie close to the upward-sloping line, indicating that a larger share of employment in services and higher income go hand in hand.

Barry Eichengreen and Poonam Gupta (2009) undertake a more sophisticated analysis of the relationship between the employment share of the service sector and income per capita, and they, too, find a positive correlation overall. But they also find that the relationship does not hold for all services. Decomposing the service sector into three groups of activities, they observe that a group they call "traditional services" (retail and wholesale trade, transport and storage, and public administration and defense) actually has a negative relationship with income per capita. They observe a positive relationship for the other two groups: The first is a mixture of traditional and modern services consumed primarily by households (education, health and social services, accommodations and restaurants, and other personal services), and the second is composed of modern services that are primarily business services (including financial intermediation, computer services, communication services, and legal and technical services).

It is worth underscoring that this positive relationship is not necessarily evidence of a causal relationship in either direction. There could exist complex relationships between fundamental features of an economy that drive both income per capita and the share of employment in the service sector upward.

Figure 1.3   Labor force shares of major sectors in selected countries

percent

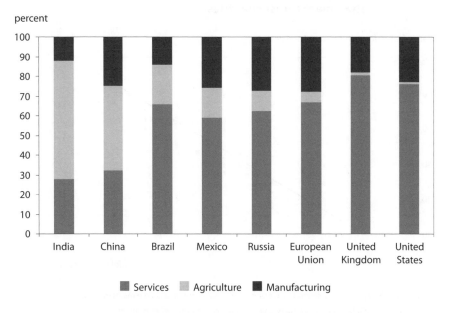

Source: CIA, *The World Factbook*, www.cia.gov/library/publications/the-world-factbook.

Figure 1.4   Labor force share of the service sector and income per capita across countries

share of labor force in services (percent)

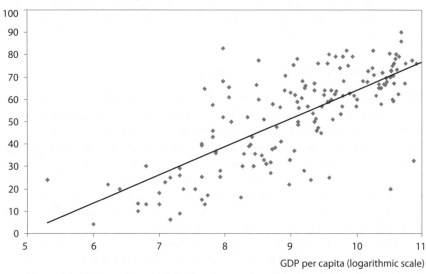

Source: CIA, *The World Factbook*, www.cia.gov/library/publications/the-world-factbook.

Figure 1.5   Labor force share of the service sector and educational attainment across countries

share of labor force in services (percent)

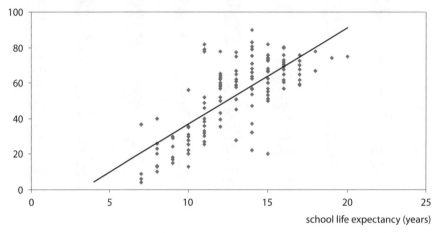

Note: School life expectancy is defined as average number of years that a child remains in school.

Source: CIA, *The World Factbook*, www.cia.gov/library/publications/the-world-factbook.

One such feature is educational attainment. Figure 1.5 shows a positive relationship between the level of educational attainment (measured here as "school life expectancy," or the average number of years that a child remains in school) and the service sector's share of employment. Again, it is difficult to disentangle which, if either, causes which, but later chapters show that many service activities—and tradable service activities in particular—require high levels of educational attainment.

A First Look at Trade in Services

The service sector is large and growing, both in the United States and in many other countries. Countries with high average incomes and high average educational attainment tend to have higher shares of employment in the service sector. The service sector is not made up of just a myriad small firms paying mostly low wages, but it includes some large producers offering relatively high-wage employment opportunities; many service sector jobs—particularly in business services—are good jobs that provide good wages. All these facts taken together demonstrate that the service sector is important and deserves significantly more attention than it has tended to receive.

These facts do not necessarily mean, however, that *trade* in services is important. It is possible that the service sector, however large, is largely insulated from the international economy and that most services are not tradable.

Indeed, services have long been thought of as nontradable, because the typical service requires a face-to-face presence of buyer and seller. This section shows, however, that this has always been a misconception, or at best an oversimplification, and today it is an increasingly inappropriate one. Falling costs of travel, communications, and computers and increasing access to the internet have vastly expanded the opportunities for trading services across long distances, including across borders. And, indeed, official statistics suggest that US service trade is increasing rapidly.

But what is service trade? This section describes what the term means and gives a number of examples. It then documents the falling costs of computer hardware, communications, and travel and the increasing access to the internet, which are facilitating ever-greater trade in services. I also examine official US government statistics for evidence of increasing trade in services—and point to some of the shortcomings in those statistics.

What Is Trade in Services?

Most of us are accustomed to thinking of trade as trade in goods. Commodities such as wheat, copper, and crude oil, as well as manufactured goods such as clothing, furniture, consumer electronics, automobiles, and jet aircraft, have long been shipped all over the world. One can visit any port or border crossing and see evidence of this kind of trade. Or one can visit the nearest mall or big-box superstore and find an abundance of goods bearing the label "Made in _____," where the blank might be filled in by the name of virtually any country in the world. So when one speaks of "trade in goods" or "merchandise trade," it is not difficult to conjure up a clear mental image.

Trade in services, however, is somewhat harder to conceptualize. Because services are intangible, the image of a service being traded comes less readily to mind. Yet services are traded, and in a variety of ways. The General Agreement on Trade in Services (GATS) provides a useful definition of what is meant by "trade in services":[7]

> For the purposes of this Agreement, trade in services is defined as the supply of a service:
>
> (a) from the territory of one Member into the territory of any other Member;
> (b) in the territory of one Member to the service consumer of any other Member;
> (c) by a service supplier of one Member, through commercial presence in the territory of any other Member;
> (d) by a service supplier of one Member, through presence of natural persons of a Member in the territory of any other Member.

---

7. See General Agreement on Trade in Services, available at www.wto.org.

The GATS definition embodies what are generally referred to as the four "modes" of trade in services:

- Mode 1 is cross-border provision, for example, when software is produced in one country and shipped via the internet to another.

- Mode 2 is consumption abroad, for example, when a vacationer travels to a resort in another country and purchases hotel accommodations, meals, and other services there.

- Mode 3 is commercial presence in a foreign country, for example, when a restaurant chain opens a branch outside its home country.

- Mode 4 is temporary movement of natural persons across borders, for example, when a business consultant travels to visit a foreign client.

Box 1.2 provides more specific examples of the different kinds of trade in services.

Mode 3, also called foreign direct investment—both outward investment by US companies abroad and inward investment by foreign companies into the United States—is undoubtedly beneficial. For example, the expansion of US service firms abroad allows them to take advantage of their successful business models around the world when trade in services via the other modes is not possible. Such investment increases total firm sales and generates profit flows to the US headquarters of these firms, which benefit the firms' owners and their US workers, increase the US tax base, and offer a range of other benefits both here and in the foreign markets being served. Unfortunately, identifying and measuring the impact of these benefits on the US economy is devilishly difficult. Therefore, for the sake of tractability, and because this book is primarily about the effects of service trade on US workers, I focus on the other three modes.[8] The employment effects of foreign direct investment on the home country are unlikely to be as large as the effects of the other modes. Likewise, although foreign firms that make direct investments in the United States offer new employment prospects for US workers, it seems likely that even in the absence of these investments, the level of economic activity undertaken in the United States would be similar.

Some Real-World Examples

I have reviewed some broad definitions of service trade, and box 1.2 lists a number of hypothetical examples. But do these transactions happen regularly in the real world? Are there firms out there that actually trade services internationally—besides the formerly high-flying financial service firms that crashed a

---

8. Looking at economic activity through the lens of corporate ownership, as opposed to the location of economic activity, is nonetheless a legitimate perspective for a range of questions. On this topic see Baldwin, Lipsey, and Richardson (1998). See also Graham and Krugman (1995) for a classic study of foreign direct investment and its benefits.

Box 1.2 Some examples of trade in services

The following people are all exporting services:

1. An advertising executive developing a TV commercial for a foreign client
2. A secretary at a law firm answering a call from a foreign client
3. A cabby who drives a foreign businessman from the airport to the hotel
4. The cast of a television show that will be broadcast abroad
5. A doctor operating on a foreign patient
6. The doorman and the bartender at a posh hotel serving foreign guests
7. An accountant unraveling the financial affairs of a foreign corporation
8. An engineer designing a bridge to be built in another country
9. A caterer preparing a meal to be served at a foreign embassy
10. A management consultant advising a foreign client

The following persons or companies are all importing services:

1. Every reader of this book who has taken a foreign vacation
2. An auto company that asks a foreign firm to design a new model
3. Someone who buys a ticket to a performance by a foreign orchestra
4. A student attending a foreign university
5. A businessman who extracts information from a foreign data base
6. A housewife who goes to "Jean Pierre" for the latest French hairstyling
7. A consumer who has a camera repaired abroad
8. An investor who buys securities at a foreign stock exchange
9. The actress who has her legs insured in London with a Lloyd's broker
10. A traveler who uses a credit card issued by a foreign bank.

Source: Excerpted from Feketekuty (1988).

few years ago? Are they providing good jobs at good wages for normal people in middle America? Or are they phantoms that show up only in the statistics—a figment of economists' imaginations? Although the purpose of this book is to provide as detailed a statistical portrait of the service sector and of trade in services as possible, it is also true that statistics do not always give the full picture. In an attempt to flesh out the analysis, therefore, this book also includes examples of real-life firms that are trading services.

Box 1.3 provides the first such example. The newspaper article reproduced there describes two water treatment technology companies in Wisconsin, Envirex and Zimpro, both owned by the German engineering firm Siemens. What is interesting is that not only is engineering services an important line of business for both companies, but for at least one of them, international sales make up a large part of its business: Chad Felch, a chemist at Zimpro, notes that 80 percent of the company's business was international in 2007. Also interesting is the article's observation that the global market for water and wastewater treatment systems is growing faster than the domestic market, providing expanding opportunities for exports. The article mentions that Siemens' water treatment group is growing at 30 percent per year and has more than doubled in size since Siemens purchased US Filter.

This article is one example of how US firms export services almost invisibly. Envirex and Zimpro are located deep within the American heartland. Their engineering service output is intangible, not packaged into containers and shipped to some distant port by truck or train. How many firms like these are in the US economy? How many workers do they employ? What are the skills required of their workers? Are these "good jobs at good wages"? These are some of the themes this book explores and the questions it tries to answer.

For now it is worth noting that Siemens, itself a global technology firm, purchased two companies in Wisconsin to acquire cutting-edge know-how. That those companies are now owned by Siemens does not change the fact that workers based in the United States are providing engineering services around the world. This is an example of how the United States can export high-tech, high-value services.

Factors Contributing to Growth in Service Trade

Because services are traded in so many different ways (recall the four modes listed above), a variety of different technological changes could facilitate increased trade in services. This section describes a number of these changes.

Falling Travel Costs

Because modes 2 and 4 involve the travel of either the consumer or the producer of a service, any decline in the cost of travel can lower the costs of importing and exporting services. And travel costs have indeed fallen dramatically in recent decades: As figure 1.6 shows, international passenger airfares have been cut by more than half since 1987. Lower airfares make it less expensive to travel to consume or produce services.

Falling Costs of Information and Communications Technology

The past two decades have also witnessed a revolution in information and communications technology. Three related trends have vastly increased the ability of people and firms to transfer knowledge around the world without having to go there personally. First, dramatically falling prices of information technology (IT) hardware led to the widespread adoption of personal computers, first in the developed world and now increasingly in the developing world. Second, the increased interconnectedness of all this hardware

Box 1.3   Siemens catches a wave

It's a burgeoning idea on the shores of Lake Michigan: As drinkable water becomes scarce in parts of the United States, Asia and the Middle East, demand is bound to proliferate for new technologies that can clean, conserve and recycle water.

Business leaders are trying to figure out whether metro Milwaukee's modest hub of water engineering companies can expand enough to replace a portion of the region's shrinking manufacturing base.

Siemens AG of Germany, which relies on two Wisconsin acquisitions to drive growth in its water technologies division, has already made up its mind about the state's role.

"Wisconsin easily is the most important state for us in the US because of those two companies," said Roger Radke, president and chief executive of Siemens Water Technologies Corp. in Warrendale, Pa.

Radke regularly visits those two Siemens facilities in Wisconsin: Envirex in Waukesha, Siemens' global R&D center for biological water treatment systems; and Zimpro Environmental near Wausau, which develops industrial water treatments.

Yet even within Siemens, Wisconsin is facing global competition.

Siemens—which is Europe's biggest engineering company—just opened a $36 million water technology R&D center in Singapore to help it crack booming markets such as India and China, where 15% growth rates for water technologies are triple the pace of growth in the US.

In what is shaping up as a full-blown global technology race with a profusion of rivals from China to India, Siemens is recruiting 50 additional scientists to work in Singapore. Those new engineers and researchers will complement the existing worldwide research roster of 150 at Siemens Water Technologies, which also operates big water research centers in Germany and Britain.

Nor is Siemens, with $104 billion in sales, the only globe-straddling giant that competes in water infrastructure, Radke said. General Electric Co., a US rival to Siemens in scale and scope, has its own "eco-imagination" strategy that banks on big growth in water projects.

Acquisition, innovation

Worldwide spending on water treatment is $45 billion a year and growing, Radke estimates. Hot technologies from Siemens include membrane filters and "closed-loop" reactors that recycle water within factories.

Siemens entered the global water business in 2004 with the acquisition of the US Filter Corp., which had acquired Envirex and Zimpro in the mid-1990s in an early wave of consolidation.

(continued on next page)

Box 1.3   Siemens catches a wave *(continued)*

Zimpro got started in the 1930s making artificial vanilla flavoring only to learn that it could adapt its processes for treating wastewater. Today, it employs 222 people.

Siemens employs another 205 people at Envirex in Waukesha. Envirex installed its first wastewater treatment equipment more than 100 years ago and more recently has been developing biological treatment reactors that reduce the enormous volumes of sludgy byproducts, thus lowering treatment and transportation costs.

With 30% annual growth, Siemens Water Technologies has more than doubled in size since acquiring US Filter.

Siemens also has been acquiring water-technology firms in Asia, a region that lacks sufficient clean-water resources to fuel its economic and population expansion, Radke said.

Nearly all economists agree on the global scope of the water crisis.

Top World Bank officials have predicted that the wars of the 21st century will be fought over water, not oil.

Radke notes that nearly 2 billion people lack access to safe water….

Prize-winning research

Siemens drew attention to Wisconsin last month when it awarded a prestigious "Inventor of the Year" prize to a chemist at Zimpro in Rothschild, near Wausau.

Siemens—a multinational conglomerate in multiple industries that employs 55,000 scientists and researchers, spends $8 billion annually on R&D and applied for 5,060 patents last year—awards only 12 such prizes a year. In 2007, only one went to an American: Chad Felch, 35, who applied Zimpro industrial technologies to the production of crude oil from tar sands in Alberta, Canada. Felch's work, which makes the process more environmentally compatible, helped Siemens book a contract worth $60 million in Canada.

Felch said growth in the wastewater sector is being driven by companies that are trying to reduce or even eliminate the discharge of wastewater.

"They're keeping all the water in a closed loop, said Felch, who has a chemistry degree from UW-Stevens Point. "They produce water and re-use it within their facilities."

Felch said he often flies to oil-producing nations such as Norway and Bahrain. "Our business was about 80 percent international last year," he said.

(continued on next page)

Competition may be intense, Radke said, but the field is also wide open.

Water engineering remains a relatively young and fragmented industry, Radke said. Many older companies that build municipal treatment plants haven't invested in new technologies in decades. US Department of the Interior data show that US water treatment industries spend far below 1% of their sales on development of new technologies.

That means Milwaukee retains a chance to champion freshwater research, as its business leaders urge, in the way that Madison mines stem-cell technology.

Asked if the global water industry has its own Silicon Valley yet, Radke said he doesn't know of any.

That title, he said, remains up for grabs.

Source: John Schmid, "Siemens Catches a Wave," *Milwaukee Journal Sentinel,* January 20, 2008, www.jsonline.com/business/29578294.html. Reprinted with permission.

via the internet has made it nearly effortless for users of those computers to share information with each other. Third, rapidly falling telecommunications costs have enabled firms to expand the geographic reach of this technology to encompass most of the world. These related developments have created an unprecedented opportunity to exchange information across large distances economically, creating a platform for dramatically increased trade in services.

The OECD reports that prices of leased telecommunications lines have fallen significantly over the past 15 years:

> Leased lines are symmetrical transmission channels provided permanently for the duration of a contract. Leased lines are provided to businesses as a way to connect offices to each other or link back to a telecommunications provider. They are commonly used as a way for companies to manage their own telecommunications services. However, leased lines are also used by alternative carriers as an element of their own networks until they become full facilities-based operators....
>
> The price for a 2Mbit/s leased line has fallen dramatically over the past 14 years. A two-kilometre line in 2006 is 64% less expensive than it was 14 years ago in nominal terms. Longer-distance connections have fallen even further. The price of a 200 kilometre line in 2006 is only 27% of the price a company would pay in 1992." (*OECD Communications Outlook 2007*, p. 224)

Figure 1.7 confirms this decline in telecommunications costs, showing that billed revenue per minute for international telecommunication services provided in the United States has declined sharply since 1992.

Figure 1.6   US international airfares, 1987–2007

index (1999 = 1.0)

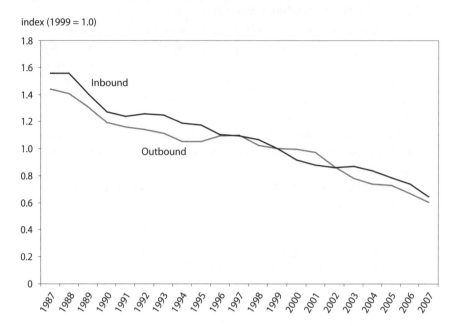

Source: Bureau of Labor Statistics, www.bls.gov.

IT hardware costs have also fallen dramatically. As figure 1.8, from Mann and Kirkegaard (2006), illustrates, both personal computers and semi-conductor memory chips have decreased significantly in price since 1992. These falling prices have led to broader adoption of IT hardware across the US economy and around the world. As this hardware becomes ever cheaper, it becomes easier and cheaper to digitize and store ever-greater quantities of information—information that can then be exported.

A closely related technological development that has influenced the tradability of services is increasing access to the internet. Table 1.5 shows the significant increase over the past decade in the number of people around the world who can access the internet. Internet penetration in developed economies is already quite high, and it is growing rapidly in developing countries as well. Caroline Freund and Diana Weinhold (2002) find that increased access to the internet increases service trade, both exports and imports, even after controlling for changes in GDP and for exchange rate movements.

All of these technological changes, combined with the fact that the service sector now accounts for more than three-quarters of employment in many countries, create potential for increasing service trade. The next section examines the growth of trade in services that has already occurred in the United States.

Figure 1.7   Price of a one-minute international telephone call, 1992–2007

current US dollars

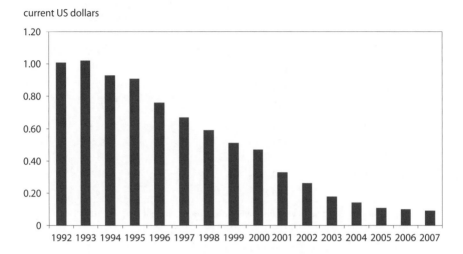

Source: Federal Communications Commission, International Telecommunications Data, June 2009.

Figure 1.8   Prices of personal computers and dynamic random access memory chips (DRAMs), December 1992–February 2005

index

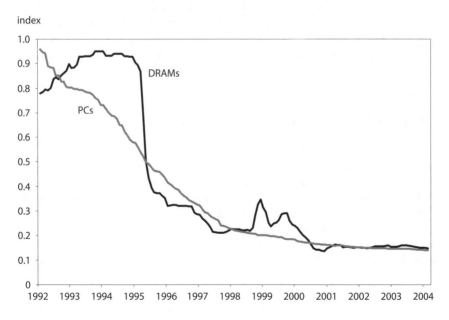

Note: Data are Bureau of Labor Statistics price series PCU334413344131A101 (DRAMs) and PCU33411133411171 (PCs), plotted semiannually (June and December).

Source: Mann and Kirkegaard (2006).

Table 1.5 Internet usage by world region, 2009

Region	Thousands of internet users	Internet penetration (users as percent of total population)	Growth in internet users, 2000–09 (percent)
Africa	54,172	6	1,100
Asia	657,171	17	475
Europe	393,373	49	274
Middle East	45,861	23	1,296
North America	251,290	74	133
Latin America and Caribbean	173,619	30	861
Australia/Oceania	20,783	60	173
World	1,596,270	24	342

Source: Internet World Stats, www.internetworldstats.com. Copyright © 2000–2010, Miniwatts Marketing Group. All rights reserved worldwide.

Growth in Service Trade

Figure 1.9 shows that US service trade increased steadily over the decade ending in 2007. Both service exports and service imports roughly doubled, with exports growing slightly faster in the last few years of the period. Service exports now account for almost 30 percent of US exports; service imports account for about 15 percent of US imports. Their sum, total service trade, now accounts for slightly over 20 percent of US trade.[9] The figure also shows that the United States has consistently maintained a positive trade balance in services, with service exports exceeding service imports. This suggests that the United States has comparative advantage in tradable services.

Composition of US Service Exports and Imports

Which industries are contributing to the growth in service trade, and which services are being traded? The Bureau of Economic Analysis (BEA) divides private services into five main groups: travel, passenger fares, other transportation, royalties and license fees, and "other private services" (OPS), a catchall category that includes education, financial services, insurance services, telecommunications, and business, professional, and technical services. This book focuses on OPS for two reasons: It is an important contributor to overall growth in service trade, and it is the area that raises most concern regarding

---

9. Lipsey (2009) reports that services' share of total trade has been roughly 20 to 30 percent for decades. Service trade is growing rapidly, but so is merchandise trade, so that the share of service trade in total trade is not changing. What is changing, however, is the composition of service trade.

Figure 1.9   US service trade, 1997–2007

billions of current dollars

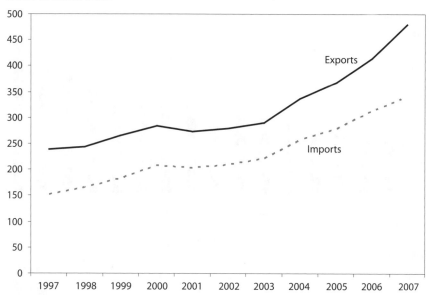

Source: Bureau of Economic Analysis, ww.bea.gov.

the impact of trade in services. Such concern seems to focus on sectors like engineering and computer services, not travel and tourism.

Figure 1.10 shows the composition of US service exports and imports by the BEA's categorization from 1992 to 2007. Although all of the categories show growth over the period, OPS grew the fastest, with both imports and exports more than doubling. OPS also contributed the most to overall service growth, accounting for more than half of the increase in service exports and about half of the increase in service imports.

Import and export data for the components of OPS are available only starting in 1997; these data are shown in figure 1.11. Business, professional, and technical services (BPTS) is the largest of these at the end of the period and contributed the most to OPS growth over the period, for both imports and exports. Financial services and insurance services also enjoyed significant growth over the period, and indeed both grew faster than BPTS, but neither contributed as much to total growth in OPS as did BPTS.[10]

Together, BPTS, financial services, and insurance services account for a significant share of service sector growth over the past 15 years.

---

10. Financial services and insurance services both present even greater measurement challenges than other types of services. See Borga (2009) for more information on how the BEA constructs estimates of insurance and financial services trade.

Figure 1.10   Composition of US service trade, 1992–2007

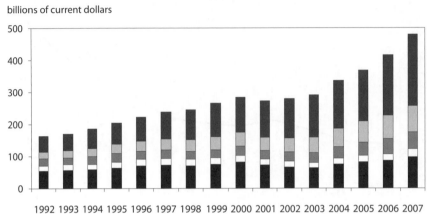
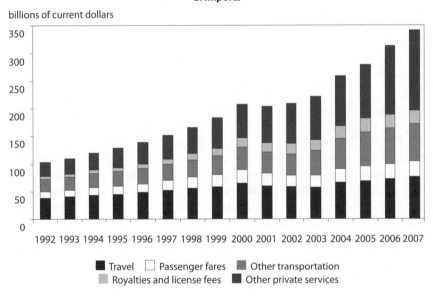

a. Exports

billions of current dollars

b. Imports

billions of current dollars

■ Travel   □ Passenger fares   ▨ Other transportation
▨ Royalties and license fees   ■ Other private services

Source: Bureau of Economic Analysis, www.bea.gov.

Shortcomings of Service-Sector Data

While the aggregate data on trade in services used in previous sections are instructive, to truly understand the potential impact of trade in services on the US economy requires significantly more detailed data for a longer period of time. To understand how increased trade in services has affected and is likely

Figure 1.11   Composition of US "Other Private Services" trade, 1997–2007

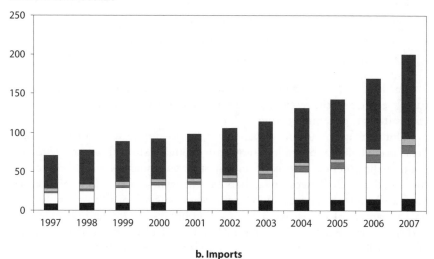

a. Exports

billions of current dollars

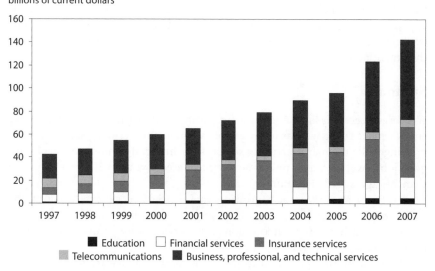

b. Imports

billions of current dollars

■ Education   ☐ Financial services   ▨ Insurance services
▨ Telecommunications   ■ Business, professional, and technical services

Source: Bureau of Economic Analysis, www.bea.gov.

to affect the US economy requires both more detailed information on trade flows than is currently available and the ability to link it to detailed information on domestic producers.

For example, to understand how increased trade in services might affect the US economy, international trade theory and previous empirical work in the manufacturing sector stress some key information needs:

- prevalence of trade in services (how many activities?), scale (how much is being traded?), and direction (who is trading with whom?) of trade in services;
- how trade in services has evolved over time;
- intensities of the factors used in service provision; and
- factor intensity differences across locations.

As discussed in chapter 4, this type of data is available for the manufacturing sector, and the research community has learned a great deal about how trade affects the manufacturing sector.

Unfortunately, currently available data do not provide anywhere near detailed enough data on trade in services or enough historical data to adequately examine the potential impact of trade in services. Appendix A briefly describes the significant challenges researchers face in trying to analyze the potential impact of trade in services and provides some suggestions for improvement. As an example of the issues, a comparison between merchandise trade data and service trade data is instructive. Currently, data on exports and imports of over 8,000 product categories are published monthly for goods trade of most countries. In contrast, only recently have about 30 categories of service trade become available for a far more limited set of countries (see table A.1 in appendix A). The next chapter introduces a methodology to construct data to overcome existing inadequacies; subsequent chapters use these data to examine the potential impact of trade in services on the US economy.

Summary

The service sector is large and growing. Business services, a focus of this book, employ more than twice as many people as the manufacturing sector and are growing while the manufacturing sector is shrinking. Business service jobs are good jobs: Average wages in business services are more than 20 percent higher than average wages in manufacturing.

Trade in services is also growing rapidly. Service exports account for almost 30 percent of US exports. The category of service trade ("other private services") that has contributed the most to service export growth consists of the types of services produced by business service firms.

To understand the implications of increased service trade for the US economy, higher resolution is needed about which activities are being traded and, perhaps more important, which activities could be traded. The next chapter develops a methodology to identify at a very detailed level which service activities are being traded within the United States and thus are, at least in principle, tradable internationally. Subsequent chapters utilize this methodology and examine tradable service activities and the implications of increased trade in services in more detail.

2

A New Approach to Identifying Tradable Services

The previous chapter highlighted a seemingly insurmountable obstacle to understanding the potential of trade in services. Information on the domestic activities of service firms is minimally sufficient for analysis, but data on international service flows are wholly unsatisfactory. Which industries and occupations are likely to be most affected by increased service trade? How large an impact will such trade have on service production and employment in the United States? Which service activities are likely to be offshored to lower-cost countries, and which are likely to be "inshored" to the United States? As chapter 1 showed, services are an important part of the economy, dominating all other sectors in terms of output and jobs both in the United States and in most other advanced economies. Chapter 1 also documented that service trade is growing, and there is potential for more rapid growth with active, liberalizing policy support. But who knows without data?

To address this data gap, I develop a concept called "tradability" and apply it empirically to a range of service industries and occupations. The concept of tradability is based on the geographic concentration of production within the United States. Using geographic concentration as an indicator of international trade potential, one can arguably measure what has so far gone unmeasured: identify at a detailed level which service activities appear to be "traded" within the United States and thus "ought" to be traded internationally. These are the activities that this book claims are tradable.

Of course, this method does not measure exactly what is desired but only an indicator of it. But when coupled with the other components of this mosaic, this component, too, tells a story. Being able to identify which activities are potentially tradable is a crucial piece of the mosaic.

New Methodology

The methodology described in this chapter is novel and relies on the geographic concentration of production within the United States to identify industries and occupations that appear to be "traded" within the United States.[1] The basic idea is simple. If one observes more of a service produced in one location than consumers in that location are likely to want to consume, then the excess services must be consumed elsewhere. This implies that the service is somehow being "shipped" to a different location. If a service can be shipped from one US location to another, there is no inherent reason why it cannot be shipped from a US location to a foreign location—that is, traded. Therefore that service is, in principle, tradable.

An important advantage of this methodology is that it can identify both service industries *and service occupations* that appear to be traded within the United States. This matters because many of the service activities that are reportedly being offshored are tasks within larger production processes. For example, bank call centers can be relocated offshore without entire banks or the banking industry moving offshore. Occupations correspond more closely to these distinctions between activities than do industries.

Having used the methodology to classify industries and occupations as tradable or nontradable, one can then examine how large a swath of US service activity is potentially exposed to import competition—and which service activities offer prospects for increased exports. One can also observe the number of workers employed in these activities. Later chapters use this classification system to reveal fascinating patterns in service tradability and trade potential.

The Intuition behind the Approach

Goods that are traded tend to be geographically concentrated (whether to capitalize on increasing returns to scale, or to gain access to inputs like natural resources or workers with specific skills, or for other reasons), whereas goods that are not traded tend to be more evenly distributed across geographic space, or, more precisely, to be distributed coextensively with demand.

The notion of using geographic concentration to identify tradable activities is related to a long tradition among geographers and regional economists of using the geographic concentration of economic activity to identify a region's export or manufacturing base. The idea is that if a region specializes in a manufacturing activity—think Boeing and airplanes in Seattle—it is likely to export the product in which it specializes.

---

1. Sections of this chapter draw heavily on Jensen and Kletzer (2006). Here and later, when for brevity's sake I say that an industry or occupation is "tradable," I of course mean that its output is tradable.

The measure used to determine whether a region specializes in a particular activity is typically some variant of a location quotient. A location quotient measures a region's share of industry output or employment and compares that share with (that is, divides it by) a measure of the region's share of overall demand (typically measured using the region's share of total population or of total employment, as in table 2.1). If a region has a larger share of an industry's activity than is predicted by demand in the region, the region is considered to be specialized in the activity.

The example of aircraft production in Seattle can be used to illustrate this concept. Seattle's share of US aircraft manufacturing employment is about 11 percent, and its share of total US employment is about 1.6 percent. Thus, Seattle has a much greater share of aircraft production employment than of total employment: Its location quotient for aircraft production is 11 divided by 1.6, or about 6.9. It is safe to assume that this concentration of aircraft production is not due to people in Seattle consuming more airplanes than other parts of the country; rather, they "export" planes to the rest of the country and export them to other countries in exchange for other goods and services. One can be quite comfortable thinking of Seattle as specializing in aircraft production and exporting aircraft.

Table 2.1 reports location quotients for selected large metropolitan areas and selected industries in the United States. It shows clearly that several other manufacturing industries are geographically concentrated just as aircraft is in Seattle (the location quotients for these are highlighted in the table). For example, motor vehicle production is concentrated in the Detroit area, with a location quotient of 11.5. Again, this is not because people in the Detroit area purchase 11.5 times more cars than the rest of the country, but because Detroit has specialized in motor vehicle production and exports cars in exchange for other goods.

Table 2.1 also shows that some manufacturing industries do not exhibit geographic concentration. For example, in none of the metropolitan areas listed do structural metals have a location quotient above 1; the location quotient for gypsum and lime production exceeds 1 in only two areas and never exceeds 2.[2] Both of these industries produce goods with relatively low value by weight, which suggests that shipping them from city to city may be too costly to be worthwhile. Whatever the reason, these manufacturing industries appear to be nontraded.

Economists have long thought of services as nontradable because many services require, or seem to require, face-to-face interaction. The quintessential services of this type are personal services like haircuts or visits to the dentist's office. Because these services are difficult to provide at a distance, they

---

2. The area with the largest location quotient for this industry, Las Vegas, was experiencing a construction boom in 2007, when these data were gathered. Gypsum and lime are important inputs to construction. Thus, in this case the relatively high location quotient could be due to unusually high local demand for the industry's goods.

Table 2.1 Location quotients for selected industries and US metropolitan areas

Industry	Boston	New York	Raleigh-Durham	Detroit	Las Vegas	Seattle	San Francisco	Los Angeles
Cement, concrete, lime, and gypsum manufacturing	0.5	0.4	0.9	0.4	1.8	1.3	0.4	0.7
Structural metals and tank and shipping container manufacturing	0.7	0.4	0.7	0.7	0.7	0.9	0.6	0.7
Aircraft and parts manufacturing	0.9	0.5	0.3	0.4	0.2	6.9	0.2	1.8
Motor vehicles and equipment manufacturing	0.1	0.1	0.3	11.5	0.1	0.3	0.3	0.4
Grocery stores	1.0	1.0	1.4	1.0	0.9	0.9	0.9	0.9
Software	3.5	0.7	3.9	0.8	0.1	6.9	4.7	1.0
Motion picture and video industries	0.7	1.8	0.5	0.7	0.9	0.7	1.6	5.7
Internet service providers	1.0	0.7	1.3	0.3	0.8	2.2	7.2	1.4
Securities, commodities, funds, and other financial investments	2.5	3.2	0.6	0.6	0.5	0.7	1.5	0.9
Scientific research and development services	2.9	0.9	4.8	0.6	0.3	1.4	3.1	0.9
Travel arrangements and reservation services	1.3	1.2	0.5	1.0	3.0	1.8	1.0	1.3
Offices of dentists	1.1	1.1	1.2	1.3	1.2	1.3	1.4	1.1
Other amusement, gambling, and recreation industries	0.8	0.7	0.7	1.0	7.1	1.4	1.0	1.2
Barber shops and beauty salons	1.0	1.0	0.8	1.1	0.9	0.9	1.0	1.1

Source: Author's calculations using data from the 2007 American Community Survey.

tend to be distributed in proportion to the population in a region—one does not see large concentrations of these service activities in one place. Hence their location quotients are uniformly low. For example, table 2.1 shows that the location quotients for grocery stores, dentists' offices, and barber shops and beauty salons are all close to 1, indicating that these services are not being traded across metropolitan areas.

But other services do not require face-to-face interaction, and many of these do appear to be traded within the United States. For example, in addition to its concentration in aircraft production, Seattle has a disproportionate share of US employment in software publishing, with a location quotient for that industry of about 6.9. Boston, Raleigh-Durham, and San Francisco also show large concentrations of software production activity. Again, this is not because people in Seattle or these other regions consume more software than do people in other parts of the country; rather, Microsoft and other software publishers based in Seattle and these other cities (the San Francisco metro area includes San Jose and Silicon Valley) produce software and then export it in exchange for other goods and services. Software is thus a service that is traded with other regions.[3] (Box 2.1 reports on one San Francisco–area company's success in exporting computer-assisted design software, and box 2.2 describes the international activities of several Bay Area architecture and urban planning firms.)

Nor is it just software and other information media (such as movies in Los Angeles) that are geographically concentrated. Table 2.1 reports several other examples, including internet service providers (concentrated in Seattle and San Francisco), scientific R&D services (Boston, Raleigh-Durham, and San Francisco), and travel arrangements and reservation services (Las Vegas, which, not surprisingly, also has a significant concentration of "other amusement, gambling, and other recreation activities"). Although not reported in the table, travel arrangements and reservation services, which are very similar in nature to call center operations, are also concentrated in some small cities in the upper Great Plains like Minot, North Dakota, and Aberdeen, South Dakota.

One can use the geographic concentration of production to distinguish between service activities that are tradable and those that require face-to-face interaction and are thus less likely to be traded. Again, the idea is that when something, whether a good or a service, is traded, its production can be concentrated in a particular region to take advantage of any economies in production. As a result, most regions will not support local production of the good or service, while one or a few will devote a disproportionate share of their

---

3. Software and other types of media "goods" have always been a bit in between categories. For example, book publishing used to be classified as a manufacturing industry, but with the introduction of the NAICS, it is now categorized in the information sector (NAICS 51), along with software publishing and other types of publishing (newspapers, greeting cards, databases). The reasoning is that the "information" content of a book (the service) is much more valuable than the physical medium (the paper and binding). A case could be made for placing books and various other "goods" in either the goods or the service category. This book takes the categorization as given and thus treats publishing activities as part of the service sector.

Box 2.1   Exporting by design: Autodesk taps the global market for CAD software

Autodesk, Inc. is a computer-assisted design (CAD) software firm based in San Rafael, California. The company is a leader in engineering software for the manufacturing, building, and construction industries and in entertainment software for the media and entertainment industries. The firm reports that "Fortune 100 companies—as well as the last 14 Academy Award winners for Best Visual Effects—use Autodesk software tools to design, visualize and simulate their ideas to save time and money, enhance quality, and foster innovation for competitive advantage."

Autodesk employs approximately 7,800 people worldwide and had revenue of $2.32 billion in 2009, according to its annual report, with sales outside of North America accounting for two-thirds of its revenue.

Examples of Autodesk's foreign projects include the following:

- Autodesk has combined its Buzzsaw project management suite with Japanese construction and civil engineering firm Maeda Corporation's Naoshiya Matabee facilities management service to manage and share project and facilities data—permits, schedules, estimates, budgets, inspection reports, construction and design documents—across Seven Eleven's network of 10,000 stores in Japan. Seven-Eleven has brought the two companies in to help implement its expansion into China.

- AREP, a French engineering design and architectural firm affiliated with SNCF, the French public railroad company, has used Buzzsaw to communicate, share documents, simultaneously review and modify plans, and otherwise collaborate with Chinese local design institutes over a secure, multilingual platform, on projects such as the Beijing Museum and the Shanghai Railway Station.

- The Chengdu Hydroelectric Investigation and Design Institute utilized Autodesk's Civil 3D mapping and design modeling program to visualize and analyze the terrain and rock structure of the steep mountain gorge along the Yalong River, in the construction of the Jinpin hydropower plant. The $2 billion phase one project includes a 3,600-megawatt power station and a 305-meter double-arched dam, the world's largest.

Source: Excerpted from Bay Area Council Economic Institute (2006, 84–85); Autodesk (2009).

Box 2.2   How US architecture and engineering firms are helping India plan for growth

San Francisco architecture/design firm Gensler decided in 2006 that it needed to be in India, as many US clients, such as Legg-Mason, UBS, and Goldman Sachs, had been expanding their presence there. Managing principal Daniel Winey says the firm first contacted Indian interior design and space planner Space Matrix, using them as architect-of-record in India. (Foreign architecture firms are required to work with Indian counterparts beyond the design drawing phase in a project; Indian firms typically take the completed design drawings and work with developers from that point on, preparing final construction drawings and assisting with permits as needed.)

Gensler is a participant—along with San Francisco landscape architects Hargreaves Associates, New Delhi–based Creative Group, and lead architectural firm Frederic Schwartz Architects of New York—in the expansion and modernization of the Chennai International Airport. The $300 million project's sustainable design will increase capacity and improve security and circulation through a wing-like design centered around two landscaped gardens. Terminal and garage roofs are designed to capture and store rainwater for airport use.

Winey says Gensler is also "short-listed" to design a 10 million-square foot mixed residential, office, and commercial project, to be developed by DLF Ltd., and is in project discussions with the Reliance Group and an India REIT managed by Warburg-Pincus. The firm is exploring several new projects this year with top-tier clients, though Winey adds that "a week doesn't go by when we don't get maybe ten requests for proposals in India.…"

Skidmore Owings & Merrill (SOM) partner Gene Schnair points to a satellite photo of the project site for a planned community, Pioneer Park, in Gurgaon. Much of the site is farmland that has to be acquired from individual small landholders in one-acre plots that had been given to them by the government years ago, and, despite official government support, there has been no eminent domain to help jump-start later stage negotiations or keep costs down. A road bisecting the site cannot be moved due to perpetual easement rights of a nearby village. While plans are on the drawing boards for a metro line, modern transit service does not yet extend from Delhi out to Pioneer Park, a 15-mile trip. Nor does utility service—the project will have its own dedicated water, sewage treatment, and electricity service.

Indian developer Pioneer Urban intends to build a new, sustainable urban community on the 75-acre site, including high-rise residential towers with 3, 4, and 5-bedroom condominiums, a hotel, a high-end shopping complex, and a 10-acre park with sports fields and clubhouse facilities. Designs call for an

(continued on next page)

Box 2.2   How US architecture and engineering firms are helping India plan for growth *(continued)*

ecological community incorporating co-generation and centralized utility services to reclaim energy; use of local materials in buildings and landscaping;
and structures ranging from 4 to 49 stories that induce cooling breezes and
provide shade to public spaces. It is SOM's first master planning project in India,
although the firm is well-established in India through its New York office.

Among the firm's other India projects are:

- a 75-acre special economic zone (SEZ) with a combined 8 million square
  feet of office and industrial space, built in conjunction with the 85-acre
  Maytas Hill County integrated township near Hyderabad;

- the Jet Airways headquarters building in Mumbai; and

- Unitech's Santa City project, for which SOM will design replacement housing for 22,000 slum dwellers (a task involving master planning, new housing prototypes, and a team of sociologists and anthropologists working
  with slum residents)….

Three Bay Area firms are among ten global architecture and design consultants hired by Unitech for its ambitious $3 billion, 347-acre Unitech Grande
project along the Western Expressway in Mumbai. HOK is designing the floor
plans, while San Francisco-based EDAW Inc. and Sausalito-based SWA Group
will serve as landscape architects. The project is to feature 12 residential towers,
with 100 acres of themed gardens, plus shopping, restaurants, theaters, and
recreational facilities.

HOK is also designing the residential and social amenities zone for a Mahindra Group new township project in New Chennai, Mahindra World City. The
50-acre project features 750 residential apartments along with retail and recreational facilities. A joint development of the Mahindra group and the Tamil
Nadu Industrial Development Corporation (TIDCO), it has three sector-specific
SEZs for information technology, auto ancillaries, and apparel and fashion ac-
cessories.

Finally, HOK is preparing the master plan for a 10,000-acre hill station—a
term from the British colonial era to describe the hill towns where colonial officials moved to escape the heat and humidity of the lowlands—Lavasa, located
between Pune and Mumbai. The new community will be roughly the size of
Paris and is the vision of Ajit Gulabchand, managing director of Indian engineering and construction firm HCC.

Source: Excerpted from Randolph and Erich (2009, 166–69).

productive activity to the good or service and then trade it.[4] This book uses the geographic concentration of a service within the United States as an indicator that the service is traded within the United States and thus potentially tradable internationally.

This intuition is conveyed more descriptively by Paul Krugman (1991, 65):

> In the late twentieth century the great bulk of our labor force makes services rather than goods. Many of these services are nontradable and simply follow the geographical distribution of the goods-producing population—fast-food outlets, day-care providers, divorce lawyers surely have locational Ginis pretty close to zero. Some services, however, especially in the financial sector, can be traded. Hartford is an insurance city; Chicago the center of futures trading; Los Angeles the entertainment capital; and so on.... The most spectacular examples of localization in today's world are, in fact, services rather than manufacturing.... Transportation of goods has not gotten much cheaper in the past eighty years.... But the ability to transmit *information* has grown spectacularly, with telecommunications, computers, fiber optics, etc.

The "locational Gini," or locational Gini coefficient, to which Krugman refers is another measure of geographic concentration. It is a way of summarizing the location quotients from many regions into one statistic that describes the distribution of location quotients across regions. The locational Gini ranges from zero to 1: the higher the Gini, the more concentrated the industry in one or a few locations.[5] The rest of this chapter extensively uses this measure.

Adjusting for Demand-Induced Concentration and Intermediate Services

First, however, I address one more technical issue. The measure of concentration just described does not distinguish among the many possible reasons an activity is concentrated. It does not tell us whether a given activity is concentrated because of the location of natural resources, or because of increasing returns to scale, or because of spillovers of technical know-how due to the presence of many workers in the same industry or occupation in close proximity. All the measures indicate is that much of the good or service is being produced in a location different from where most of it is consumed.

---

4. The relationship between the geographic concentration of production and trade, particularly exports, has a long tradition in both economic geography (where the measure used is the location quotient) and trade analysis (where the measure used is revealed comparative advantage). The measure of economic concentration used here is different from both these measures, but all the measures have a similar flavor in that they compare the share of production (or exports) in a particular region to an "expected" baseline.

5. Gini coefficients can be used to measure many other kinds of concentration or dispersion besides that by location—perhaps its most common use is in measuring the distribution of income.

In general, the reasons for the concentration do not matter for the purposes of this book. But in one instance the reason does matter. If *demand* for a service is concentrated because industries using that service as an input are concentrated, then that service industry may be geographically concentrated even if it is not tradable. If the concentration measure were used without taking this possibility into account, one might incorrectly infer that the service is tradable.

A paper that I cowrote with Lori Kletzer (Jensen and Kletzer 2006) shows how to correct for this possibility. If a nontradable industry provides intermediate inputs to a downstream industry, one will expect the geographical distribution of the nontraded intermediate industry to follow the distribution of the downstream industry. Instead of being distributed with income, the nontraded good or service will be distributed in proportion to the geographical distribution of demand for that industry. The implementation of this correction is described in appendix D.

Implementing the Method

In that same paper, Kletzer and I implemented our geographic concentration measures using employment information from the 2000 Decennial Census of Population Public Use Micro Sample (PUMS) files. We defined geographic areas using the Census-defined Metropolitan Statistical Areas (MSAs) and Consolidated Metropolitan Statistical Areas: A worker's MSA is the one where that worker reports himself or herself as working. We then constructed Gini coefficients of geographic concentration for each industry,[6] using the formula described in appendix D.

Our use of worker-level data to investigate economic concentration is somewhat unusual. We pursued this strategy because, as mentioned above, we are interested in both industrial concentration and occupational concentration.

Classifying Industries and Occupations by Tradability

Industries

Having constructed the locational Gini coefficient for each industry and occupation, we also had to specify the level of geographic concentration that indicates that an industry or occupation is tradable. In our 2006 paper, Kletzer and I first explored where to set the threshold for industries, because we have a much better sense of which industries, especially goods-producing industries, are tradable than of which occupations are tradable.

---

6. For regions we used the Place of Work Consolidated Metropolitan Area (POWCMA5) field on the decennial PUMS. When a POWCMA is coded as a nonmetropolitan area or as a mixed area, we concatenated the Place of Work state code with the POWCMA5 code. For more information on the 5 percent sample PUMS, see www.census.gov/Press-Release/www/2003/PUMS5.html.

We initially sorted industries into three roughly equal groups: those with a locational Gini coefficient of less than 0.1 (the least geographically concentrated, which we called class 1), those with Ginis between 0.1 and 0.3 (class 2), and those with Ginis of 0.3 or above (class 3, the most geographically concentrated). Approximately 36 percent of industries are in class 1, about 37 percent are in class 2, and 27 percent are in class 3.

Panel A of figure 2.1 plots the Gini coefficients from the Decennial Census data for all industries by their two-digit NAICS codes. The resulting pattern is generally consistent with our expectation that industries known to be tradable will be geographically concentrated. For example, industries in the goods-producing sectors (agriculture, mining, and manufacturing) are typically in the top two Gini classes. Only 5 of the 92 industries in these sectors are in class 1: cement and concrete, machine shops, miscellaneous manufacturing, structural metals and tanks, and printing and related activities. All of these industries seem to be nontraded either because of a high weight-to-value ratio (such as cement and concrete) or because they include a range of potentially dissimilar activities (miscellaneous manufacturing). Most agriculture, mining, and manufacturing products are considered tradable; so, as a first approximation, defining only the lowest geographic concentration category (class 1) as nontradable seems appropriate for these sectors.

Another check on the industry classification is to examine how the geographic concentration of manufacturing industries correlates with the level of trade intensity in those industries—that is, the degree to which trade actually occurs in them. In our paper, Kletzer and I calculated the mean industry trade share as follows:

trade share = (imports + exports)/domestic production.

The shares thus calculated were 0.40, 0.57, and 0.71 for classes 1, 2, and 3, respectively. (If manufacturing machinery not elsewhere classified is removed from class 1, on the grounds that it includes a broad range of unrelated activities, the mean trade share for that class falls to 0.35.) As expected, the mean trade share rises as one goes from Gini class 1 to Gini class 3. This evidence supports the idea that geographic concentration is a useful proxy for identifying activities that are tradable.

Although manufacturing industries tend to be more geographically concentrated than industries in the service sector, many service industries also exhibit levels of concentration consistent with their being traded within the United States. In addition, these same industries conform to expectations about which service activities might be tradable. For example, software publishing, sound recording, motion picture production, and securities and commodities trading all exhibit high geographic concentration. By contrast, retail banking and videotape rental exhibit low geographic concentration, again consistent with what one would expect.

Using a Gini coefficient of 0.1 as the threshold for tradability seems to make sense in other sectors as well. Industries in the retail trade sector

Figure 2.1 Geographic concentration of industries in the United States

a. Using worker-level data

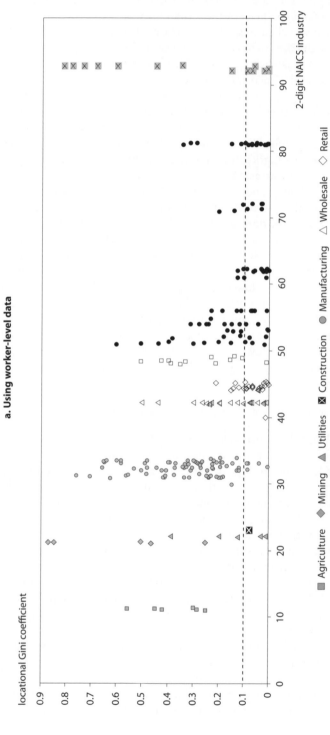

locational Gini coefficient

2-digit NAICS industry

■ Agriculture ◆ Mining △ Utilities ● Manufacturing ◯ Construction ◇ Retail
□ Transportation ● Services ▣ Public administration

NAICS = North American Industry Classification System

Source: Author's calculations using 2000 Decennial Census of Population.

b. Using establishment-level data

locational Gini coefficient

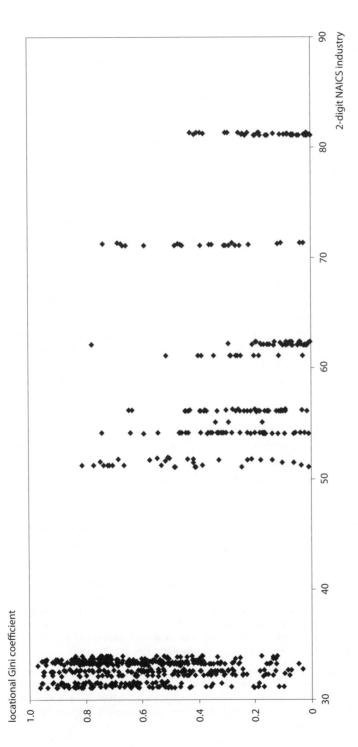

NAICS = North American Industry Classification System

Source: Author's calculations from 2002 Economic Census data.

(which includes grocers, clothing stores, and the like) are primarily classified as nontradable by this threshold. Industries in the transportation sector are mostly classified as tradable. Within public administration, most activities are nontradable except for public finance and the military. Within the service sector, industries are fairly evenly divided between nontradable and tradable. Table 2.2 provides a complete list of service industries by two-digit NAICS sector and Gini class.[7]

Table 2.3 shows the shares of employment classified in tradable industries by NAICS major group. Again the results across categories and industries conform to expectations. All employment in the agriculture and mining sectors, as well as most manufacturing employment, is classified as tradable. Utilities are mostly nontradable, and construction is entirely nontradable.

The evidence above suggests that a threshold of "tradability" of 0.1 in terms of the locational Gini coefficient is reasonable. Therefore, we categorized industries with a Gini below 0.1 as nontradable and those with a Gini greater than or equal to 0.1 as tradable.[8]

As an alternative to the worker-level data analyzed above, I also calculate locational Gini coefficients for manufacturing and service industries using employment information at the establishment level from the Census Bureau (specifically, from the Business Register, the Census of Manufactures, and the Census of Services, all from the 2002 vintage). These data have the advantage of having more-detailed industry classifications than those available for the worker-level data. These Gini coefficients use the labor market areas defined by the Bureau of Economic Analysis (BEA) as the unit of geography, instead of the Place of Work data reported in the Decennial Census used in the previous analysis. Each labor market area, of which there are 183 in all, consists of a metropolitan area and its surrounding counties. For this book I constructed Gini coefficients of the concentration of employment at the six-digit NAICS industry level. Panel B of figure 2.1 plots the resulting geographic concentration measures by two-digit NAICS industry. The main patterns are very similar to the Gini coefficients constructed using the worker-level data.

Although Gini coefficients for manufacturing industries tend to be higher than those for service industries, a number of service industries have relatively high Gini coefficients. These are evidence of significant geographic concentra-

---

7. Higher education may appear misclassified in table 2.2 as a nontradable service industry. US colleges and universities, particularly research institutions, do attract many foreign students and have acknowledged global comparative advantage. However, the sector also includes community colleges, which are, by design, geographically dispersed. Also, the types of specialized scientific occupations associated with research institutions (the ones most likely to "export" educational services) are geographically concentrated and thus considered tradable.

8. Although the choice of threshold for nontradable versus tradable is inherently arbitrary, we ran a number of robustness checks on the results reported in the paper (Jensen and Kletzer 2006) to see whether alternative choices made much of a difference in the results. With the exception of the share of employment in the tradable sector (which decreases as the threshold is increased), the results are robust to the choice of threshold.

Table 2.2   Locational Gini classes for individual service industries

Two-digit NAICS code	Industry	Locational Gini class (1 = least tradable)
	Information	
51	Newspaper publishers	1
51	Radio and television broadcasting and cable	1
51	Libraries and archives	1
51	Wired telecommunications carriers	2
51	Data processing services	2
51	Other telecommunication services	2
51	Publishing except newspapers and software	2
51	Other information services	3
51	Motion pictures and video industries	3
51	Sound recording industries	3
51	Software publishing	3
	Finance and insurance	
52	Savings institutions, including credit unions	1
52	Banking and related activities	1
52	Insurance carriers and related activities	2
52	Nondepository credit and related activities	2
52	Securities, commodities, funds, trusts, and other financial investments	3
	Real estate and rental	
53	Video tape and disk rental	1
53	Other consumer goods rental	1
53	Commercial, industrial, and other intangible assets rental and lease	2
53	Real estate	2
53	Automotive equipment rental and leasing	2
	Professional, scientific, and technical services	
54	Veterinary services	1
54	Accounting, tax preparation, bookkeeping, and payroll services	1
54	Architectural, engineering, and related services	2
54	Other professional, scientific, and technical services	2
54	Legal services	2
54	Specialized design services	2

(continued on next page)

Table 2.2 Locational Gini classes for individual service industries (continued)

Two-digit NAICS code	Industry	Locational Gini class (1 = least tradable)
Professional, scientific, and technical services (continued)		
54	Computer systems design and related services	2
54	Advertising and related services	2
54	Management, scientific, and technical consulting services	2
54	Scientific research and development services	3
Management		
55	Management of companies and enterprises	2
Administrative support		
56	Waste management and remediation services	1
56	Business support services	1
56	Services to buildings and dwellings	1
56	Landscaping services	1
56	Employment services	2
56	Other administrative and other support services	2
56	Investigation and security services	2
56	Travel arrangement and reservation services	2
Education		
61	Elementary and secondary schools	1
61	Colleges and universities, including junior colleges	1
61	Other schools, instruction, and educational services	1
61	Business, technical, and trade schools and training	2
Health care and social services		
62	Hospitals	1
62	Nursing care facilities	1
62	Vocational rehabilitation services	1
62	Offices of physicians	1
62	Outpatient care centers	1
62	Offices of dentists	1
62	Offices of optometrists	1
62	Residential care facilities, without nursing	1
62	Child day care services	1
62	Home health care services	1
62	Other health care services	1
62	Office of chiropractors	1

(continued on next page)

Table 2.2 Locational Gini classes for individual service industries *(continued)*

Two-digit NAICS code	Industry	Locational Gini class (1 = least tradable)
Health care and social services *(continued)*		
62	Individual and family services	1
62	Community food and housing, and emergency services	2
62	Offices of other health practitioners	2
Arts, entertainment, and recreation		
71	Bowling centers	1
71	Other amusement, gambling, and recreation industries	1
71	Museums, art galleries, historical sites, and similar institutions	2
71	Independent artists, performing arts, spectator sports, and related	2
Accommodation		
72	Drinking places, alcoholic beverages	1
72	Restaurants and other food services	1
72	Recreational vehicle parks and camps, and rooming and boarding houses	1
72	Traveler accommodation	2
Other services		
81	Beauty salons	1
81	Funeral homes, cemeteries, and crematories	1
81	Personal and household goods repair and maintenance	1
81	Automotive repair and maintenance	1
81	Barber shops	1
81	Religious organizations	1
81	Commercial and industrial machinery and equipment repair and maintenance	1
81	Drycleaning and laundry services	1
81	Car washes	1
81	Electronic and precision equipment repair and maintenance	1
81	Civic, social, advocacy organizations, and grantmaking and giving	1
81	Nail salons and other personal care services	2
81	Other personal services	2
81	Business, professional, political, and similar organizations	2

(continued on next page)

Table 2.2   Locational Gini classes for individual service industries
(continued)

Two-digit NAICS code	Industry	Locational Gini class (1 = least tradable)
	Other services *(continued)*	
81	Labor unions	3
81	Footwear and leather goods repair	3
	Public administration	
92	Justice, public order, and safety activities	1
92	Administration of human resource programs	1
92	Other general government and support	1
92	Executive offices and legislative bodies	1
92	Military Reserves or National Guard	1
92	Administration of economic programs and space research	1
92	Administration of environmental quality and housing programs	1
92	Public finance activities	2
92	National security and international affairs	3
92	US Armed Forces, branch not specified	3
92	US Coast Guard	3
92	US Air Force	3
92	US Army	3
92	US Navy	3
92	US Marines	3

NAICS = North American Industry Classification System

Source: Jensen and Kletzer (2006).

tion of employment, sufficient to suggest that these services are traded within the United States. In addition, the industries within both services and manufacturing that have high Ginis conform to expectations about which service activities are likely to be tradable and which manufacturing industries are less likely to be tradable, again because they have high ratios of trade costs to value. For example, the five manufacturing industries with the lowest Ginis are "other" concrete product manufacturing, fabricated structural metal manufacturing, concrete block and brick manufacturing, wood container and pallet manufacturing, and ready-mix concrete manufacturing. All of these are characterized by low value-to-weight ratios and thus are less likely to be traded.

Within the information sector, the industries with the lowest Ginis are newspaper publishers, motion picture theaters except drive-ins, television broadcasting, radio stations, and wired telecommunication carriers. These all tend to rely heavily on local inputs or require a physical presence to provide the service. The information industries with the highest Ginis are record produc-

Table 2.3   Employment in NAICS sectors by degree of tradability
(percent)

NAICS code	Sector	Locational Gini class (1 = least tradable)		
		1	2	3
11	Agriculture	0	88	12.1
21	Mining	0	24.2	75.8
22	Utilities	80.9	15.3	3.8
23	Construction	100	0	0
31	Manufacturing	0	40.4	59.6
32	Manufacturing	22	44.9	33.1
33	Manufacturing	14.4	65.4	20.2
3M	Manufacturing	0	100	0
42	Wholesale trade	45.8	50.6	3.6
44	Retail trade	81.7	18.3	0
45	Retail trade	88.7	11.4	0
4M	Retail trade	100	0	0
48	Transportation and warehousing	42.8	22	35.2
49	Transportation and warehousing	0	100	0
51	Information	33.3	50.4	16.4
52	Finance and insurance	32.1	51	17
53	Real estate and rental and leasing	9.1	90.9	0
54	Professional, scientific, and technical services	14	79.9	6.2
55	Management of companies and enterprises	0	100	0
56	Administrative support and waste management and remediation	59.5	40.5	0
61	Education	99	1.1	0
62	Health care and social assistance	97.8	2.2	0
71	Arts, entertainment, and recreation	67.4	32.7	0
72	Accommodation and food services	81.9	18.1	0
81	Other services (except public administration)	79.8	9.9	10.4
92	Public administration	71.7	4.6	23.7
	All industries	60.8	29.8	9.4

NAICS = North American Industry Classification System; M = miscellaneous

Source: Jensen and Kletzer (2006).

Table 2.4 Correlations between geographic concentration and export measures for manufacturing and business services

Sector	Number of industries	Correlation between locational Gini coefficient and	
		Exports-to-sales ratio	Share of establishments that export
Manufacturing	473	0.255	0.440
Business services	125	0.436	0.523

Note: All correlations are statistically significant at p < 0.0001.

Source: Author's calculations using data from the 2002 Census of Manufactures and the 2002 Census of Service Industries.

tion, music publishers, cable and other subscription programming, integrated record production and distribution, and "other motion picture and video industries."

Within professional, scientific, and technical services, some of the low-Gini industries are portrait photography studios and veterinary services. High-Gini industries in this group include payroll services and R&D in the social sciences and humanities. These results are also consistent with our expectations about the ability to provide these services over distances. Industries within the educational, health service, and "other services (except public administration)" sectors tend to have low Gini coefficients, suggesting low tradability.

As another check on the usefulness of geographic concentration in identifying tradable activities, table 2.4 reports, for 473 six-digit NAICS manufacturing industries, the correlations between the locational Gini coefficient and the exports-to-sales ratio and between the Gini and the share of establishments that export. The correlations are strong, providing further evidence that geographic concentration is a useful proxy for tradability.

For a subset of business service industries, those in NAICS sectors 51, 54, and 56, similar export information is available. Table 2.3 reports the same correlations for these industries as for the manufacturing industries above. Again the correlations are very strong.

Again, these results suggest that a number of service industries are tradable within the United States. For at least some of these, international trade seems technologically feasible.

Occupations

So far I have been seeking to identify service industries that are potentially tradable. I am also interested in identifying tradable occupations within service industries because, at least according to anecdotal reports in the press, some inputs into service production might be tradable even though the service industry to which those inputs contribute is not. For example, retail banking is classified as a nontradable industry because it has low geographic concentration. Yet one might think of some of the activities at a typical retail bank—especially back-office operations like accounting but also customer support—as at least potentially tradable. Thus, looking at occupations as well as industries yields a different perspective on economic activity and tradability—another piece of the mosaic.

To classify occupations into tradable and nontradable categories, Kletzer and I (2006) used a methodology similar to that for industries. We constructed a demand-weighted Gini coefficient for each occupation as described in appendix D and used the same threshold (a Gini of 0.1) to distinguish between tradable and nontradable occupations. Figure 2.2 shows the results by major occupational group. Examples of occupations that are highly geographically concentrated include marine engineers and naval architects, actors, economists, actuaries, brokerage clerks, medical scientists, and financial analysts. Occupations with low geographic concentration include retail salespeople, dental hygienists, secondary school teachers, bartenders, child care workers, and pharmacists.

Table 2.5 reports the share of employment in each two-digit Standard Occupational Classification (SOC) group by Gini class. Once again the groupings are largely consistent with expectations. For example, 68 percent of employment in business and financial operations is in detailed occupation categories classified as tradable (66 percent in Gini class 2 and 2 percent in Gini class 3). Computer and mathematical occupations are all classified as tradable. The architecture and engineering category has 64 percent of its employment in tradable occupations. Almost all employment—96 percent—in legal occupations is classified as tradable.

Notable occupational groups that are nontradable include education and library occupations, where 99 percent of employment is in occupations classified as nontradable; health care practitioners, where 87 percent of employment is so classified; health care support, 97 percent nontradable; and food preparation and serving, 96 percent nontradable. Among blue-collar occupations, 90 percent of employment in installation, maintenance, and repair occupations is classified as nontradable, as is 80 percent of employment in production occupations and 89 percent in transportation and material moving occupations. The result for production occupations may at first seem counterintuitive, given the manufacturing industry results. However, production occupations are typically not industry specific but instead are functional activities and are thus distributed more broadly. For example, production occupations include occupations like "extruding and drawing machine setters, operators, and tenders, metal and plastic" or "cutting, punching, and press machine setters, operators, and tenders, metal and plastic" and "tool and die makers"—all of which could be found in a number of manufacturing industries. Thus, even though the aircraft industry or the automobile industry might be concentrated in a particular region, the production occupations of many of their workers are not, because many other manufacturing industries also employ workers in these occupations. This shows why it is important to look at tradability from both an industry perspective and an occupation perspective.

Figure 2.2   Geographic concentration of occupations in the United States

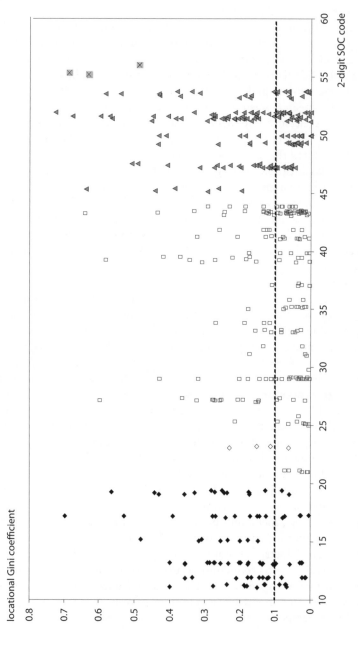

locational Gini coefficient

2-digit SOC code

◆ High-end services   □ Other services   ◇ Legal   ◀ Production related   ⊠ Military specific

SOC = Standard Occupational Classification

Note: "Other services" includes SOC major categories 21 and 25–43 (see appendix C for a list of major categories).

Source: Author's calculations using 2000 Decennial Census of Population.

Table 2.5   Employment in SOC occupations by degree of tradability
(percent)

SOC code	Occupation	Locational Gini class (1 = least tradable)		
		1	2	3
11	Management	34.5	61.2	4.4
13	Business and financial operations	31.7	66	2.3
15	Computer and mathematical	0	73.1	26.9
17	Architecture and engineering	36	58.3	5.7
19	Life, physical, and social sciences	16.3	58.6	25.1
21	Community and social services	100	0	0
23	Legal	3.8	96.2	0
25	Education and library	99.5	0.5	0
27	Arts, design, and entertainment	17.1	75	7.9
29	Health care practitioners and technologists	86.6	13.1	0.3
31	Health care support	96.7	3.3	0
33	Protective service	59.8	40.2	0
35	Food preparation and serving	95.7	4.3	0
37	Building maintenance	98.5	1.5	0
39	Personal care services	82.6	7.2	10.1
41	Sales and related	75.4	21.8	2.8
43	Office and administrative support	93.1	6.7	0.2
45	Farming, fishing, and forestry	0	81	19
47	Construction and extraction	61.4	36.2	2.5
49	Installation, maintenance, and repair	90	8.9	1.1
51	Production	80.3	17.2	2.6
53	Transportation and material moving	89.2	5.9	5
55	Military specific	0	0	100
	All occupations	71.7	24.9	3.5

SOC = Standard Occupational Classification

Source: Jensen and Kletzer (2006).

Summary

This chapter began by bemoaning the fact that data for service trade are nowhere as detailed as for the manufacturing sector. The rest of the chapter has shown, however, that this obstacle need not be insurmountable. The chapter presented a methodology for identifying, at a detailed level, industries and occupations whose outputs appear to be traded within the United States and thus, at least in principle, are tradable internationally. The intuition behind this methodology relies on a long-standing measurement tradition in economic geography and produces results very much in line with what one would expect given the nature of the different service activities examined. In addition, to the extent possible with existing data, the chapter reported results of validity checks on the relationship between geographic concentration and trade, which further suggest that the method is useful. Chapter 3 examines the next piece of the mosaic on trade in services, exploring the characteristics of workers in tradable activities.

3

Characteristics of Workers in Tradable Service Industries

The previous chapter described a methodology for overcoming the paucity of data on trade in services so as to identify, at a detailed level for both industries and occupations, which activities appear to be traded within the United States. The industries and occupations thus identified are, at least in principle, tradable internationally.

The ability to identify which service activities are tradable and which are not is important because it allows a better understanding of which services are likely to be traded, which services the United States is likely to import and which it is likely to export, and what the implications of increased trade in services are likely to be. Having more resolution on the types of activities that can be provided at a distance is necessary for determining the size and scope of tradable services.

The ability to identify the number of workers in tradable activities is also important to the evolving mosaic of trade in services. Tradable activities (both industries and occupations, across all sectors) employ approximately half of the US workforce. Tradable services account for a significant share of these workers. In fact, the number of workers in tradable business services alone exceeds that in the entire manufacturing sector. Clearly, what happens with trade in services could have very broad implications for the economy as a whole.

Given the large number of workers in tradable activities and the broad range of those activities, generalizations about how workers in tradable activities differ from workers in nontradable activities are hard to come by. Yet understanding these differences is another important piece of the mosaic.

This chapter explores these differences in worker characteristics across a number of different dimensions to gain insight into whether tradable activities are significantly different from nontradable activities and, if they are, how the differences might affect US firms and workers as trade in services increases. Using the detailed classifications of tradable and nontradable activities developed in the previous chapter, this chapter presents information on the educational attainment and earnings of workers in tradable activities across a range of sectors.

The bottom line is this: Workers in tradable activities are indeed different from workers in nontradable activities, and the differences are striking. Workers in tradable service activities are, on average, more educated (and apparently more skilled) than those in nontradable activities. The share of workers with a college degree in tradable services is double that in nontradable services (and double that in manufacturing); the share of tradable service workers with advanced degrees is also double that in these other sectors. Moreover, workers in tradable activities have significantly (more than 30 percent) higher earnings, on average, than workers in nontradable activities. This qualitative finding holds not only in the aggregate but also across similar industries within the same sector and across detailed occupations within major occupational groups, although the exact numbers differ. The earnings differences persist even after controlling for detailed worker characteristics that typically explain such differences. These differences have important implications for whether increased trade in services will have an adverse impact on the US economy or on US workers—a topic taken up in the next chapter.

How Many Workers Are Employed in Tradable Services?

Using the methodology described in the previous chapter, Lori Kletzer and I (Jensen and Kletzer 2006) identified industries and occupations that exhibit a level of geographic concentration in excess of demand that suggests that these activities are traded within the United States. These activities span the economy and include many within both manufacturing and services. Table 3.1 reports the shares of total employment in tradable and nontradable industries in each major sector and shows that a large share—almost 40 percent—of US employment is in industries classified as tradable.

Chapter 1 discussed how services have been traditionally characterized as nontradable. Yet, box 3.1 provides a profile of a California-based advertising firm that is providing marketing services to companies based on both sides of the Pacific. Dae Advertising may seem like a niche player. Is it therefore the exception that proves the rule that tradable services are rare? No, the data show quite the contrary. Table 3.1 shows that, in contrast to traditional characterizations of services as predominantly nontradable, a significant share of total employment is in tradable service industries. For example, more workers are in tradable industries in the business service sector alone (14 percent of all workers) than in tradable manufacturing industries (10 percent). True, some large service subsectors (such as education, health care, personal services, and public administration) have low shares of employment in tradable industries. However, because the service sector is much larger than the manufacturing

Table 3.1   Shares of US employment in nontradable and tradable industries by sector (percent)

NAICS code	Sector	Share of economywide employment	
		Nontradable industries	Tradable industries
11	Agriculture, forestry, fishing, and hunting	0	1
21	Mining, quarrying, and oil and gas extraction	0	0
22	Utilities	1	0
23	Construction	8	0
31–33	Manufacturing	2	10
42	Wholesale trade	2	2
44–45	Retail trade	9	2
48–49	Transportation and warehousing	1	3
50–56	Business services	6	14
61–81	Personal services	31	3
92	Public administration	4	2
	Total	64	37

NAICS = North American Industry Classification System

Source: Author's calculations using data from the 2007 American Community Survey.

sector, the number of workers potentially exposed to international trade in services is actually larger than the number of workers exposed in manufacturing.

The significant share of workers in tradable service industries is only part of the story, however. As discussed in chapter 2, it is not only whether a worker's industry is tradable that matters, but also whether that worker's occupation is tradable. A service worker can face potential competition from service imports if his or her industry *or* occupation is tradable. Thus, to get a more complete sense of how many workers are likely to face competition from trade in services, one needs to examine workers in tradable occupations as well.

Table 3.2 shows that, for the economy as a whole, only about 12 percent of all US workers are in occupations classified as tradable but in industries classified as nontradable. To the extent that firms can disentangle intermediate service inputs from the rest of their business, workers in these tradable occupations are vulnerable to trade, even though their industry is not tradable. Thus, the industry results above on the share of workers potentially vulnerable to trade are understated. What these numbers imply is that close to half of all workers in the United States are potentially exposed to international trade either through their industry or through their occupation, or both. These workers include not only the manufacturing workers traditionally thought of as exposed to trade, but also a large number of service workers.

Box 3.1   How one US advertising firm sells brand recognition to would-be Chinese exporters

San Francisco-based Dae Advertising was formed in 1990 by a group of friends to serve what 1990 US Census Bureau figures revealed to be a burgeoning Asian-American consumer market defined by relatively high disposable incomes, education and consumer expenditures. Dae worked with clients ranging from Miller Brewing to Wells Fargo Bank to Albertson's, tailoring campaigns to Asian-American tastes, aesthetics and aspirations.

Dae cofounder Wei-Tai Kwok notes that more than a third of the 12.5 million Asian-Americans in the United States are in California. Roughly 22 percent of the Bay Area's population is of Asia-Pacific origin, and about 8 percent are ethnic Chinese, according to US Census Bureau 2005 data. That, he says, has led to a cross-cultural understanding here that aids businesses in tapping markets on either side of the Pacific.

Dae's first major Chinese client was 999 Pharmaceutical, a maker of powdered ginseng, echinacea and other herbal medicines owned by the People's Liberation Army. 999 hoped to establish a retail brand presence in the United States in 1996, and Kwok bought space on a huge billboard in Times Square promoting the company. Eventually 999 became a listed company and a supplier to health food store chains and pharmacies, and the sign remained prominent in Times Square for several years.

Dae also helped Hong Kong-based Vitasoy market its soy milk products in the United States by first selling to an Asian-American customer base. Kwok sees opportunity in large Chinese manufacturers trying to build global brand identity in the United States, as Lenovo has done by purchasing the PC unit of IBM and as appliance-maker Haier attempted in its bid to acquire Whirlpool. Another such company in Dae's sights, Konka, is among the largest television manufacturers in the world and a supplier to Sharp, Toshiba and other brands, but remains unknown outside China. It is not lost on these firms that most of the end user value is not in the physical production of their goods but in design, marketing, advertising and branding. It is inevitable, Kwok believes, that those firms will be looking to go beyond a supplier role and raise their profiles globally.

Source: Excerpted from Bay Area Council Economic Institute (2006).

Further, table 3.2 shows, for many business and professional occupations, the share of workers in tradable occupations but nontradable industries is much larger than the economywide share of such workers. For example, 28 percent of employment in business and financial operations occupations,

Table 3.2   Shares of US employment in tradable occupations and industries (percent)

Category	Nontradable occupations	Tradable occupations
All occupations		
Nontradable industries	51.4	11.7
Tradable industries	19.6	17.3
Management occupations (SOC group 11)		
Nontradable industries	24	28.7
Tradable industries	8.6	38.7
Business and financial operations occupations (SOC group 13)		
Nontradable industries	13.3	28.1
Tradable industries	17.5	41.1
Computer and mathematical occupations (SOC group 15)		
Nontradable industries	0	28.9
Tradable industries	0	71.1
Architecture and engineering occupations (SOC group 17)		
Nontradable industries	7.9	12.3
Tradable industries	27.1	52.6
Life, physical, and social sciences occupations (SOC group 19)		
Nontradable industries	7.7	32.8
Tradable industries	9.3	50.3
Legal occupations (SOC group 23)		
Nontradable industries	0	22.7
Tradable industries	0	77.3

SOC = Standard Occupational Classification

Source: Author's calculations using data from the 2007 American Community Survey.

and 29 percent of employment in computer and mathematical occupations, are in tradable occupations but nontradable industries. These tradable occupations that support nontradable industries increase the share of workers involved in tradable service activities—making tradable services potentially even more important.

Characteristics of Workers in Tradable Industries and Tradable Occupations

I now turn to fleshing out the picture of workers in tradable activities, by examining the characteristics of these workers in some detail and comparing them with workers in nontradable activities. I start at the most aggregated level, first comparing tradable and nontradable industries and then comparing tradable and nontradable occupations. The top panel of table 3.3 reports the total number of workers in tradable and nontradable industries in all sectors and the educational characteristics and average earnings of each group. Workers in tradable industries are more likely to have a college degree, 34 percent compared with 28 percent. The share of workers with advanced degrees, however, is the same for both groups. Consistent with this higher average educational attainment in tradable industries, workers in those industries have significantly (almost 40 percent) higher earnings than their counterparts in nontradable industries.

The top panel of table 3.4 reports similar aggregate information for workers in tradable and nontradable occupations. Again the workers in tradable activities have different characteristics: They are almost twice as likely to have a college degree and twice as likely to have an advanced degree. And again, given these large differences in educational attainment, it is not surprising that workers in tradable occupations have higher earnings. What is surprising is the size of the earnings differential. Workers in tradable occupations earn 88 percent more, on average, than workers in nontradable occupations.

This broad-brush evidence suggests that workers in tradable activities, whether tradable industries or tradable occupations, differ in important ways from workers in nontradable activities. They are more educated and earn higher wages. However, because these categories are so broad and encompass such a wide range of activities, it is possible that these findings do not hold for a broad range of industries and occupations, but instead result from some very large differences in a small number of industries or occupations.

In this context, it is interesting that the share of workers in tradable occupations is higher in tradable industries than the comparable share in nontradable industries (table 3.3) and that the share of workers in tradable industries is higher in tradable occupations than the share in nontradable occupations (table 3.4). Given the overlap of workers in tradable industries and tradable occupations, it is possible that a few industry-occupation groups could be so different from the rest that they are driving the aggregate results for both occupations and industries. It will be interesting to see whether the earnings premiums observed for workers in tradable activities are also found across more detailed groupings.

Table 3.3   Characteristics of US workers in tradable and nontradable industries (percent except where stated otherwise)

Sector and characteristics	Nontradable industries	Tradable industries
All sectors		
Number of workers (thousands)	83,174	48,600
Average annual earnings (dollars)	38,270	53,230
Share with bachelor's degree	28	34
Share with advanced degree	11	11
Share in tradable occupations	19	47
Manufacturing (NAICS 30s)		
Number of workers (thousands)	2,235	12,994
Average annual earnings (dollars)	44,014	49,952
Share with bachelor's degree	16	24
Share with advanced degree	3	7
Share in tradable occupations	26	34
Business services (NAICS 50s)		
Number of workers (thousands)	8,038	18,430
Average annual earnings (dollars)	42,226	66,454
Share with bachelor's degree	29	50
Share with advanced degree	7	17
Share in tradable occupations	31	60
Information (NAICS 51)		
Average annual earnings (dollars)	46,963	62,346
Share with bachelor's degree	43	44
Share with advanced degree	11	12
Share in tradable occupations	36	56
Finance and insurance (NAICS 52)		
Average annual earnings (dollars)	53,356	74,370
Share with bachelor's degree	38	50
Share with advanced degree	8	12
Share in tradable occupations	43	48
Real estate (NAICS 53)		
Average annual earnings (dollars)	26,565	53,777
Share with bachelor's degree	16	34
Share with advanced degree	2	8
Share in tradable occupations	15	62

(continued on next page)

Table 3.3   Characteristics of US workers in tradable and nontradable industries (percent except where stated otherwise) *(continued)*

Sector and characteristics	Nontradable industries	Tradable industries
Professional, scientific, and technical (NAICS 54)		
Average annual earnings (dollars)	56,235	74,824
Share with bachelor's degree	54	64
Share with advanced degree	18	27
Share in tradable occupations	47	71
Management (NAICS 55)		
Average annual earnings (dollars)	n.a.	77,909
Share with bachelor's degree	n.a.	52
Share with advanced degree	n.a.	16
Share in tradable occupations	n.a.	56
Administrative support and waste remediation (NAICS 56)		
Average annual earnings (dollars)	29,132	37,515
Share with bachelor's degree	12	26
Share with advanced degree	2	6
Share in tradable occupations	16	50

n.a. = not applicable
NAICS = North American Industry Classification System
Source: Author's calculations using data from the 2007 American Community Survey.

Characteristics of Industry-Occupation Combinations

Because workers in official surveys (such as the American Community Survey) report both the industry in which they work and their occupation, one can classify workers according to the tradability of both their occupation and their industry. One can compare workers in nontradable industries and nontradable occupations with workers in tradable industries and tradable occupations and with workers in the other two combinations as well.

Table 3.5 reports the share of employment, the share of workers with a college degree, the share of workers with an advanced degree, and average earnings for each of these four groups of workers: those in nontradable industries and nontradable occupations, those in nontradable occupations and tradable industries, those in tradable occupations and nontradable industries, and those in tradable occupations and tradable industries. The results are interesting because they demonstrate that workers in the different occupation-industry combinations have different earnings and educational profiles, and

Table 3.4   Characteristics of US workers in tradable and nontradable occupations (percent except where stated otherwise)

Occupation category and characteristics	Nontradable occupations	Tradable occupations
All occupations		
Number of workers (thousands)	93,564	38,210
Average annual earnings (dollars)	34,920	65,500
Share with bachelor's degree	24	47
Share with advanced degree	8	17
Share in tradable industries	28	60
Management (SOC 11)		
Average annual earnings (dollars)	63,690	87,392
Share with bachelor's degree	51	52
Share with advanced degree	22	17
Share in tradable industries	26	57
Business and financial operations (SOC 13)		
Average annual earnings (dollars)	56,994	69,227
Share with bachelor's degree	49	67
Share with advanced degree	12	19
Share in tradable industries	57	59
Computer and mathematical (SOC 15)		
Average annual earnings (dollars)	n.a.	69,095
Share with bachelor's degree	n.a.	64
Share with advanced degree	n.a.	20
Share in tradable industries	n.a.	71
Architecture and engineering (SOC 17)		
Average annual earnings (dollars)	50,420	80,595
Share with bachelor's degree	30	81
Share with advanced degree	6	28
Share in tradable industries	77	81
Life, physical, and social sciences (SOC 19)		
Average annual earnings (dollars)	36,281	67,274
Share with bachelor's degree	40	86
Share with advanced degree	12	54
Share in tradable industries	55	61

(continued on next page)

Table 3.4   Characteristics of US workers in tradable and nontradable occupations (percent except where stated otherwise) *(continued)*

Occupation category and characteristics	Nontradable occupations	Tradable occupations
Legal (SOC 23)		
Average annual earnings (dollars)	n.a.	102,397
Share with bachelor's degree	n.a.	77
Share with advanced degree	n.a.	63
Share in tradable industries	n.a.	77
Health care practitioners (SOC 29)		
Average annual earnings (dollars)	52,355	170,442
Share with bachelor's degree	49	98
Share with advanced degree	18	95
Share in tradable industries	5	5
Health care support (SOC 31)		
Average annual earnings (dollars)	22,413	23,906
Share with bachelor's degree	9	29
Share with advanced degree	2	8
Share in tradable industries	3	65
Production (SOC 51)		
Average annual earnings (dollars)	33,765	31,687
Share with bachelor's degree	7	6
Share with advanced degree	1	1
Share in tradable industries	68	76

n.a. = not applicable
SOC = Standard Occupational Classification

Source: Author's calculations using data from the 2007 American Community Survey.

in particular that one group of workers—those in tradable industries *and* tradable occupations—is different from the other three.

As the table shows, average earnings are highest for workers in this last group. The next highest earnings are for workers in tradable occupations and nontradable industries. Not surprisingly, these two categories also have the highest shares of college-educated workers and the highest shares of advanced degrees.

What is surprising is that workers in nontradable industries and nontradable occupations have higher average educational attainment, but lower average earnings, than workers in tradable industries but nontradable occupations. Among the first group of workers, the share with a college degree is 25 percent, compared with 19 percent in the second. Yet average earnings for the second group are almost 20 percent higher than for the first.

Table 3.5 Characteristics of US workers by industry-occupation group
(percent except where stated otherwise)

Worker group	Share of total employment	Share with bachelor's degree	Share with advanced degree	Average annual earnings (dollars)
Nontradable occupation, nontradable industry	51	25	9	33,342
Nontradable occupation, tradable industry	20	19	4	39,062
Tradable occupation, nontradable industry	12	41	16	59,916
Tradable occupation, tradable industry	17	51	18	69,279

Source: Author's calculations using data from the 2007 American Community Survey.

This difference is likely due to the fact that many workers in nontradable occupations within tradable industries are manufacturing workers. The kinds of occupations that production workers in the manufacturing sector perform are generally classified as nontradable, even though most manufacturing industries are classified as tradable. Of the 8.8 million US workers in these production occupations, 83 percent are in nontradable occupations—only 1.5 million workers in production occupations are in occupations classified as tradable. Further, a relatively small share of manufacturing sector employment (about one-third) is classified as employed in tradable occupations, even though over 80 percent of manufacturing workers are classified as being in a tradable industry.

This makes sense. Production workers need to be present along with other inputs—capital and materials—to make whatever it is they are producing. Yet because the products themselves are tradable, even if the occupation is not, production workers are vulnerable to offshoring. This underscores the point that it is insufficient to look at the characteristics of an industry or occupation alone; it is the combination of the tradability of the industry and the tradability of the occupation that more accurately describes how tradable an activity is. The fact that many production occupations are nontradable, yet many manufacturing sector workers feel exposed to competition from international trade, highlights the point that if *either* a worker's industry or the worker's occupation is tradable, the activity is potentially affected by international trade.

To further explore the differences between workers in the manufacturing sector and workers in tradable services, the second and third panels of table 3.3 break out the manufacturing sector (NAICS 30s) and the business service sector (NAICS 50s) separately and report worker characteristics for each. The table shows that only 34 percent of workers in tradable manufacturing industries are in tradable occupations—this even though 85 percent of manufacturing workers are in tradable industries. The table also confirms the notion that manufacturing workers have relatively high earnings: The average worker in a tradable manufacturing industry earns about $50,000 per year.

Yet manufacturing jobs are not the only "good jobs with good wages." Workers in tradable service jobs also have very high average earnings. In fact, the average worker in a tradable business service industry earns more than $66,000 per year—fully a third more than the average worker in a tradable manufacturing industry. And this large earnings premium is not attributable to a small, select group of business service industries being classified as tradable. Over 18 million workers are in such industries—over 40 percent more than in the entire manufacturing sector.

A large contributor to the earnings differentials between manufacturing and business services is undoubtedly the significant differences in their average level of education: As noted previously, the shares of workers in tradable business service industries with bachelor's and advanced degrees are double those in tradable manufacturing industries. (As an aside, it is interesting that workers in nontradable business services also have significantly more education than their counterparts in nontradable manufacturing.)

The results in table 3.3 turn conventional wisdom on its head. The tradable business service sector is much larger than the tradable manufacturing sector, and its workers earn significantly higher wages than workers in the tradable manufacturing sector. Tradable business service industries thus offer "good jobs at good wages." The sector is important and should receive more attention.

Detailed Industry and Occupation Profiles

The business service sector is large and made up of diverse industries. Thus, it is still possible that a few industries are accounting for the large earnings and education differentials between tradable and nontradable services (and between tradable services and manufacturing). To further explore the robustness of the relationship between tradable activities and educational attainment and earnings, I examine worker demographic characteristics by two-digit NAICS sector and major occupational category.

Table 3.3 reports the characteristics of workers in tradable and nontradable industries within each two-digit NAICS business service sector, and figure 3.1 shows the differences in earnings within each sector. (The figure also presents results for the manufacturing sector as a benchmark, representing the earnings typically associated with trade-affected workers.) Workers in tradable service industries in each of the two-digit business service sectors (with one exception: administrative support and waste remediation, NAICS 56) are, on average, more highly paid and more educated than workers in tradable manufacturing industries. Within business services, the most striking result is the difference in annual earnings between tradable and nontradable industries: Across all major groups in the business service sector, workers in tradable

Figure 3.1 Average annual earnings in tradable and nontradable industries in US manufacturing and business services

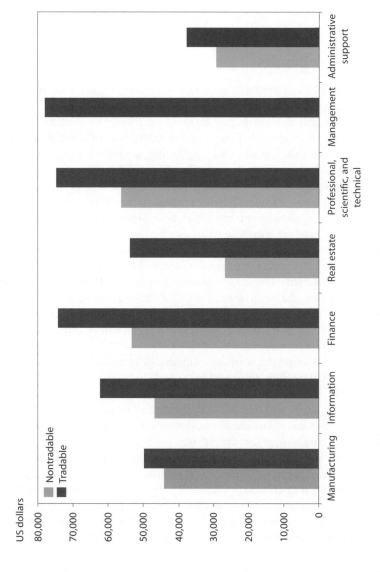

Source: Author's calculations using data from the 2007 American Community Survey.

industries earn appreciably higher wages. Workers in tradable industries also tend to have higher educational attainment.

The story is very similar for service-oriented occupational categories. Figure 3.2 presents average earnings information for selected major occupational categories within services. As in the case of industries, the tradable occupations all have higher earnings than closely related nontradable occupations. Table 3.4 reports educational attainment for the same set of occupations.

The results presented in this section suggest that workers in tradable and nontradable activities differ across a broad range of industries and occupations. Even when related activities are compared (industries within a sector, or detailed occupations within a major occupation group), workers in tradable activities are, on average, significantly better educated and have significantly higher earnings.

Regression Results

Because workers in tradable activities have both higher educational attainment and higher earnings, on average, than workers in nontradable activities, it is possible that the higher earnings are merely a reflection of the higher educational attainment, rather than a characteristic of tradable activities per se. To explore this further, this concluding section of the chapter presents regression-based evidence on earnings differences across tradable industries and occupations for the whole economy and for select groups of industries and occupations. Essentially, the regression analysis controls statistically for educational attainment and other possibly confounding variables in the data. The procedure thus allows an estimation of how much more or less a worker with a given set of these characteristics, working in a tradable activity, would earn than another worker with identical characteristics but working in a nontradable activity These regressions estimate the effect of worker, industry, and occupation characteristics on worker earnings using data from the 2007 American Community Survey. The focus of the analysis is to determine whether workers in tradable activities earn significantly different wages from similar workers in nontradable activities.

Figure 3.3 shows the resulting estimated differences in earnings. It compares the earnings of workers employed in tradable industries and nontradable occupations, those in nontradable industries and tradable occupations, and those in tradable industries and tradable occupations, all relative to workers in nontradable industries and nontradable occupations (called the omitted category). The first set of bars shows the simple average differences, before controlling for worker characteristics. It shows that the average worker in a tradable industry and tradable occupation earns over 70 percent more than the average worker in a nontradable industry and nontradable occupation. Workers in tradable industries and nontradable occupations have about 20 percent higher earnings than workers in the omitted category, and the earnings of workers in nontradable industries and tradable occupations are more than 50 percent higher. These

Figure 3.2   Average annual earnings in tradable and nontradable US service occupations

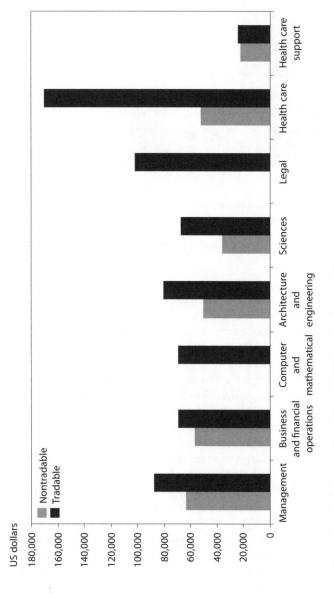

Source: Author's calculations using data from the 2007 American Community Survey.

Figure 3.3   Estimated US average earnings differentials across industry-occupation categories

percent

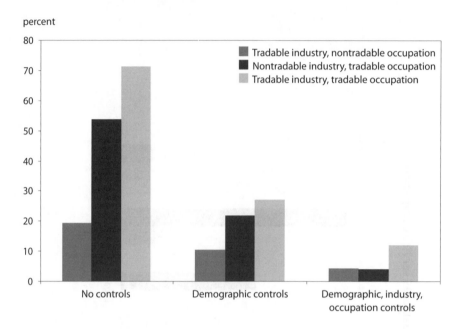

Legend:
- Tradable industry, nontradable occupation
- Nontradable industry, tradable occupation
- Tradable industry, tradable occupation

X-axis categories: No controls · Demographic controls · Demographic, industry, occupation controls

Note: Bars indicate the earnings premium for a worker in the indicated industry-occupation combination over a worker in a nontradable industry and nontradable occupation.

Source: Author's calculations using data from the 2007 American Community Survey.

differences are very large but, again, could be driven by the fact that workers in tradable activities have significantly higher educational attainment than workers in nontradable activities.

The second set of bars in figure 3.3 reports earnings differences between tradable and nontradable activities from a regression that controls for workers' level of education and other demographic characteristics (race, sex, age, and hours and weeks worked). The differences are significantly smaller than the simple averages, suggesting that a large part of the earnings differences is indeed due to differences in the characteristics of workers in tradable service activities. But much of the difference in earnings remains: Workers in tradable industries and tradable occupations have more than 25 percent higher earnings than workers with the same demographic characteristics in nontradable industries and nontradable occupations, working the same number of hours. In other words, if one were to compare two workers of the same age, race, sex, and educational attainment, both working the same amount of time, the worker in an industry and occupation classified as tradable would on average have 25 percent higher earnings than the worker employed in a nontradable industry and occupation. This is a remarkably large difference.

The third set of bars in figure 3.3 reports earnings differences between

Table 3.6 Estimated US earnings premiums in tradable and nontradable activities (percent)

Worker industry and occupation[a]	Sample		
	All workers	Workers in business service sector	Workers in "high-end" occupations[b]
Nontradable industry, tradable occupation	4	13	13
Tradable industry, nontradable occupation	4	14	11
Tradable industry, tradable occupation	12	21	20
N	1,266,977	253,185	376,714
Weighted N	1.32×10^8	2.64×10^7	3.70×10^7
R^2	0.6	0.57	0.48

a. Dummy variables indicate to which industry and occupation combination a worker belongs; nontradable industry, nontradable occupation is the omitted category.

b. Occupations in the following Standard Occupational Classification (SOC) groups: management (SOC 11), business and financial operations (SOC 13), computer and mathematical (SOC 15), architecture and engineering (SOC 17), life, physical, and social sciences (SOC 19), legal (SOC 23), health care practitioner and technical (SOC 29), and health care support (SOC 31).

Note: The dependent variable is the logarithm of employment income in dollars per year. Results measure the wage premium earned by a worker in the indicated industry-occupation combination over an otherwise identical worker in a nontraded industry and nontraded occupation. All regressions control for level of education, race, sex, age, and hours and weeks worked and include fixed effects for two-digit NAICS industry and two-digit SOC occupation.

Source: Author's calculations using data from 2007 American Community Survey.

tradable and nontradable activities from a regression that controls for workers' level of education, other demographic characteristics, and the worker's sector (NAICS two-digit industry) and major occupation group (SOC two-digit occupation group). This essentially compares earnings differences between workers in tradable and nontradable activities with the same demographic characteristics and the same education level, working in the same major industry and occupation categories. These earnings differentials are smaller still, but still sizable at 10 percent for tradable industries and tradable occupations within the same industry and occupational groups.

The above results are for workers in all industries, and table 3.6 examines whether the same effects of being in a tradable industry and occupation hold within business service industries and white-collar service occupations, too. Within the business service sector, and within a group of service occupations classified as "high-end,"[1] the effect of being in a tradable industry and a trad-

---

1. These are occupations in the following Standard Occupational Classification (SOC) groups: management (SOC 11), business and financial operations (SOC 13), computer and mathematical

able occupation is larger. A worker in a tradable industry and a tradable occupation within the business service sector receives 17 percent higher wages than a demographically identical worker in a nontradable industry and a nontradable occupation *within the same sector*. Within "high-end" service occupations, the difference is almost as large: almost 16 percent.

These results demonstrate that tradable industries and occupations pay higher wages, even after controlling for observable characteristics. Working in a tradable industry is associated with higher wages, and working in a tradable occupation is associated with higher wages. Moreover, these effects appear to be independent: Working in both a tradable industry and a tradable occupation is associated with a larger (almost double) income premium than being in either a tradable industry or a tradable occupation alone. This suggests that tradable services are consistent with US comparative advantage: Compared with both manufacturing and nontradable service activities, these are high-skill and high-wage activities.

(SOC 15), architecture and engineering (SOC 17), life, physical, and social sciences (SOC 19), legal (SOC 23), health care practitioner and technical (SOC 29), and health care support (SOC 31).

4

Comparative Advantage: Lessons from Manufacturing

Chapter 3 examined evidence that a large share of total US employment is in service activities that appear to be tradable, and that the workers in these activities are qualitatively different from workers in nontradable services—and from workers in manufacturing. Workers in tradable services tend to have more education and higher earnings than other workers. If these high-wage, high-skill jobs are tradable, is the United States likely to lose them to large, low-wage, labor-abundant countries?

Some argue that this is indeed likely. For example, Alan Blinder writes in *Foreign Affairs* (2006) that

> Changing trade patterns will keep most personal-service jobs at home while many jobs producing goods and impersonal services migrate to the developing world…. In the first place, rich countries such as the United States will have to reorganize the nature of work to exploit their big advantage in nontradable services: that they are close to where the money is. That will mean, in part, specializing more in the delivery of services where personal presence is either imperative or highly beneficial.

The underlying assumption here seems to be that because wages in the United States are higher than wages in, say, India, the United States will lose tradable service jobs to India, just as it has lost many manufacturing jobs to low-wage competition from China. The United States will import manufactured goods from China and tradable services from India and specialize in nontradable services provided to domestic customers.

These fears ignore over a century of international trade theory and empirical research. They ignore the role of productivity differences across countries and across sectors and how these differences influence trade patterns. They also ignore the basic logic of accounting. How could the United States import everything that it consumes that is tradable and produce only nontradable products and services for domestic consumption? What would the United States exchange for the goods and services it imports, if it produces only nontradable services? Moreover, these fears focus primarily (indeed, almost exclusively) on the competitive threat posed by imports while completely overlooking the opportunities presented by exports.

Perhaps most important, these fears ignore the facts.

The United States runs a persistent trade surplus in services (in marked contrast to its persistent trade deficit in goods) and is the world leader in service exports. As seen in chapter 3, many service activities require high levels of skill, and the United States has an abundance of skilled workers. When the United States does import services, it tends to import them from other high-wage, high-skill countries. These facts indicate that the United States has comparative advantage in tradable services.

This chapter explores the conceptual framework of international comparative advantage—and the real-world evidence that supports it—to begin to explain why fears about the widespread loss of US service jobs are unfounded. The most straightforward way to do this would be by examining data on the service sector directly. However, as chapter 2 showed, data on trade in services are not as complete or detailed as one would like. On the other hand, researchers do have a pretty good picture of how increased international trade has influenced the US manufacturing sector. Therefore I examine evidence on the manufacturing sector, with an eye to understanding how increased trade in services is likely to play out in the US service sector. I look at both aggregate information on manufacturing and a growing body of microdata research in manufacturing. These data show that imports from low-wage countries are indeed creating dislocations in some US manufacturing industries but also that other US manufacturing industries are under little pressure from low-wage imports and continue to export—indicating global competitiveness in these industries. Chapter 5 then considers whether the same patterns are likely to appear in the service sector.

Comparative Advantage

International trade theory emphasizes the role of comparative advantage in determining which activities countries undertake. Comparative advantage stresses that countries produce and export goods that they are *relatively* more efficient at producing than other countries. This notion of relative (or comparative) advantage is crucial to understanding how trade influences the composition of economic activity in a country, that is, which goods are produced and which are imported. But—and this point proves important—the theory says *only* that trade influences the composition of activity, and not the *level* of activity. In particular, trade does not influence how many workers the economy as a whole will employ, nor does it affect the unemployment rate.

Box 4.1 David Ricardo on comparative advantage

If Portugal had no commercial connexion with other countries, instead of employing a great part of her capital and industry in the production of wines, with which she purchases for her own use the cloth and hardware of other countries, she would be obliged to devote a part of that capital to the manufacture of those commodities, which she would thus obtain probably inferior in quality as well as quantity.

The quantity of wine which she shall give in exchange for the cloth of England, is not determined by the respective quantities of labour devoted to the production of each, as it would be, if both commodities were manufactured in England, or both in Portugal.

England may be so circumstanced, that to produce the cloth may require the labour of 100 men for one year; and if she attempted to make the wine, it might require the labour of 120 men for the same time. England would therefore find it in her interest to import wine, and to purchase it by the exportation of cloth.

To produce the wine in Portugal might require only the labour of 80 men for one year, and to produce the cloth in the same country might require the labour of 90 men for the same time. It would therefore be advantageous for her to export wine in exchange for cloth. This exchange might even take place, notwithstanding that the commodity imported by Portugal could be produced there with less labour than in England. Though she could make the cloth with the labour of 90 men, she would import it from a country where it required the labour of 100 men to produce it, because it would be advantageous to her rather to employ her capital in the production of wine, for which she would obtain more cloth from England, than she could produce by diverting a portion of her capital from the cultivation of vines to the manufacture of cloth.

Thus England would give the produce of the labour of 100 men, for the produce of the labour of 80.

Source: Excerpted from Ricardo (1821, chapter 7).

The principle of comparative advantage was first elaborated by the English economist David Ricardo, in his classic work *On the Principles of Political Economy and Taxation* (1821), some key paragraphs of which are excerpted in box 4.1. Ricardo's crucial insight was that it is not absolute differences in productivity between countries that matter for whether and what they trade, but rather *relative* differences.

One might think that if a country was capable of producing goods of all types more efficiently than another country, it would not bother to trade with that country—it could produce everything it needed or wanted more cheaply at home. Ricardo showed that trade even between two such countries can still be beneficial to both, as long as the second country is *relatively* more efficient at producing some goods. Then, if each country devotes its scarce resources to producing just those goods that it can produce *most* efficiently, each can sell some of those more cheaply produced goods to the other, freeing up resources in the other country to make what that country produces most efficiently. Each country's inhabitants can then consume more of the goods they desire, and trade thus makes each country better off.

Ricardo explained this concept with the example of trade between England and Portugal. Suppose that Portugal is more efficient than England at producing both wine and cloth, but that it is far more efficient than England at producing wine and only somewhat more efficient than England at producing cloth. For example, it might take five English workers to produce as much wine as two Portuguese workers could produce in the same amount of time, but only four English workers to produce as much cloth as three Portuguese workers. Although Portugal can thus produce both wine and cloth more cheaply than England, it can consume more wine *and* more cloth if it specializes in producing wine and trades some of the wine to England in exchange for cloth. Likewise, England can consume more wine and more cloth if it specializes in cloth and trades some of it to Portugal for wine.

A crucial point—and an important piece in the mosaic—is that although England is less efficient at producing both goods, England does not import all its consumption of both goods from Portugal. Opening to trade with a country that is more efficient at producing everything does not result in the more efficient country doing all the exporting and the less efficient one doing all the importing. It would not make sense for Portugal to "trade" with England and get nothing in return. England needs to have something to give to Portugal in exchange for wine—otherwise Portugal will have no interest in trade. So England produces the good in which it has a smaller productivity gap with Portugal, namely, cloth. Under this arrangement, both countries are better off: Both can consume more wine and more cloth than they could without trade.

Factor Abundance, Factor Intensity, and Comparative Advantage

Ricardo's insight was essential to understanding the forces that drive international trade. Yet his theory of comparative advantage—that it is relative productivity differences that matter—does not explain *why* differences in productivity exist between countries; those differences are simply assumed to exist.

The key complementary insight into why certain countries export and import some goods rather than others was developed in the early 20th century by Eli Heckscher (1919) and Bertil Ohlin (1933). Heckscher and Ohlin start by observing that different products have different input intensities. Some are labor intensive—that is, they require a large amount of labor in their production relative to other factors such as raw materials or capital or energy (think of an intricately carved piece of wood, for example), while others are intensive in these other factors. They also observed that countries differ in their relative abundance of these factors. For example, some countries have an abundance of capital (such as industrial plants, equipment, and infrastructure) relative to the size of their workforce, while other countries have a greater relative abundance of labor. In Heckscher and Ohlin's theory, these differing factor intensities and abundances interact to determine comparative advantage: Countries have comparative advantage in those products (or services) that are intensive in the use of inputs that are abundant in the country. For example, countries that have an abundance of low-cost labor have an advantage in producing labor-intensive products, such as apparel, and countries with an abundance of low-cost electricity (perhaps because they have large rivers that they have dammed to produce hydroelectricity) have comparative advantage in producing energy-intensive products like aluminum.

One important factor on which countries differ is skilled labor: Some countries have many highly skilled workers, while others have mostly unskilled workers. Although skill is very difficult to measure, one tends to think of more-educated workers as possessing greater skills. Educational attainment can thus be used as a proxy for skill. Figure 4.1 compares average educational attainment (average years of schooling for people over the age of 25) and GDP per capita for a group of 25 countries as of 1985. Each bubble represents a country, and the size of the bubble represents that country's population.

One thing the figure shows is that even compared with other developed economies, the United States is skill abundant. The United States' skill abundance relative to China and India, two very populous countries where average educational attainment was very low in the mid-1980s, is even greater. Because the United States is (and in fact has historically been) a relatively skill-abundant country, the theory of comparative advantage, as extended by Heckscher and Ohlin, suggests that the United States should produce and export skill-intensive goods and activities and import goods and activities intensive in low-skilled labor.

Figure 4.1 also shows that skill abundance is closely correlated across countries with income per capita. This point proves important when I examine the effects of increased trade on US service sector workers.

It is true that China and India and many other countries are improving their educational systems, so that their relative lack of skill abundance is surely less today than it was in 1985. However, because of the nature of education and the fact that most people over the age of 25 do not return to school, it is difficult to make dramatic changes in average educational attainment for the entire workforce over short periods of time. As a result, the relationships depicted in the figure are undoubtedly key factors in explaining trade patterns over the past 30 years and are likely to shape these countries' comparative advantage even today.

Figure 4.1 Average educational attainment and GDP per capita in selected countries, 1985

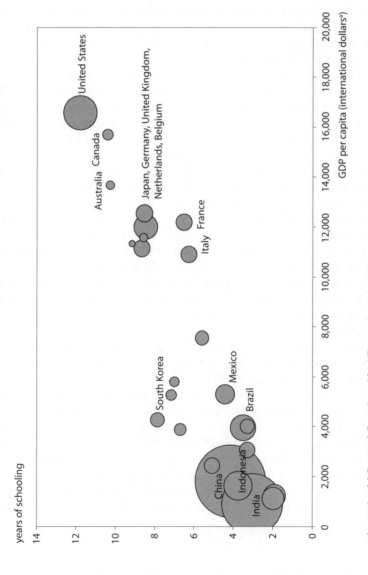

years of schooling

a. International dollars are dollars adjusted for differences in purchasing power across countries.

Note: Bubbles are sized proportionally to country populations. Data for China exclude Taiwan.

Sources: Barro and Lee (1993) and Penn World Tables Version 5.5, 1993.

I will soon show that these patterns have influenced US imports and exports in the past and continue to do so today. Comparative advantage is alive and at work influencing trade flows for both goods and services. Heckscher and Ohlin's concept, that it is the interaction of the factor abundance of countries and the factor intensity of products and services that determines countries' comparative advantage in various industries, is crucial to the emerging mosaic of how increased service trade will play out.

A Key Assumption: The Long Run

An important assumption underlies this model of trade and its determinants, namely, that the economies of both trading countries are operating at full capacity. This assumption, implicit in Ricardo's work and explicit in Heckscher's and Ohlin's, means that the theory is a theory of the long run. In a long-run model there is no concept of inadequate aggregate demand. If a shortfall of demand leads to unused productive capacity over more than a short period, the owners of that spare capacity will most likely reduce the price they charge for it so as to ensure its productive use, or convert it to other uses or abandon it. (If the unused capacity consists of workers' human capital rather than physical capital, the workers will either see their wages reduced or retrain or exit the labor force.) Thus any such shortfall of demand must be temporary: Over time, prices adjust to ensure that supply and demand are in balance. In the long run, then, it is assumed that all physical capital in the economy and all workers still in the labor force are fully employed. In other words, the model does not take into account the business cycle, that is, the possibility of recession or unemployment. This assumption is crucial to understanding the gains from trade and why economists believe that, in the long run, trade does not affect the aggregate number of jobs in an economy but instead affects only their composition across industries or occupations.

It is also an assumption that drives critics of free trade crazy (and, as box 4.2 shows, sometimes its supporters!). It seems to assume away precisely the problem that many of the critics are concerned about, namely, lost jobs and output. They point, for example, to the long-running US trade deficit as evidence that free trade has siphoned away output and therefore jobs. But no country can run a trade deficit with the rest of the world in the long run—that would be like Portugal exporting wine and cloth to England and never getting anything in return. Eventually any such global trade deficits must be offset by trade surpluses. And "eventually" is what one means by the long run.

The notion that trade does not affect aggregate employment, but instead influences the composition of economic activity, is difficult for some people to accept. It is beyond the scope of this book to address this topic in depth, but figure 4.2 presents one piece of evidence: the relationship over time between the trade deficit (as a share of GDP) and the unemployment rate in the United States.

Box 4.2 Paul Krugman on Ricardo and employment

Krugman, in an article much-cited but apparently never published in print, discusses the relationship between trade and employment in this way:

> The standard textbook version of the Ricardian model assumes full employment in both countries. But in reality unemployment is constantly a concern of economic policy—so why is this the usual assumption? There are two answers. One—the answer that Ricardo would have given—is that international trade is a long-run issue, and that in the long run the economy has a natural self-correcting tendency to return to full employment. The other, more modern answer is that countries have central banks, which try to stabilize employment around the NAIRU [the non-accelerating-inflation (or natural) rate of unemployment]; so that it makes sense to think of the Federal Reserve and its counterparts acting in the background to hold employment constant. This is not at all the way that non-economists think about the issue. Both supporters and opponents of free trade normally claim that their preferred policies will create jobs; free-traders are forever warning that the Smoot-Hawley tariff caused the Great Depression. And the alternative view does not come at all naturally. During the NAFTA debates I shared a podium with an experienced, highly regarded U.S. trade negotiator, a strong NAFTA supporter. At one point a member of the audience asked me what I thought the effect of NAFTA would be on the number of jobs in the United States; when I replied "none," based on the standard arguments, the trade official exploded in anger: "It's remarks like that which explain why people hate economists!"

Source: Paul R. Krugman, "Ricardo's Difficult Idea," available at web.mit.edu/krugman/www/ricardo.htm.

If trade deficits caused unemployment, one would expect to see a positive correlation between the two series: When trade deficits are high, unemployment will be high as well. But as the figure shows, over intervals of five years or more, the trade deficit is not correlated at all with the unemployment rate. If anything, the contrary is true: Periods of high unemployment tend to occur along with, or slightly after, periods of *smaller* trade deficits (for example, in 1975, 1983, and 2009). And vice versa: From 2002 through 2007, for example, the trade deficit was large but unemployment was low.

The point is worth repeating: International trade in general and the trade deficit in particular do not influence the total *number* of jobs in the economy. Shortfalls of demand for labor are short-run phenomena, whereas the impact of trade is felt over the long run. However, trade does influence the *composition* of activities in an economy—what kinds of goods and services are produced—and thus will influence the sectoral composition of employment, that is, the *kinds of jobs* that are available over the long run. The next section explores how comparative advantage has shaped the composition of activities within the US manufacturing sector.

Figure 4.2   US unemployment rate and trade deficit, 1970–2010

percent

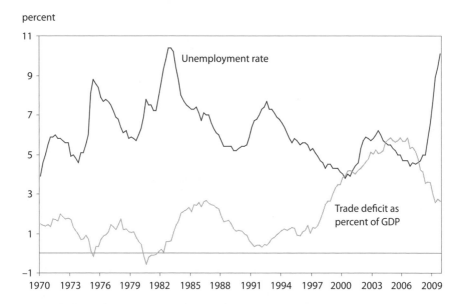

Sources: Bureau of Economic Analysis, www.bea.gov; Bureau of Labor Statistics, www.bls.gov.

Comparative Advantage across Industries in Manufacturing

Changes in the US manufacturing sector over the past 40 to 50 years reveal a lot about how comparative advantage has shaped the economy. Manufacturing is often seen as a poster child for the negative economic impact of trade on the United States. It is often asserted that trade has "hollowed out" the US manufacturing sector and destroyed millions of "good jobs at good wages." The US experience of increasing international trade in manufacturing, especially trade with low-wage, labor-abundant countries, is often invoked as a cautionary tale regarding increased trade in services.

The full picture is richer than these impressions, however. This section explores developments in US manufacturing with an eye to how trade and other factors have influenced the composition of activity and employment in that sector. The next chapter does the same for services, showing that many of the patterns seen in manufacturing in recent decades are being repeated in the service sector today. This repetition of patterns is important to the development of the mosaic.

Figure 4.3 traces US manufacturing employment over the past 50 years: The solid line shows the total number of manufacturing workers and the dotted line the manufacturing sector's share of total nonagricultural employment. As discussed in chapter 1, manufacturing's share of employment has

Figure 4.3　US manufacturing employment, 1960–2007

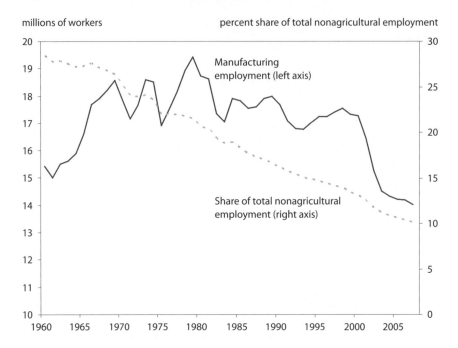

millions of workers　　　　　　　　　　　　percent share of total nonagricultural employment

Source: Economic Report of the President, 2009.

been on a secular decline for several decades, falling from close to 30 percent in 1960 to about 10 percent in 2007. The total number of manufacturing workers has also fallen, and it has fallen especially sharply over the past decade: In 2000 the manufacturing sector still employed over 17 million workers, but by 2007 that number had decreased to about 14 million. These facts are relatively well known and are part of the narrative that suggests that trade has played a destructive role in the US economy.

A more complete picture shows, however, that rumors of US manufacturing's demise have been greatly exaggerated. Although *employment* in US manufacturing has decreased, US manufacturing *output* has increased and is still increasing. Indeed, the United States still produces a far larger share of global manufacturing output (more than 20 percent) than its global population share (less than 5 percent) would indicate. As figure 4.4 shows, US growth in manufacturing output compares favorably in absolute terms with growth in several countries widely regarded as the United States' manufacturing rivals, such as Japan, Germany, and even China (although Chinese manufacturing output is growing faster in percentage terms, so that the gap is narrowing). India, meanwhile, lags far behind, with only 2 percent of world manufacturing output (yet nearly 20 percent of the world's population), and the gap in absolute terms between India and the United States is widening.

Figure 4.4   Real manufacturing output in selected countries, 1970–2007

billions of 1990 dollars

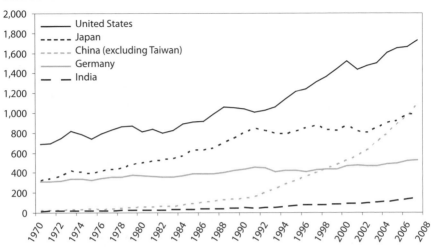

Source: UN National Accounts Statistics database.

In short, both in absolute terms and on a per capita basis, US manufacturing output remains strong. And the reason for that strength is also the reason that manufacturing employment has decreased: Manufacturing *productivity,* or output per worker, has been increasing dramatically over the last several decades. As a result, US manufacturers today are able to produce much more output than they did in 1960 despite employing far fewer workers.

Figure 4.5 documents the strong labor productivity growth experienced by the US manufacturing sector over the past 40 years, relative to aggregate US productivity growth. Between 1970 and 2007, output per worker in manufacturing roughly tripled in constant dollars (that is, after adjusting for inflation), while for the economy as a whole (including the manufacturing sector), productivity grew by only about 50 percent. This dramatic increase in labor productivity in manufacturing explains both the strong and continuing growth in US manufacturing output and part of the decline in manufacturing employment.

What accounts for the spectacular rise in US manufacturing productivity? One important source is technological advancement: New technologies, including computers, have allowed many tasks to be automated. Another is the emergence of specialization by comparative advantage, promoted by freer trade, as discussed above: If trade allows US firms to produce more of the goods that they produce more efficiently, and fewer of the goods that they produce less efficiently, average productivity must necessarily rise.

How much of the total rise in productivity is due to technology, and how much to increased trade? Unfortunately, disentangling the two is very difficult. Technological improvements and international trade are intimately linked,

Figure 4.5   US output per worker, overall and in manufacturing, 1970–2007

index (1970 = 1.0)

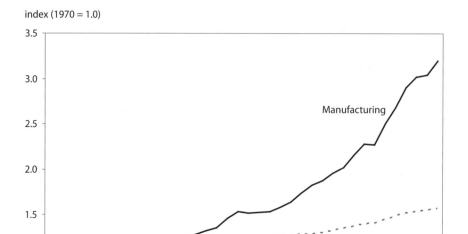

Sources: UN National Accounts Statistics database; *Economic Report of the President*, 2009.

making it hard to empirically identify how much productivity growth is attributable to either source independent of the other. One can, however, look for evidence of comparative advantage in shaping employment patterns (and productivity growth) in the US manufacturing sector. I take this up in the next few sections.

Education, Skills, and Earnings in Manufacturing

Recall that Heckscher and Ohlin argued that countries will have comparative advantage in activities that are intensive in the use of factors that are relatively abundant in the country. So, countries with a relatively abundant supply of low-wage, low-skill labor will have comparative advantage in activities that are intensive in the use of such labor. Countries that have relatively abundant skilled labor will have comparative advantage in activities that are intensive in the use of that kind of labor.

The United States is relatively skill abundant: The share of US workers with a high level of skill, as proxied by education, is relatively high. To investigate whether comparative advantage explains the pattern of US trade, one needs information on the skill intensity of US industries. I consider the information on skill intensity in the manufacturing sector here and in the service sector in chapter 5.

Table 4.1   Educational attainment and earnings in selected US manufacturing industries, 2007

| Industry | Percent with | | Average annual earnings (dollars) |
	Bachelor's degree	Advanced degree	
Animal slaughtering and processing	7	1	28,826
Fiber, yarn, and thread mills	9	3	29,462
Carpet and rug mills	9	1	32,654
Cement, concrete, lime, and gypsum product manufacturing	9	2	43,451
Prefabricated wood buildings and mobile homes	9	1	35,721
Machine shops; turned product; screw, nut and bolt manufacturing	9	1	42,421
Apparel accessories and other apparel manufacturing	10	3	25,456
Retail bakeries	10	1	25,525
Sawmills and wood preservation	10	2	37,999
Veneer, plywood, and engineered wood products	11	2	38,787
Agricultural chemical manufacturing	31	8	55,764
Petroleum refining	33	9	79,353
Industrial and miscellaneous chemicals	34	11	64,154
Aircraft and parts manufacturing	35	11	62,509
Medical equipment and supplies manufacturing	36	11	59,704
Navigational, measuring, electromedical, and control instruments manufacturing	41	13	62,008
Electronic component and product manufacturing, n.e.c.	44	17	68,797
Communications, audio, and video equipment manufacturing	48	20	72,361
Computer and peripheral equipment manufacturing	56	22	81,075
Aerospace products and parts manufacturing	56	22	77,350

n.e.c. = not elsewhere classified

Source: Author's calculations from data in the 2007 American Community Survey.

The manufacturing data show that there is considerable variation in skill intensity across industries within the sector. Table 4.1 reports the share of US workers with a bachelor's degree and the share with an advanced degree, for US manufacturing industries. Some industries have very low average educational

**Figure 4.6   Educational attainment and average earnings by US
manufacturing industry, 2007**

annual earnings (dollars)

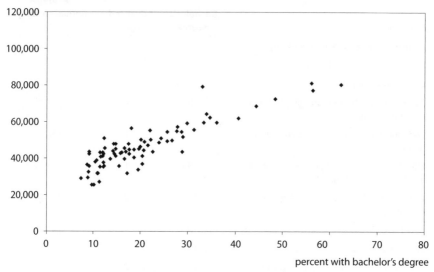

percent with bachelor's degree

Note: Each dot represents one NAICS manufacturing industry.

Source: Author's calculations using data from 2007 American Community Survey.

attainment: For example, only 7 percent of workers in animal slaughtering and processing have a college degree, and only 1 percent have an advanced degree. At the other extreme, 56 percent of workers in the aerospace products industry have a college degree, and 22 percent have an advanced degree.

Table 4.1 also shows that average earnings tend to be higher in industries with higher educational attainment—an observation that parallels the relationship between education and income per capita that is seen across countries in figure 4.1. Indeed, the relationship is quite strong statistically, as figure 4.6 shows. This relationship is useful for this study's purposes because some data sources lack information on educational attainment, requiring use of average wages as a proxy for skill. Figure 4.6 shows that the average wage is a useful proxy for skill in the manufacturing sector.

Comparative Advantage and US Manufacturing Imports

The United States has a relative abundance of skilled labor, whereas many of the countries typically viewed as a threat to US jobs have an abundance of low-skilled labor. Some manufacturing industries are more skill intensive than others. The theory of comparative advantage predicts that the United States should therefore export skill-intensive manufactured goods while importing

**Figure 4.7   Average earnings and low-wage country import penetration
by US manufacturing industry**

low-wage-country share of US imports (percent)

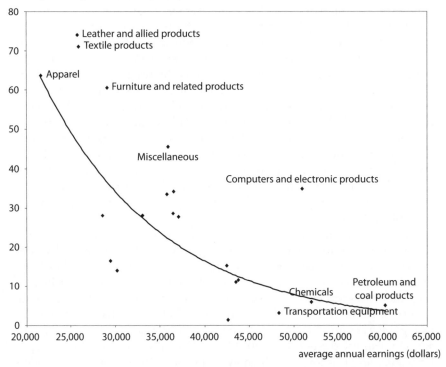

Note: Low-wage countries are those where income per capita is less than 5 percent of US income per capita. The curve is fitted from an exponential regression of the low-wage-country import share on earnings ($y = 3.0996\ e^{(-7E-05x)}$, $R^2 = 0.467$).

Source: Author's calculations using data from the 2002 Economic Census, the 2006 US Imports of Merchandise, and the World Bank.

manufactures that are intensive in low-skilled labor. Does the theory hold up in the data? When one examines the profile of US manufacturing imports that come from low-wage, labor-abundant countries, the empirical evidence suggests that comparative advantage indeed seems to hold for US manufacturing.

Figure 4.7 shows, for each US manufacturing industry, the share of US imports in that industry that originate in low-wage countries and the average wage in that industry. (Recall that the close relationship between education and wages allows use of wages as a proxy for education and thus for skill.) It is clear that imports from low-wage, labor-abundant countries (like China) into the United States are concentrated in low-wage, labor-intensive industries such as apparel, leather goods, and furniture. These are the industries in which US firms and workers face stiff competition from low-wage imports. By contrast, high-wage, high-skill industries like transportation equipment, chemicals, and petroleum and coal products (i.e., refining) face very little competition from low-wage imports.

The only real exception to this relationship is computers and electronic equipment, an industry that has high average wages and relatively high penetration by low-wage-country imports. This is likely due to the increased fragmentation of consumer electronics production, where the design and production of the underlying components (such as microprocessors), high-wage, high-skill activities, occur in the United States and the products are then shipped to China for low-wage, labor-intensive assembly. If this sector could be separated into two pieces, the assembly portion would likely move toward the upper left corner of figure 4.7, and the microprocessor fabrication portion would move toward the lower right corner, thus lining up with the other industries.[1] (Perhaps reflecting this logic, one important US-based producer of computers and other electronic equipment, IBM, has largely divested itself of its hardware business, much of which has moved abroad, while retaining its more skill-intensive operations such as consulting, as box 4.3 explains.)

One can summarize figure 4.7 as saying that US manufacturing industries with average annual wages above roughly $40,000 face very low levels of low-wage import competition. Obviously, there is no sharp cutoff, but firms in industries that pay wages below that level are more likely, and higher-wage industries less likely, to face strong import competition from low-wage countries. To put it more accurately, the risk of a US manufacturing industry facing low-wage import competition decreases with that industry's skill intensity. One can use the notional $40,000 cutoff as shorthand for this concept.[2] Understanding this low-wage/high-wage distinction is important for understanding the labor market implications both of manufacturing trade and of increased trade in services.

Figure 4.7 thus provides evidence that supports the theory of comparative advantage as it applies to US manufacturing. But it does so in snapshot fashion, showing the predicted relationship between factor abundance and trade patterns at a moment in time. The theory of comparative advantage also has a dynamic aspect: It suggests that when countries open to trade, they tend to shift resources among industries, increasing output in those in which they are relatively more efficient, while the output of comparatively less efficient industries shrinks. As the US economy has opened to imports from low-wage countries, the resulting increase in trade should have caused a reallocation of economic activity away from manufacturing industries in which the United

---

1. Academic studies document similar patterns using more disaggregated data. See, for example, Bernard, Jensen, and Schott (2002) and Krugman (2008).

2. Average annual earnings in the United States are approximately $44,000, according to the 2007 American Community Survey.

Box 4.3 IBM evolves

International Business Machines Corp., better known as IBM, has long been a world leader in the manufacture of computer hardware. Yet in its 2009 annual report, IBM reported that hardware accounted for only 7 percent of its pretax income—down from 24 percent as recently as 2000. Software and other services (such as consulting, infrastructure, and hosting) accounted for 84 percent. The report explains:

> To capture the emerging higher-value opportunities, IBM divested commoditizing businesses like personal computers and hard disk drives, and strengthened its position through strategic investments and acquisitions in areas such as analytics, next-generation data centers, cloud computing and green solutions. ....This has changed our business mix toward higher-value, more profitable segments of the industry.

IBM is thus a good example of a US firm that has switched its product line away from increasingly commoditized tangible goods and toward activities consistent with its comparative advantage. The company also exemplifies the transition going on within the US economy away from low-skill, labor-intensive activities and toward high-skill activities, a large share of which consists of services.

Source: IBM, 2009 Annual Report, available at www.ibm.com/annualreport/2009.

Table 4.2 Changes in employment and output in US manufacturing industries by level of import exposure, 1972–2001 (percent)

Initial exposure to low-wage-country imports	Average change	
	Employment	Real output
Low	2.3	38.7
Medium	−4.4	32.4
High	−12.8	15.0

Source: Bernard, Jensen, and Schott (2005).

States has comparative *dis*advantage (mainly low-wage, low-skill industries like apparel) and toward manufacturing industries where the United States has comparative advantage (mainly high-wage, high-skill industries).

Is there evidence of such a reallocation? Over the 30 years from 1972 to 2001, US manufacturing industries that faced import competition from low-wage countries experienced lower net employment growth than other manufacturing industries (Bernard, Jensen, and Schott 2005). Table 4.2 shows the average change in employment over those three decades for three groups of

Figure 4.8   US manufacturing employment by major industry group, 1963 and 2007

millions of workers

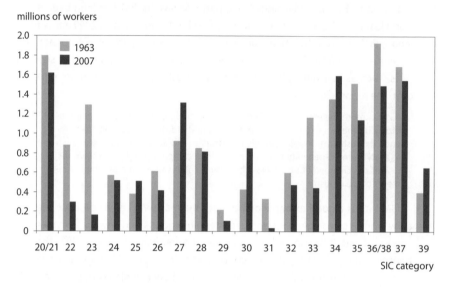

Note: The Standard Industrial Classification (SIC) categories on the horizontal axis are as follows: 20/21, food, beverage, and tobacco products; 22, textiles; 23, apparel; 24, wood products; 25, furniture and related products; 26, paper; 27, printing and publishing; 28, chemicals; 29, petroleum and coal products; 30, rubber and plastic; 31, leather; 32, nonmetallic mineral products; 33, primary metals; 34, fabricated metals; 35, industrial machinery; 36/38, electronic and electric machinery and instruments; 37, transportation equipment; and 39, miscellaneous.

Source: 1963 and 2007 Economic Censuses.

manufacturing industries, ranked by their level of exposure to low-wage-country import competition. Manufacturing industries that faced strong import competition from low-wage countries experienced large net employment losses, while industries that faced little low-wage import competition (these tended to be high-wage industries) actually increased employment and significantly increased output. As figure 4.7 showed, imports from low-wage countries tend to be more prevalent in low-wage, labor-intensive industries. This explains some of the shift in the allocation of employment across industries in US manufacturing: Comparative advantage has shaped the allocation of employment across manufacturing industries as trade has expanded.

Another perspective is provided in figure 4.8, which compares employment by two-digit NAICS manufacturing industry in 1963 and 2007. Most industries experienced decreases in employment over the period: Only printing and publishing (NAICS 27), rubber and plastic products (30), fabricated metal products (34), and miscellaneous manufacturing (39) experienced increases. In contrast, four industries—textiles (22), apparel (23), leather and allied products (31), and primary metals manufacturing (33)—experienced extraordinary job losses of greater than 60 percent, and together they account for over three-quarters of the total decrease in manufacturing employment. (Textiles and apparel alone account for nearly half.)

These findings bolster the argument that comparative advantage has shaped the allocation of economic activity across manufacturing industries. Typically, low-wage, labor-intensive (and low-labor-productivity) industries have faced the greatest import competition from low-wage, labor-abundant countries. Because the United States is a relatively skill-abundant country, these are not industries in which the United States has comparative advantage. Increased trade with low-wage countries has reduced activity in these comparative-disadvantage industries.

Comparative Advantage and US Manufacturing Exports

Comparative advantage also shapes which products the United States exports. Manufacturing industries vary considerably in terms of average wages and also differ in capital intensity and productivity. For example, apparel production tends to be labor intensive and to pay relatively low wages, whereas chemicals and transportation equipment production tend to be capital intensive and to pay high wages. As the previous section showed, apparel producers face stronger competition from low-wage imports than do higher-skill, higher-wage industries like aircraft production. But the theory of comparative advantage also holds that high-skill manufacturing industries in the United States should export more than other industries. I examine next whether the facts bear out this prediction as well.

Figure 4.9 shows a strong positive relationship between average wages and exports per worker for US manufacturing industries. Manufacturing industries that pay relatively high wages (which, again, I interpret as being highly skill intensive) tend to export more than lower-paying industries, as is consistent with the theory of comparative advantage.

As in figure 4.7, it appears that an average annual wage of about $40,000 can serve as a notional cutoff between US manufacturing industries that are internationally competitive and those that are not. When the skill level in an industry reaches a level consistent with an average annual wage of about $40,000, export intensity increases significantly.

Wages are not the only industry characteristic that varies systematically across industries in manufacturing in a manner related to exporting. Within manufacturing, there is considerable variation in relative factor intensities, mean plant size, and productivity across industries. Some industries have characteristics more consistent with US comparative advantage and others less so, and these differences are systematically related to industry export behavior.

Table 4.3 reports correlation coefficients between a number of industry-level measures, including average wage, other inputs per worker, labor productivity, and exports as a share of sales, for US manufacturing industries. As the table shows, there are strong positive correlations between export participation, whether measured in terms of the exports-to-sales ratio or in terms of

Figure 4.9   Average earnings and exports per worker in US manufacturing industries, 2002

exports per worker (thousands of dollars)

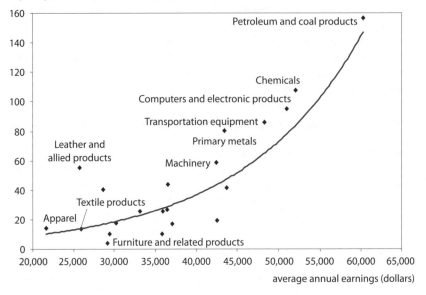

Note: The curve is fitted from an exponential regression of exports per worker on earnings ($y = 2.3723 \ e^{(7E - 05x)}$, $R^2 = 0.5364$).

Source: Author's calculations using data from 2002 Economic Census.

the share of plants that export, and the other measures. Industries that have higher export participation measures tend to have larger plants, higher average wages, higher other inputs (fixed costs) per worker, and higher labor productivity; they also tend to be more geographically concentrated, as measured by their locational Gini coefficient. These correlations are consistent with the notion that the United States has comparative advantage in activities that are capital intensive (larger average plant size, higher other inputs) and skilled labor intensive (higher wages) and in those activities in which US producers are more efficient (higher productivity).

Comparative Advantage within Manufacturing Industries

The cross-industry evidence presented above, which shows that high-skill, high-wage US manufacturing industries have higher export participation, is not the only evidence consistent with the United States having comparative advantage in high-skill, high-wage activities. There is strong within-industry evidence as well.

Table 4.3 Correlations between selected industry characteristics in US manufacturing, 2002
(correlation coefficients)

Characteristic	Exports as share of sales	Share of firms exporting	Gini coefficient
Share of firms exporting	0.5516		
Gini coefficient	0.25505	0.43985	
Labor productivity	0.14143[a]	0.31121	0.29783
Other inputs per worker	0.1216[b]	0.29658	0.30075
Average wage	0.40856	0.51312	0.18732
Average plant size	0.21713	0.50045	0.56675

Characteristic	Labor productivity	Other inputs per worker	Average wage
Share of firms exporting			
Gini coefficient			
Labor productivity			
Other inputs per worker	0.99693		
Average wage	0.63105	0.5840	
Average plant size	0.4261	0.4294	0.36909

a. $p = 0.002$.
b. $p = 0.0081$.

Note: The probability p that the measured correlation would occur by chance is less than 0.0001 in all cases except where noted otherwise.

Source: Author's calculations using data from the 2002 Economic Census.

A large and growing body of recent empirical work emphasizes the potential for comparative advantage to work within as well as across industries. This research uses microdata—data at the plant and firm level rather than industry aggregates—from the manufacturing sector to demonstrate that the traditional assumption of a "representative" firm in an industry is not appropriate for many research questions. Even within narrowly defined industries, plants and firms exhibit considerable heterogeneity both in their cross-sectional characteristics and in their behavior over time. This heterogeneity of plants and firms and the variation in their responses to globalization have clear implications for the impact of trade in both manufacturing and services.

Within-Industry Heterogeneity

Bernard and Jensen (1995) provided the first plant-level results on US exporters and found that exporters are relatively rare. Even in industries in which the United States has comparative advantage, the majority of plants do not export. (Conversely, even in sectors facing strong import competition, like textiles and apparel, some firms still do export.) In addition, plants that export tend as a group to be strikingly different from other plants in the same industry. They are, on average, significantly larger, more capital intensive, and more skilled worker intensive, and they pay higher wages than plants of similar size in the same industry, even in the same state. Exporters are also more productive than nonexporters in the same industry and region.

The desirable characteristics of exporting plants and firms in the manufacturing sector are now well known.[3] Work subsequent to Bernard and Jensen (1995) has confirmed that US manufacturing exporters pay significantly higher wages and are more productive, more skill intensive, and more likely to survive and grow than nonexporters in the same industry (see Bernard and Jensen 1999, 2007; Bernard, Jensen, Redding, and Schott 2007). In addition, because exporters have higher growth and survival rates, their growth is associated with a reallocation of economic activity that improves aggregate productivity (Bernard and Jensen 2004). Figure 4.10 reports results from a regression using microdata from the 2002 Economic Census on several desirable characteristics of exporters in the manufacturing sector. It shows that exporters in this sector tend to be larger than nonexporters in the same industry: On average, they have 80 percent higher employment and double the sales. They also pay over 10 percent higher wages and have 20 percent higher sales per employee (a measure of labor productivity). Comparing averages without controlling for industry, exporters are more than twice the size of nonexporters.[4] Bernard and Jensen (1999, 2007) also show that manufacturing exporters are more likely to survive and have more rapid employment growth than nonexporters of similar size in the same industry in the same region.

Because exporters have different characteristics than nonexporters, and because they have different growth and survival rates, the potential exists for the behavior of exporters to contribute to a reallocation of economic activity

---

3. For examples of reviews of the academic literature, see Tybout (2003), Helpman (2006), and Bernard, Jensen, Redding, and Schott (2007). For examples of the policy-related literature, see Richardson and Rindal (1995, 1996) and Lewis and Richardson (2001).

4. The coefficients reported in figure 4.10 are mean log differences and can be interpreted as the percentage difference between exporters and nonexporters.

Figure 4.10   Exporter premiums in US manufacturing

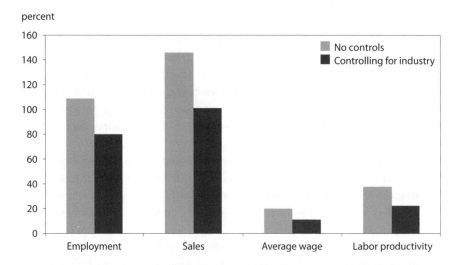

Note: Each bar represents the percentage by which the performance of the average exporter exceeds that of the average nonexporter in the same industry. Results are derived from a regression of the form log(y) of the indicated measure on a dummy variable identifying whether the establishment exports and a set of industry controls (or no controls).

Source: Author's calculations using microdata from the 2002 Economic Census.

away from firms with weaker performance on the measures cited above. Such a reallocation would improve aggregate measures such as industry and aggregate productivity and boost the demand for and returns to the factors of production (such as skilled workers) that exporters use intensively.

A New Conceptual Framework of Trade at the Firm Level

Economists are now incorporating these observed empirical regularities into models of international trade and investment that focus specifically on firms and firm differences, as opposed to traditional trade theory's focus on industries and countries.[5] The key insight from this literature is that firms need to pay additional costs—either a one-time, sunk cost or an ongoing, distance-related cost—to become exporters (see box 4.4). The presence of these additional costs, in a world with producer heterogeneity even within industries, means that only the most productive firms will find it profitable to export to foreign markets.

The implications of this can be seen in figure 4.11. An important dimension along which firms vary is productivity. One can think of a distribution of producers within an industry according to their level of productivity. The

---

5. For example, see Bernard, Eaton, Jensen, and Kortum (2003), Melitz (2003), and Bernard, Redding, and Schott (2007). See also Bernard, Jensen, Redding, and Schott (2007) for a review of this literature.

Box 4.4 Sunk costs and iceberg costs

The types of sunk costs that exporting firms must pay include the time and effort to identify appropriate foreign markets, the expense of ensuring that their products meet any product standards in the foreign market (both the testing itself and any resulting modifications to the product), and the costs of finding a distributor in the foreign market. These are fixed costs that must be incurred before entering the market, and if, in the end, the decision is made not to enter the foreign market, these costs are not recoverable—that is why they are called "sunk" costs.

Iceberg costs are trade costs that are proportional to the distance a good travels or to the value of the good. They are so called because just as an iceberg shrinks from melting as it floats ever farther from its glacier, so the profit from a product "melts" away as the product incurs ever greater costs the farther it is shipped. Although this is a simplification of a variety of costs that firms face— for example, ad valorem tariffs are, by definition, proportional to the value of the good, and shipping costs are often distance related—it is frequently used in models of international trade, because the costs can be simply modeled as a fraction of the value of the product itself, again just as the meltwater comes from the iceberg.

For an example of a trade model with sunk trade costs, see Meltiz (2003); for a model with distance-related trade costs, see Bernard, Eaton, Jensen, and Kortum (2003).

distribution is typical of most statistical distributions: There are a few very productive firms (in the right tail of the curve in figure 4.11), a mass of firms with more or less average productivity, and a few firms with low productivity (the left tail). Even without international trade, normal competition within the industry will force the lowest-productivity firms out of business. These firms are represented by the area under the curve to the left of the "Before trade" survival threshold in figure 4.11. At the other end of the curve, if there are additional costs to exporting (whether sunk costs or iceberg costs), then only the most productive firms will find it profitable to incur these costs and export. This group of firms is represented as the area under the curve to the right of the "Before trade" export threshold in figure 4.11.

Now imagine that the cost of exporting falls for all firms in this industry, domestic and foreign, for example, because an advance in technology lowers transport costs, or because tariffs are eliminated bilaterally, or because a bilateral change in trade policy lowers sunk costs. Whatever the cause, when the cost of exporting decreases, a number of things will happen. First, the profits that existing exporters can earn in foreign markets will rise, encouraging them to

**Figure 4.11   Productivity distribution of firms before and after a
decrease in trade costs**

number of firms

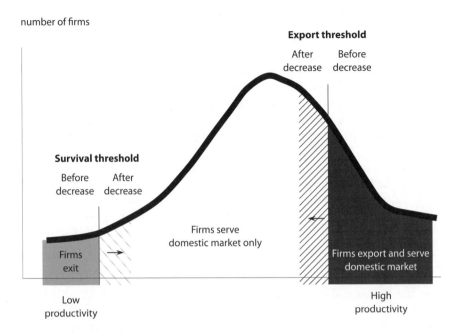

Note: The figure illustrates how before a decline in trade costs, the threshold for the level of productivity necessary for a firm in a given industry to survive is lower and that for a firm to be successful at exporting is higher, than after the decline. The left shaded area represents the additional firms that are driven by import competition to exit the industry after trade costs fall, and the right shaded area the additional firms that are able to export because of falling costs.

increase their exports. The increase in profits to exporting will also encourage nonexporting firms that until now were just below the level of productivity marked by the export threshold to begin exporting. This increase in the number of exporters is represented by the leftward shift in the export threshold in figure 4.11. Second, and similarly, a larger number of foreign firms than before will now find it profitable to enter the home market, making it more competitive. The increased competition will induce the least productive domestic producers that previously were just able to survive to exit the industry. This is represented by the rightward shift in the survival threshold in figure 4.11.

Although these heterogeneous-firm trade models differ in their details, they have several shared implications:

- Exporters are rare.
- Exporters are more productive than nonexporters.
- As trade costs fall, low-productivity nonexporters are more likely to fail.

- As trade costs fall, high-productivity nonexporters are more likely to start exporting.
- As trade costs fall, existing exporters should increase their exports.

Another important implication of this model is that increased trade increases aggregate productivity, even if no individual plant experiences productivity growth. The reallocation of economic activity from low-productivity nonexporters to high-productivity exporters is sufficient to increase aggregate productivity. The shutdown of low-productivity producers increases average productivity for the industry as a whole, as does the increase in activity by both the high-productivity existing exporters and the firms becoming exporters for the first time.

These models and the related empirical work on heterogeneous firms using plant-level microdata provide a rich description of how international trade and comparative advantage work to shape the allocation of economic activity both across and within industries. The next section reviews results that examine the impact of international trade on US manufacturers explicitly.

Falling Trade Costs

Bernard, Jensen, and Schott (2006b) examined the impact of falling trade costs (both tariffs and transportation costs) on US manufacturers. We found that when trade costs in an industry fall, plants within that industry are more likely to close. This is consistent with the above model: Lower trade costs increase imports, which compete with the output of the lower-productivity firms in the same industry, forcing some to close.

Imports increase and plants close when trade expands. This implication of trade creates considerable discomfort, but it is a fact. However, the story does not end there. We also found that when trade costs fall, industry productivity growth increases. This is one of the main sources of the gains from trade: Productivity growth drives increased living standards.

There are a number of channels by which reduced trade costs increase productivity. The first is the one just discussed: When trade costs fall and imports increase, it is the lower-productivity plants that close. Falling trade costs thus raise aggregate productivity both by eliminating the low-productivity firms that were pulling down the average, and by allowing firms toward the higher end of the productivity distribution to expand their market share. In addition, nonexporters with relatively high productivity in the industry are more likely to start exporting. Their expansion also causes average productivity to rise. Finally, existing exporters increase their shipments abroad as trade costs fall. Since these firms have the highest productivity of all, their expansion raises aggregate productivity yet further. On top of all this, there is also evidence of productivity growth *within* plants in response to decreases in industry-level trade costs. Plants seem to respond to increased import competition by increasing their productivity (Bernard, Jensen, and Schott 2006b).

Not surprisingly, given the number of channels by which falling trade costs shift the distribution of economic activity toward more productive plants, and given the plant-level productivity improvements associated with falling trade costs, entire industries experiencing relatively large declines in trade costs exhibit relatively strong productivity growth compared with other industries.

Competition from Low-Wage Countries

In separate but related work, Bernard, Jensen, and Schott (2006a) examined the role of import competition from low-wage countries on the reallocation of US manufacturing within and across industries from 1977 to 1997. Motivated by the Heckscher-Ohlin factor proportions framework and by the significant increases in import shares from low-wage countries like China, that study focused on where imports originate, in addition to their overall level. The use of plant-level data allowed a richer examination of US producer responses to international trade, including plant exit and product switching, than is possible with more aggregate data. Specifically, the analysis identified whether reallocation within industries is consistent with US comparative advantage.

The results show that low-wage-country import shares and overall penetration vary substantially across both industries and time. Both tend to be higher and to increase more rapidly among labor-intensive industries such as apparel and leather. Other industries such as textiles see only modest rises in both series. Finally, more capital- and skill-intensive sectors such as transportation and industrial machinery experience rapid growth of import penetration but little or no increase in the share of imports from low-wage countries.

The study exploited this variation in low-wage import penetration across industries and over time to investigate the impact of import competition from very low wage countries. We found that plant survival and employment growth are negatively associated with industry exposure to low-wage-country imports. In addition, even for plants in the same industry facing the same level and type of import competition, plants that are more labor intensive are more likely to close and have lower employment growth.

In unpublished results from that same project, we found that changes in import shares from developed countries—those with endowments and comparative advantage similar to those of the United States—are less disruptive than imports from low-wage countries. This is an important point because the United States tends to import services from countries that are similar in income and relative factor abundance to itself.

Last, plants that face more low-wage import competition are more likely to change the products they produce and more likely to switch to an industry that is more capital and skill intensive (Bernard, Jensen, and Schott 2006a). These results suggest that trade with low-wage countries is causing US manufacturing to shift toward activities that are consistent with US comparative advantage—that is, toward capital- and skill-intensive products and production techniques.

Conclusion

International trade, and specifically trade with low-wage, labor-abundant countries like China, has shaped the allocation of economic activity within the US manufacturing sector, and even within manufacturing industries, in ways that are consistent with US comparative advantage. The United States tends to import low-wage, labor-intensive products from low-wage, labor-abundant countries and to export products that are relatively skill intensive.

In chapter 5 I argue that there is little reason to expect decreasing impediments to trade to play out any differently in the service sector than in manufacturing. Increased trade in services should foster the same type of reallocation, across and within industries, as it has in manufacturing. Low-productivity service producers will be more likely to close, high-productivity nonexporters will be more likely to start exporting (and to grow), and existing exporters will be more likely to increase their exports (and to grow). The reallocation associated with these changes will tend to increase productivity in the tradable service sector. In addition, the increased competitive pressure will likely foster productivity growth *within* service producers. Although disruptive to both the affected firms and their workers, all of these responses to increased trade will have the positive impact of increasing productivity growth—and raising living standards—in the United States and its trading partners.

5

Comparative Advantage: Prospects for the Service Sector

Much of the discussion of service offshoring has focused on the potential loss of US service jobs to low-wage, labor-abundant countries like India. The fear is that tradable services now produced in the United States will migrate to these countries because they can be produced more cheaply there. This chapter uses concepts and empirical findings from the previous chapter, on manufacturing, to consider whether this fear of competition from low-wage countries in the service sector is warranted.

Much less is heard in the current debate about the prospects for increased *exports from* the US service sector. Rather, the conventional wisdom seems to have shifted abruptly from the view that services are nontradable to the view that, yes, services are very tradable, but primarily *importable*. What the public discussion typically overlooks is that the United States is actually quite well positioned to export services. In fact, the United States today has a large *positive* trade balance in services, and many tradable services seem consistent with US comparative advantage. This suggests that the US service sector is likely to benefit, rather than suffer, from increased trade in services.

Chapter 4 showed how comparative advantage has influenced the allocation of output and employment within the US manufacturing sector. The United States imports mainly low-wage, low-skilled-labor-intensive manufactured goods from low-wage, low-skilled-labor-abundant countries and exports high-wage, high-skill-intensive manufactures to the rest of the world. This is just what the theory of comparative advantage, as extended by Heckscher and Ohlin, predicts: The United States has an abundance of skilled labor, and therefore it trades products that are intensive in skilled labor for products that are not. Many if not most tradable services are likewise skill intensive, and again because the United States is a skill-abundant country, comparative advantage predicts that the United States is likely to continue to run a trade surplus in services in the future, just as it does today.

Moreover, this chapter shows that the services that the United States does import tend to come from other advanced, high-wage economies—not from low-wage, labor-abundant countries like India. Yet again, this is consistent with the notion that most tradable services are skill intensive, which means that other skill-abundant countries have comparative advantage in them as well. Even when one looks at the vertically integrated service affiliates of US multinationals—those that one might expect to be quickest to take advantage of low wages abroad—one finds that they tend instead to be in high-wage locations and pay higher than average wages.

Finally, this chapter also examines the empirical evidence *within* the service sector for clues as to how increased trade in services might influence the composition of activities that US service firms perform—what services the United States is likely to import (and from where), and what services the United States is likely to export. The chapter's bottom line is this: Tradable services are consistent with US comparative advantage. As a result, it is reasonable to expect that the United States stands to gain from increasing trade in services.

Comparative Advantage across Sectors: US Trade Balances in Goods and Services

The place to start is with some basic facts about US service trade. Figure 5.1 traces the US trade balances in goods and in services over the past 20 years. The figure shows that whereas the United States has a large and (until very recently) growing trade deficit in goods, the US trade balance in services has been persistently positive. Although little detail is available within the service trade balance, it is noteworthy that the balance for the "other private services" category (see chapter 1), which includes education, finance and insurance, and business, professional, and technical services, more than doubled over the period and contributed about a third of the overall growth in the service trade surplus.

The United States is, in fact, the global leader in business service exports. The OECD (2007) reports that the United States accounts for about 13 percent of the world total and is the world's leading exporter of business services. At the same time, the United States accounts for approximately 10 percent of world business service imports. Other countries with a disproportionate share of service exports relative to their population are mostly other developed economies, including France, Germany, Ireland, the Netherlands, and the United Kingdom. China and India each account for less than 4 percent of global business service exports—much lower than their shares of global population.

Figure 5.1   US balances of trade in goods and services, 1992–2009

billions of current dollars

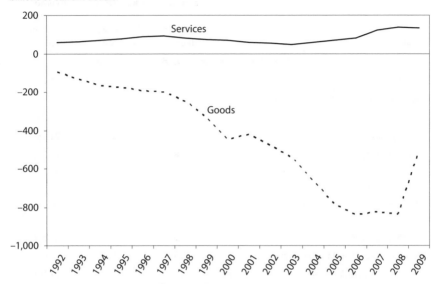

Source: Bureau of Economic Analysis, US International Trade in Goods and Services, www.bea.gov.

Education, Skills, and Earnings in Services

As described in the last chapter, the key concepts for understanding how international trade shapes the composition of economic activity are the theory of comparative advantage and the Heckscher-Ohlin relationship between factor intensity and factor abundance. Heckscher and Ohlin argued that countries will have comparative advantage in activities that are intensive in the use of factors that are relatively abundant in the country. Chapter 4 showed that this prediction holds true for the US manufacturing sector; here I will show whether it holds in services as well.

Although the United States is relatively skill abundant overall, that does not imply that the skill intensity of all US industries is high. However, workers in tradable service activities tend to have higher—often much higher—educational attainment than manufacturing workers, and this indicates that tradable services are generally *more* skill intensive than manufacturing. It is also true that there is considerable variation in skill intensity across industries *within* the service sector.

Table 5.1 shows the shares of workers with a bachelor's degree and with an advanced degree in a select set of service industries, some with low average educational attainment (the top panel) and some with high (the bottom panel). There is significant variation across these two groups. For example, only 5 percent of workers in barber shops have a college degree, and only 1 percent have an

Table 5.1   Educational attainment and earnings for selected US service industries, 2007

Industry	Percent of workers with		Average annual earnings (dollars)
	Bachelor's degree	Advanced degree	
Low-skill, low-wage industries			
Barber shops	5	1	24,257
Automotive repair and maintenance	6	1	33,948
Car washes	6	2	23,783
Beauty salons	7	2	22,157
Bowling centers	8	0	21,220
Services to buildings and dwellings (excluding cleaning during construction)	8	1	24,622
Waste management and remediation services	8	1	40,781
Landscaping services	9	1	25,656
Restaurants and other food services	10	1	19,636
Videotape and disk rental	10	1	17,176
High-skill, high-wage industries			
Advertising and related services	59	9	64,502
Architectural, engineering, and related services	60	20	67,652
Colleges and universities, including junior colleges	61	38	39,215
Legal services	63	47	87,844
Computer systems design and related services	67	22	79,773
Internet publishing and broadcasting	67	20	66,910
Securities, commodities, funds, trusts, and other financial investments	70	23	110,184
Scientific research and development services	70	37	69,836
Management, scientific, and technical consulting services	71	30	83,156
Software publishing	76	27	95,685

Source: Author's calculations using data from the 2007 American Community Survey.

advanced degree. In contrast, 76 percent of workers in software publishing have a college degree, and 27 percent have an advanced degree. (For an example of a US service exporter with a high share of highly educated workers, see box 5.1.)

The table also shows that within this set of industries, earnings are uniformly higher in the industries with higher educational attainment. In

Box 5.1 Tapping the global market for satellite imaging

GeoEye is a satellite imaging, imagery information products, and image processing services firm based in Dulles, Virginia. The firm, which owns and manages several satellites, has developed an advanced information technology infrastructure for capturing, receiving, processing, and distributing high-resolution and low-resolution imagery from these satellites to private-sector and government customers around the world.

The company's website states:

> We operate in three areas of the geospatial information services market: imagery collection, geospatial and imagery production and information services. Our capabilities serve market demand worldwide for imagery and information products to map, measure and monitor the Earth for a wide variety of applications including:
>
>   Defense and intelligence sectors
>   National mapping market
>   On-line mapping customers
>   Mining markets
>   Oil and gas markets
>   Architecture, engineering and construction companies
>   Monitoring
>   Forestry industry
>   Environmental assessment market.

The firm operates a number of facilities around the United States, including, besides its Dulles headquarters, Thornton, Colorado; St. Louis, Missouri; and Mission, Kansas.

Like many US service firms, GeoEye is growing rapidly. Revenue in 2009 was $272 million, up from $151 million in 2006. The firm has about 530 employees, most of them highly skilled, with more than 20 percent holding advanced degrees.

Although the US government is an important customer for GeoEye, exports make up a significant share (27 percent in 2009) of the company's sales, and that share is likely to grow over time.

Source: GeoEye website and annual report, www.geoeye.com.

fact, the relationship between educational attainment and average earnings in a given industry in the service sector as a whole is quite strong statistically, just as it is in the manufacturing sector (recall figure 4.6 in chapter 4). Figure 5.2 plots the share of workers with a bachelor's degree in a given service industry against average earnings in that industry. There is obviously a fairly tight relationship.

Figure 5.2　Educational attainment and average earnings in US service industries, 2007

average annual earnings (dollars)

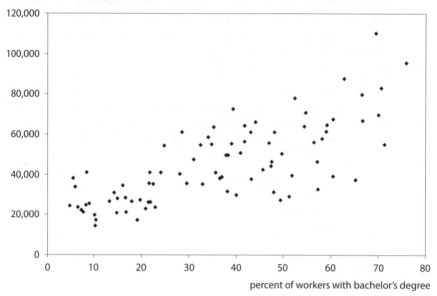

percent of workers with bachelor's degree

Note: Each dot represents one NAICS service industry.

Source: Author's calculations using data from the 2007 American Community Survey.

Comparative Advantage and Exports across Service Industries

As chapter 4 showed exports per worker are significantly higher in US manufacturing industries with relatively high wages, indicating a positive relationship between worker skills and export intensity. Also, US import shares from low-wage countries are significantly higher in relatively low wage manufacturing industries. This is consistent with comparative advantage and with the Heckscher-Ohlin model. The model also predicts that the same should be true in the tradable service sector, because these services also tend to be skill intensive. But does what holds in theory hold in reality? Here I examine evidence on how export intensity varies across industries within the tradable service sector, to see whether skill intensity is in fact a good predictor of US service exports across industries.

Unfortunately, detailed information on exports is available only for a subset of service industries. The US Census Bureau collects information on exports only for a few service subsectors, namely, information (NAICS 51), professional, scientific, and technical industries (NAICS 54), and administra-

Figure 5.3 Average earnings and exports per worker in US business service industries, 2002

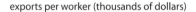

exports per worker (thousands of dollars)

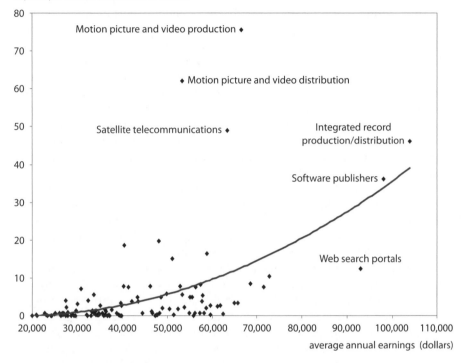

average annual earnings (dollars)

Note: The trend line is fitted from a polynomial regression using the plotted data ($y = 5E - 09x^2 - 0.0002x + 1.3732$, $R^2 = 0.2946$).

Source: Author's calculations using data from the 2002 Economic Census.

tive support and waste remediation industries (NAICS 56). Although these three NAICS subsectors are a small part of what many people consider the service sector, together they employ more workers in the United States than the entire manufacturing sector. Figure 5.3, the analogue for services to figure 4.9 for manufacturing, plots the relationship between export intensity and skill intensity (as measured by average wages) for individual industries within these three business service subsectors. The figure shows that, just as in manufacturing, service industries that pay higher wages tend to have higher exports per worker. This is strong evidence that the United States does have comparative advantage in high-wage, skill-intensive services.

Another similarity with manufacturing is that beyond a level of annual earnings of about $40,000, service industries tend to have much higher exports per worker. Although $40,000 a year is again not a sharp threshold, this finding suggests that across service industries, as across manufacturing industries, those that use more-skilled workers are more consistent with US comparative advantage and more likely to export.

It is also useful to note that many of the United States' export-intensive industries are industries where intellectual property is important. Motion pictures, sound recording, and software are all highly export intensive industries where intellectual property rights are important for producers. Because the output from these service industries can be digitized, the threat of piracy is high—and a continuing concern to these producers.

Table 5.2, which is the analogue of table 4.3 for manufacturing, reports correlation coefficients between certain key characteristics of business service industries and their export participation. These correlations are generally quite high, further supporting the idea that the United States has comparative advantage in high-skill, high-wage services. Several of the correlations are particularly interesting. First, industries with higher exports-to-sales ratios and a higher share of establishments that export tend to be more geographically concentrated: The correlations between these measures and the locational Gini coefficient are high (second row of the table). This is consistent with geographic concentration being a useful indicator of tradability. Recall from chapter 2 that geographic concentration indicates that there is no inherent obstacle to these services being provided at a distance.

The table also provides evidence (third row) that business service industries with higher labor productivity are more likely to export. This, too, is consistent with the claim that the United States has comparative advantage in skill-intensive business service industries: Firms in such industries generally produce more output per worker than do firms where workers are less skilled. Business service industries that make more intensive use of other inputs are also more likely to export (fourth row). Although this correlation is similar to that for manufacturing, in the case of business services it is not exactly clear what these fixed costs represent. Presumably they are not materials costs, but they may be costs of either physical capital or intangible assets such as brands or other intellectual property. Finally, the table reports (fifth row) that business service industries that pay higher average wages are more likely to export. To the extent that wages correlate with skill, this is yet again consistent with the claim that these industries are ones in which the United States has comparative advantage.

Together these results demonstrate that the United States tends to export services in a manner consistent with US comparative advantage. Tradable service activities in general are high-skill, high-earnings activities, and the direct evidence from selected US service industries suggests that high-wage services are more likely to be exported. Taken together, these results argue strongly that the United States can benefit from expanded service trade.

Table 5.2 Correlations between selected industry characteristics in US services, 2002
(correlation coefficients)

Characteristic	Exports as share of sales	Share of firms exporting	Gini coefficient
Share of firms exporting	0.55479		
Gini coefficient	0.43616	0.52284	
Labor productivity	0.37735	0.49168	0.48887
Other inputs per worker	0.32229[a]	0.42311	0.3833
Average wage	0.37415	0.44083	0.44902

	Labor productivity	Other inputs per worker
Share of firms exporting		
Gini coefficient		
Labor productivity		
Other inputs per worker	0.94977	
Average wage	0.74043	0.56375

a. $p < 0.0002$.

Note: The probability p that the measured correlation would occur by chance is less than 0.0001 except where noted otherwise.

Source: Author's calculations using data from the 2002 Economic Census.

Comparative Advantage within Service Industries

A closer look at the data on business service industries reveals more about their characteristics. Table 5.3 presents summary statistics on the manufacturing sector and the three subsectors of the business service sector discussed above. One striking fact that emerges is that these business service industries pay average wages that exceed those in the manufacturing sector by 20 percent.[1] This subset of the service sector thus not only employs more workers than the manufacturing sector but also pays higher wages.

The table also reports the average wage paid by exporters in each sector. Chapter 4 showed that within the manufacturing sector, plants that export tend to pay higher wages (and have other desirable characteristics). Figure 5.4,

---

1. The calculations reported here are based on respondent-level microdata accessed at the Center for Economic Studies at the US Census Bureau. The data exclude establishments (respondents) that are not mailed a form and thus do not report information. These establishments tend to be much smaller than the average establishment and are more prevalent in the business service sector than in the manufacturing sector. This does bias the results obtained from these data, as a larger share of very small establishments in the business service sector is excluded from the analysis than in the manufacturing sector. Average annual establishment wages, calculated from published aggregates, are about $39,000 in the manufacturing sector and about $40,000 in the business service sector. The microdata results are used throughout this section for consistency.

Table 5.3 Characteristics of US manufacturing and business service industries, 2002

Characteristic	Manufacturing	Business services[a]
Number of establishments	146,986	390,377
Employment (thousands of workers)	11,763	14,120
Sales (billions of dollars)	3,317	1,600
Exports (billions of dollars)	316	36
Average annual wages (thousands of dollars)	35	43
Exporter annual average wages (thousands of dollars)	39	63

a. NAICS 51, 54, and 56 only.

Source: 2002 Economic Census.

which, like figure 4.10 for manufacturing, reports export "premiums" for the three business service subsectors, reveals that this is not only a manufacturing sector phenomenon. Business service exporters pay significantly higher wages than business service nonexporters, as well as higher wages than both exporters and nonexporters in the manufacturing sector.

Figure 5.4 also shows that, like manufacturing exporters, business service exporters tend to be larger in terms of both sales and employment and to have higher sales per worker than nonexporters in the same industry. A comparison of results with and without industry controls indicates that much of the effect is due to variation across industries. Business service exporters tend to be in industries characterized by high average wages and high labor productivity. Relative to nonexporters in the same industry, business service exporters have on average almost 70 percent more workers and 100 percent more sales. Exporters are also more skill intensive, paying average wages almost 20 percent higher than nonexporters in the same industry.

Establishment size is correlated with these other measures. When establishments in the same six-digit NAICS industry, in the same state, with approximately the same number of workers, are compared (results not shown), business service exporters are still significantly different from nonexporters (the same is true of manufacturers). Exporters have higher sales, pay higher average wages, and are more productive than nonexporters. As can be seen by comparing figure 4.10 and figure 5.4, exporters in the business service sector are different from business service nonexporters in many of the same ways that exporters differ from nonexporters in the manufacturing sector.

To summarize, the service establishment results discussed here suggest that US business services' export activity tends to be concentrated in high-wage, high-productivity industries. Within these industries, the establishments that export tend to be larger and more productive and pay higher wages than nonexporters. These results yet again suggest that tradable business services are consistent with US comparative advantage and, as a result, less likely to be

Figure 5.4　Exporter premiums in US business services

percent

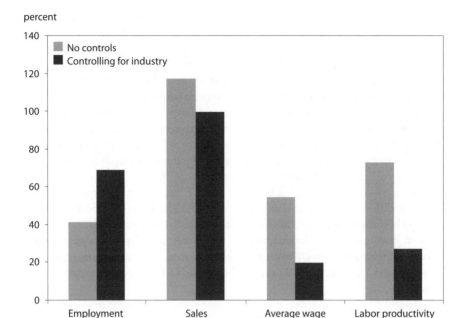

Note: Each bar represents percent by which the performance of the average exporter exceeds that of the average nonexporter in the same industry. Results are derived from a regression of the form log(y) of the indicated measure on a dummy variable identifying whether the establishment exports and a set of industry controls (or no controls).

Source: Author's calculations using microdata from the 2002 Economic Census.

vulnerable to low-wage foreign competition. To the contrary, the United States is likely to benefit from increased trade in these services.

These findings also imply that as services continue to become more tradable, the same dynamic should be observed as has played out in the manufacturing sector in recent decades. As trade costs fall, resources are likely to be reallocated across industries in accordance with comparative advantage: The United States should tend to import low-skill-intensive services from low-wage countries and export high-skill-intensive services. Within industries, relatively low productivity service producers (which are likely to pay relatively low wages) are likely to exit, while relatively high productivity nonexporters become exporters and firms that already export increase their export sales. All of this will reallocate economic activity in the United States toward relatively high-skill activities.

Comparative Advantage and US Service Imports

The previous section showed that, in services just as in manufacturing, the United States tends to export more from higher-wage industries within the sector. It is also of interest to examine whether US service *imports* likewise exhibit patterns similar to those observed in manufacturing, with higher import shares for low-wage countries in low-wage and low-skill industries.

Unfortunately, the data available for service sector imports are once again not as detailed as the information for merchandise imports—indeed, they are even less detailed than the data for service exports. As a result, one cannot construct the service sector analogue to figure 4.7, which plotted for each manufacturing industry the low-wage-country share of imports against the industry's average wages. Instead I examine what information is available to try to get a sense of where US business service imports come from: Do they come from low-wage, labor-abundant countries like India? Or do they come from other developed, skill-abundant countries? To answer this question, I look at the geographical distribution of US service imports and examine detailed information on US multinational affiliates. The information gleaned may not amount to a detailed portrait, but it adds a few pieces to the emerging mosaic.

Comparative Advantage and the Geography of Service Imports

Although the popular perception is that the United States increasingly and overwhelmingly imports services from low-wage developing countries like India, according to the theory of comparative advantage the United States is more likely to import services from other high-wage, relatively skill abundant developed countries. One reason is that, as already seen, tradable services consist largely of business services, which tend to be relatively skill intensive. Comparative advantage suggests that skill-abundant countries should produce and export such activities.

Ideally, one would want to study how the distribution of countries that export services to the United States has changed over time. Unfortunately, data on the geographic breakdown for business, professional, and technical services start only in 2006. To examine longer-term trends in the sources of US service imports, one must look instead at a more aggregated series that is available over a longer period.

As described in chapter 1, the Bureau of Economic Analysis divides private services into five main groups: travel, passenger fares, other transportation, royalties and license fees, and "other private services," which comprises education, financial services, insurance services, telecommunications, and business, professional, and technical services. "Other private services" is thus the category closest to the set of activities I have been calling "tradable business services."

Figure 5.5   Composition of US service imports, 2008

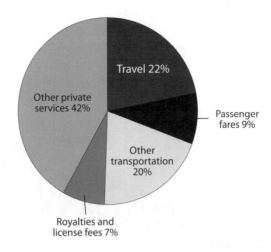

Source: Bureau of Economic Analysis, www.bea.gov.

As figure 5.5 shows, "other private services" accounted for 42 percent of all service imports in 2008, the largest share of any of the five main service groups. And as figure 1.10 in chapter 1 showed, US trade in "other private services" is growing rapidly: Both imports and exports more than doubled from 1992 to 2007. It is also the category that has contributed the most to growth in overall service trade, accounting for half of the increase in service imports and more than half of the increase in service exports. Figure 1.11 showed that, within private services, for both imports and exports, the business, professional, and technical services category was the largest at the end of the period and contributed the most to growth over the period. Financial services and insurance services also demonstrated significant growth: In fact, both had higher growth rates than the business, professional, and technical services category, but because they were smaller to begin with, they contributed less in absolute terms.[2]

Where do these service imports come from? Figure 5.6 shows that developed countries—Canada, Europe, Japan, and South Korea—accounted both for the lion's share (about two-thirds) of US imports of "other private services" at any point in time since 1992 and for most of the growth (more than 60 percent) in those imports over the period. Latin America contributed over 18 percent of service import growth, and emerging Asia (including China and India) 16 percent. The geographic distribution as of 2008 is quite similar for the subcategory of business, professional, and technical services: Figure 5.7 shows

---

2. Financial services and insurance services present even greater measurement challenges than other types of services. See Borga (2009) for more information on how the Bureau of Economic Analysis constructs estimates of trade in these services.

Figure 5.6   US "Other Private Services" imports by source country/region, 1992–2008

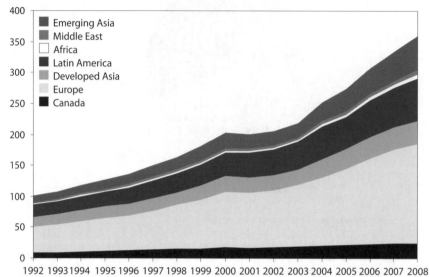

billions of dollars

Legend:
- Emerging Asia
- Middle East
- Africa
- Latin America
- Developed Asia
- Europe
- Canada

Note: Developed Asia = Australia, Japan, and South Korea. Other Asian countries are included in "emerging Asia."

Source: Bureau of Economic Analysis, www.bea.gov.

that two-thirds of US imports in this subcategory came from Canada, Europe, and developed Asia.[3] (Information for earlier years is lacking.)

These data belie the popular notion that countries like India are the primary source of increased service imports in the United States. India, which accounts for nearly 20 percent of the world's population, accounts for only about 11 percent of US imports of business, professional, and technical services—about the same as Canada, whose share of world population is about half of 1 percent. India, moreover, is an exception among developing countries in the volume of services it exports to the United States: US imports from almost all other developing countries are far lower. As an exception, it certainly deserves closer examination (which box 5.2 attempts to provide). But the rule remains as Eli Heckscher and Bertil Ohlin articulated it: Other skill-abundant countries—developed, not developing countries—are the main exporters of skill-intensive services and hence the main sources of US service imports.

---

3. This type of trade within industries between countries with similar factor endowments is observed in the manufacturing sector as well, for example, see Grubel and Lloyd (1975). Such intra-industry trade is explained by economies of scale in production and consumer preferences for variety. For example, see Krugman (1980), Helpman (1981), Ethier (1982), and Helpman and Krugman (1985).

Figure 5.7   US business, professional, and technical services imports by source country/region, 2008

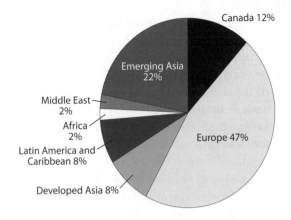

Canada 12%

Emerging Asia 22%

Middle East 2%

Africa 2%

Latin America and Caribbean 8%

Developed Asia 8%

Europe 47%

Note: Developed Asia = Australia, Japan, and South Korea. Other Asian countries are included in "emerging Asia."

Source: Bureau of Economic Analysis, www.bea.gov.

Imports of Services from Affiliates of US Multinationals

Much of the discussion in the press about service imports voices the concern that US multinationals are setting up affiliates in low-wage countries with the intention of hiring low-wage workers to replace the high-wage US workers they previously employed. Are large volumes of services being imported through this "high-bandwidth" connection between domestic parent companies and their foreign affiliates? If so, does it somehow circumvent or nullify comparative advantage? This section examines the relationships between US multinationals and their foreign affiliates with an eye to understanding whether they are an important source of service imports from low-wage countries.

One way of approaching the question is to examine where the vertically integrated service affiliates of US multinationals (that is, affiliates that primarily supply inputs to the parent) are located and to compare the results with those for affiliates in other sectors and for affiliates in the service sector that are not vertically integrated.

Table 5.4 presents some descriptive statistics on the countries in which US affiliates are located, for each major sector. It is clear that US multinationals in different sectors do vary in terms of where they choose to locate their affiliates. For example, whereas agriculture and mining affiliates tend to be located in the poorest countries, service sector affiliates tend to be located in richer countries: Across all six sectors, country income per capita is highest among service affiliates. Service affiliates also tend to be located in countries with relatively high telecommunications coverage and in countries where English is spoken. This is evidence that an advanced communications infrastructure and

Box 5.2 What explains India's success in business service exporting?

How is it that India, a country with relatively low average educational attainment, even by developing country standards, is able to produce and export business services in considerable volume to the United States and other developed countries? In this chapter I have argued that most tradable business services are relatively skill intensive and that, as a result, skill-abundant countries like the United States should have comparative advantage in these activities—and the facts show that this is true. How, then, is India able not only to compete with the United States in global trade in relatively high skilled services, but even to export such services *to* the United States?

India's workforce is relatively unskilled, where skill is proxied by educational attainment. India does have millions of well-educated workers, but it has hundreds of millions of poorly educated ones, many of whom are in fact illiterate. As a result, the *share* of the population that is highly educated is small—and it is the share of the workforce, not the sheer number, that matters for comparative advantage. According to theory, because India is a relatively unskilled country, it should be exporting low-skill, labor-intensive products and services, not high-skill business services.

Yet India does export high-skill business services. Does this mean that the theory of comparative advantage is wrong or no longer applicable in the modern global economy? No, comparative advantage is still relevant, and India may be the exception that proves the rule.

To see why, consider that, as figure 4.4 in chapter 4 showed, India produces a very small share of global manufacturing output—only about 2 percent—particularly relative to its huge share—nearly 20 percent—of the world's population. Why doesn't India produce more manufactured goods? In particular, why doesn't it produce more of the labor-intensive manufactures that would seem to be its comparative advantage? The answer, according to Arvind Panagariya (2008), is that India has stifled its manufacturing sector with intrusive regulation. Two areas of regulation in particular inhibit the size and productivity of Indian manufacturing.

The first is the small-scale industries (SSI) reservation policy. This policy, introduced in 1967 presumably with the intent to promote small business, created a list of items that by law could only be produced by small-scale firms. Once an item was placed on the SSI list, no new medium-size or large firms could enter the market, and existing large firms were prohibited from increasing their output of the item. The SSI list was expanded several times and by the late 1970s included over 500 items. As Panagariya (2008, 65) reports, "Items such as clothing,

(continued on next page)

knitted textiles, shoes, leather products, sports goods, toys, stationery, office products, furniture, simple electrical appliances, and simple extruded plastic products, which have been among the major export items of successful labor-abundant countries such as the Republic of Korea, Taiwan, and China at one time or another, have been on the list for the better part of the last several decades." Whether or not the policy succeeded in its aim of encouraging manufacturing by small businesses, it almost surely had an adverse impact on exports of these manufactures: Recall from chapter 4 that small companies tend to be less able to meet the fixed costs of exporting. They also tend to be less efficient than large companies, which can realize economies of scale—and chapter 4 showed that success at exporting depends critically on productivity.

According to Panagariya, the SSI is now being dismantled and is no longer a binding policy impediment, but its legacy continues to have a direct influence on the structure of the Indian manufacturing sector. Panagariya reports that Indian manufacturing exports, which, again, theory suggests should consist mainly of low-skill, labor-intensive products like apparel and toys, instead remain skewed toward capital- and skill-intensive products like chemicals.

The second policy impediment to realizing the potential of India's large unskilled labor force is a complex set of labor market regulations applying to manufacturing firms outside of 19 government-designated heavy investment sectors. Outside these preferred sectors, firms with 10 or more employees (if they are using electric power) or 20 employees (if they are not) are considered to be in the formal sector and thus subject to the Factories Act of 1948, which imposes a large number of limitations and costs on firms. Firms employing 50 or more workers are subject to the Industrial Disputes Act of 1947. Under this act, a firm employing more than 100 workers effectively loses the right to reassign workers to alternative tasks, to fire workers, or to close the facility. This is obviously a very stringent regulatory regime that discourages investment and strongly discourages large-scale production.

As a result of these policies, industrial production in India is highly fragmented: Very small firms produce much of the industrial output. As Panagariya (2008, 287) argues, "This is best illustrated by a comparison of the apparel firms in India with those in China, Bangladesh, and Sri Lanka. Whereas the firms in these latter countries often employ thousands of workers under a single roof, those in India remain tiny, frequently consisting of shops with less than 50 tailors." Partly as a consequence, he notes, although apparel is among India's leading exports, the country's share of the US market is approximately the same as that of neigh-

(continued on next page)

boring Bangladesh, which has about one-seventh India's population.

Policy in India has thus saddled the country with a comparative *dis*advantage in labor-intensive products, by prohibiting firms from achieving efficient scale in labor-intensive manufacturing industries.

However—and this is key—these crippling regulations do not, in general, apply to service firms. As a result, service providers are able to avoid the regulations that prevent their manufacturing counterparts from reaching efficient scale, or from managing their workforce flexibly, or in some cases even from entering the market for a potentially exportable item. In other words, it is not that the Indian service sector is necessarily more productive than those of other countries, but rather that regulation has made India's manufacturing sector far less productive than those of other countries with similar comparative advantage in low-skilled manufacturing, and the result is an artificial comparative advantage in service production: services are the relatively less expensive type of good to produce in India. The fact that India exports skill-intensive services (and manufactured goods) is the unintended consequence of government policy stifling production of the labor-intensive goods that are India's natural comparative advantage.

If and when India liberalizes its manufacturing sector, the likely result will be increased demand for people with technical skills and managerial talent to manage new and expanding manufacturing firms. This should bid up wages for skilled workers and make India's service exports less competitive, restoring the balance of comparative advantage to what one would expect it to be.

a population that speaks English facilitate trade in services. Compensation varies across sectors as well: Perhaps not surprisingly, given their location in relatively high-income countries, service affiliates pay higher average compensation than affiliates in other sectors.

Figure 5.8 looks at the same set of information from another perspective: It reports the results of a regression analysis that measures the differences between sectors on the characteristics reported in table 5.4. (The differences are expressed relative to levels for affiliates in wholesale and retail trade, which thus serve as a baseline.) Again it is clear that service affiliates differ from affiliates in the other sectors. Whereas service affiliates have compensation levels about 7 percent higher than wholesale and retail trade affiliates, manufacturing affiliates have compensation levels about 30 percent lower than the baseline. The countries in which service affiliates tend to be located again have higher income per capita—about 10 percent higher than the baseline. In contrast, manufac-

Table 5.4 Characteristics of countries hosting US multinationals' affiliates, by sector

Sector of affiliate	Number of affiliates in sample	Country characteristic			
		GDP per capita (dollars)	Telecommunications coverage[a]	English spoken[b]	Average annual compensation per employee (dollars)[c]
Agriculture and mining	1,468	15,236	0.451	0.373	47,527
Construction	205	19,824	0.579	0.456	37,040
Manufacturing	12,719	22,827	0.692	0.345	43,425
Services	13,730	26,536	0.778	0.436	67,337
Telecommunications and utilities	949	19,208	0.596	0.428	36,274
Wholesale and retail	7,336	24,522	0.750	0.355	54,710

a. Ratio of the number of telephones per 1,000 people in the host country to that in the United States.
b. Fraction located in countries where English is spoken.
c. The number of affiliates for which these figures are calculated is somewhat lower than for the other characteristics.

Source: Author's calculations from Bureau of Economic Analysis, 2004 Benchmark of Foreign Direct Investment Abroad; and World Bank, *World Development Indicators.*

130

Figure 5.8 Sectoral differences in characteristics of US affiliates and their host countries, 2004

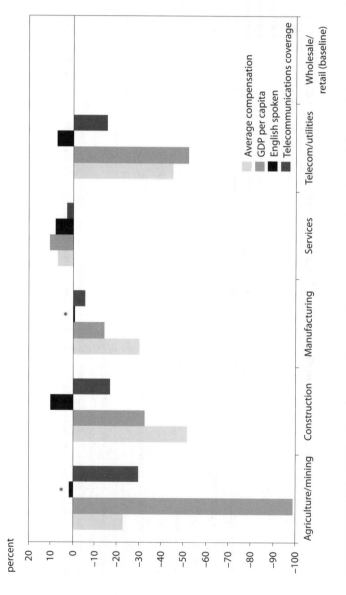

Note: Reported values are from a regression on sector dummy variables; wholesale and retail trade is the excluded (baseline) category. Characteristics are as defined in table 5.4. All coefficients are statistically significantly different from zero at the 1 percent level, except where marked by an asterisk.

Source: Author's calculations using data from Bureau of Economic Analysis, US Foreign Direct Investment Abroad.

turing affiliates are located in countries where GDP per capita is on average about 15 percent lower than the baseline. Service affiliates also are more likely than affiliates in other sectors to be located in countries with more telecommunications coverage and in countries where English is spoken.

Vertically Integrated Affiliates of US Multinationals

The finding that service affiliates tend to be located in relatively high income countries and to pay relatively high compensation suggests that the services imported by US multinationals from these affiliates come from relatively high income countries. But it is not definitive. It is possible that the affiliates that provide services to their US parents are in different locations than other service affiliates because they are different in kind from those affiliates. There are two different types of affiliates, corresponding to the two principal reasons for establishing an affiliate in a foreign country: The first is to access an important market for the parent company's products, and the second is to obtain access to lower-cost inputs. Affiliates of the first, customer demand–based type are referred to as "horizontal," and those of the second, input supply–based type are referred to as "vertical."

Multinational firms that set up horizontal affiliates typically do so because they need to be present in the foreign country to serve customers there. A local production presence could be required for a variety of reasons: for example, because the firm's product is difficult or costly to ship, or because the country imposes high tariffs or onerous regulations on imports. Firms pursuing vertical integration, in contrast, are typically seeking labor or materials inputs that are cheaper than those available at home (adjusted, of course, for the cost of shipping the product to the home country or to another destination for sale). Much of the public debate regarding offshoring and outsourcing has focused on this latter motivation.

In what follows service affiliates are classified as vertical if they export 60 percent or more of their total sales to their US parent; others are classified as horizontal affiliates. Using these definitions, table 5.5 reports, for the same major sectors as in table 5.4, the share of affiliates that export to any country, the share that export any output back to their US parent, and the share of affiliates that are vertical. The table shows that the vast majority of affiliates are predominantly horizontal: Fewer than 3 percent in any sector are vertical. However, this handful of vertical affiliates accounts for a significant share (usually more than 50 percent) of affiliated imports by US parent companies. (The exceptions are construction, where no affiliates are classified as vertical, and agriculture and mining, where vertical affiliates account for 44 percent of their parents' affiliated imports.)

Table 5.6 compares the country characteristics of horizontal and vertical affiliates in both manufacturing and services. The pattern for the vertical affiliates in manufacturing is quite different from that for services. As seen in table 5.4 manufacturing affiliates are on average located in countries with lower

Table 5.5　Export behavior of US multinationals' affiliates, by sector
　　　　　　　(percent)

Sector of affiliate	Share of affiliates that			Share of US parent affiliated imports from vertical affiliates
	Export	Export to US parent	Are vertical[1]	
Agriculture and mining	47	11	2	44
Construction	52	5	0	0
Manufacturing	76	26	3	54
Services	48	6	2	50
Telecommunications and utilities	45	8	1	52
Wholesale and retail	61	12	1	51

1. Affiliates that export more than 60 percent of their output to their US parent.

Source: Author's calculations using data from Bureau of Economic Analysis, 2004 Benchmark of Foreign Direct Investment Abroad.

income per capita than are services affiliates. Table 5.6 shows that vertical manufacturing affiliates are in countries with (on average) even lower incomes per capita: The average vertical manufacturing affiliate is in a country with GDP per capita of just $16,000. In stark contrast, the average vertical service affiliate is in a country with GDP per capita of $29,000. Vertical service affiliates also tend to be in countries with better telecommunications coverage and in countries where English is spoken.

Vertical service affiliates also pay significantly higher wages than manufacturing affiliates and other service affiliates. The average vertical service affiliate pays an average wage of about $108,000 a year, compared with $32,000 for the average manufacturing affiliate. This is a striking difference. Even compared with other service affiliates (which pay an average of $67,000 per year), vertical service affiliates offer much higher pay.

Some of the difference in compensation between vertical service and manufacturing affiliates is due to the fact that the former tend to be located in higher-income countries, where employees are able to demand higher wages. To control for this effect, table 5.7 presents results from a regression that compares average compensation at vertical affiliates to other affiliates for the manufacturing sector and the service sector. The regressions are run both with and without the industry and country terms, which control for the effects of industry and country composition.

The first and second columns of table 5.7 present regression coefficients for vertical manufacturing and service affiliates without controlling for industry or country. The average vertical manufacturing affiliate pays almost 53 percent less than the average horizontal manufacturing affiliate. In contrast, the average vertical service affiliate pays almost 55 percent more than the average horizontal service affiliate. Together with the fact, noted previously,

Table 5.6   Characteristics of countries hosting vertical affiliates of US multinationals, by sector

		Country characteristic[a]			
Sector of affiliate	Number of affiliates in sample	GDP per capita (dollars)	Telecommuni- cations coverage	English spoken	Average annual compensation per employee (dollars)[b]
Manufacturing					
Not vertical	12,391	23,002	0.70	0.35	43,731
Vertical	328	16,229	0.49	0.36	32,069
Services					
Not vertical	13,541	26,500	0.78	0.43	66,868
Vertical	189	29,096	0.84	0.55	108,216

a. See table 5.4 for definitions.
b. The number of affiliates for which these figures are calculated is somewhat lower than for the other characteristics.

Source: Author's calculations using data from Bureau of Economic Analysis, 2004 Benchmark of Foreign Direct Investment Abroad.

133

Table 5.7   Regressions investigating the effect of vertical integration on compensation

Independent variable[a]	Without controls		With country and industry controls	
	Manufacturing affiliates	Service affiliates	Manufacturing affiliates	Service affiliates
Dummy for whether affiliate is vertical	−0.525 (0.058)	0.548 (0.104)	−0.135 (0.048)	0.511 (0.093)
N	11,637	9,946	11,637	9,946

a. Table reports coefficients from regressions of the logarithm of affiliate compensation per employee on a dummy variable set equal to 1 when the affiliate is vertical. Standard errors are in parentheses. All results are statistically significant at the 1 percent level.

Source: Author's calculations using data from Bureau of Economic Analysis, 2004 Benchmark of Foreign Direct Investment Abroad.

that service affiliates in general, and vertically integrated service affiliates in particular, tend to be located in high-income countries, this finding suggests that these vertical service affiliates employ significantly more skilled workers.

The third and fourth columns of table 5.7 present results of regressions that control for industry and country effects. As seen earlier, vertically integrated manufacturing affiliates tend to be located in countries with lower income per capita than other manufacturing affiliates. For manufacturing affiliates, the country and industry effects sharply reduce the wage differential between vertically integrated manufacturing and other manufacturing affiliates, but it is still economically and statistically significant: Vertical manufacturing affiliates pay almost 14 percent less than horizontal manufacturing affiliates in the same country in the same industry. In contrast, again after controlling for industry and country effects, vertical service affiliates still pay significantly higher compensation than other service affiliates in the same country in the same industry: The compensation differential is still more than 50 percent.

To summarize, manufacturing affiliates tend to be in low-wage countries and tend to pay lower than average wages in those countries. Service affiliates, in contrast, tend to be in high-wage countries, and vertically integrated service affiliates tend to pay higher than average wages. These findings are diametrically opposite to what one would observe if most US multinationals used their foreign affiliates as a means of accessing low-cost service labor.

Conclusion

The United States has an abundance of skilled labor, and tradable services tend to be skill intensive. The range of evidence considered in this chapter—on the skill intensity of tradable services, on the export behavior of US service industries, and on the location of US service imports—all points to tradable services being aligned with comparative advantage in high-skill, high-wage countries like the United States, and not in low-wage-labor-abundant countries like India. Tradable services are consistent with US comparative advantage, and the United States will likely increase its share of global service production if trade costs in services continue to fall. Increased trade in services would allow the United States to further specialize in high-wage, high-skill activities, encouraging productivity growth both within the US service sector and in the countries to which the United States exports services.

6

Impediments to Trade in Services

There is a growing perception worldwide that services are becoming more tradable—indeed, that they are becoming as tradable as, or perhaps even more easily traded than, manufactures. Certainly trade in services is growing. Official statistics indicate that aggregate US exports and imports in "other private services," a category that includes education, finance and insurance, and business, professional, and technical services, has doubled over the past 15 years. In chapter 5 I argued that the United States has much to gain from increasing trade in services, because the United States has comparative advantage in tradable service production.

How likely is it that trade in services will continue to grow? The answer depends largely on the nature of the impediments to that growth. But what are those impediments? How much do they restrict service trade? Are they greater or smaller than the impediments to trade in goods? Are they different altogether?

These are not easy questions to answer. As previous chapters have shown, the data covering international trade in services are nowhere near as robust as the trade data for manufacturing. Not only are the data on service trade flows less detailed than the data for trade in goods, but the types of ancillary data (on transportation costs and tariffs, for example) that researchers use to measure the impediments to trade are not as well developed for services either.

To try to understand the impediments to trade in services despite the paucity of data, this chapter examines evidence on the prevalence of service trade among US firms to see whether as many firms participate in exporting or importing services as participate in importing or exporting goods. This provides a sense of how difficult it is to trade services. Participation by US firms in service trade, both imports and exports, lags their participation in goods trade.

I then turn to the nature of impediments to service trade. Services, unlike manufactured goods, do not typically face tariffs. Yet barriers to service trade do exist.

How Prevalent Is Trade in Services?

Chapter 2 showed that a wide range of service activities appear to be "traded" within the United States. Production of many services, such as software and movie production and distribution, is concentrated in one or a few regions, far from most demand for the service. These geographically concentrated services are likely to be tradable internationally: If a service produced in California can be consumed in Maine, what prevents it from being consumed in Canada or China?

This chapter considers the extent to which services actually are traded internationally, by looking at direct evidence of firms' participation in service trade. I start by reviewing the literature on trade costs and how they influence the likelihood that firms either import or export. As before, I establish a conceptual framework and then examine evidence from the manufacturing sector, where the data are better than for services. Then I examine the data that do exist for trade in services to see whether the same patterns emerge.

In chapter 4 I described a set of new economic models of how trade costs influence the types of firms that participate in exporting. Because there are costs associated with exporting (sunk costs and iceberg costs), exporters tend to be larger and more productive than nonexporters. Such firms are better able to bear these extra costs and still make a profit.

Importers and Exporters of Goods

The empirical literature on firms in international trade has been concerned almost exclusively with exporting, largely because of limitations in datasets based on censuses of domestic production or manufacturing. As a result, new theories of heterogeneous firms and trade were developed to explain observed facts about firm export behavior and yield few, if any, predictions for firm import behavior. In most of these models, consumers purchase imports directly from foreign firms, and no intermediate inputs exist—that is, firms themselves do not import.

However, researchers have started to examine the importing behavior of firms in the manufacturing sector, and the patterns they observe are similar to those for exporting. One similarity is that importers, like exporters (as chapter 4 showed), are rare. In fact, they are even rarer than exporters: In most manufacturing industries, only a relatively small number of firms import. Table 6.1, reproduced from Bernard, Jensen, Redding, and Schott (2007), shows the share of US firms that export, the share that import, and the share that both import and export, for all three-digit NAICS manufacturing industries. In every industry but one (leather and allied products, where exporters and importers are tied), even fewer firms import than export, and the difference is often wide.

We also investigated the characteristics of firms that import. Table 6.2

Table 6.1 Shares of US manufacturing firms exporting and importing goods, by industry, 1997 (percent)

Industry	Share of firms in industry that		
	Export	Import	Import and export
Food manufacturing	17	10	7
Beverage and tobacco products	28	19	13
Textile mills	47	31	24
Textile product mills	19	13	9
Apparel manufacturing	16	15	9
Leather and allied products	43	43	30
Wood product manufacturing	15	5	3
Paper manufacturing	42	18	15
Printing and related support	10	3	2
Petroleum and coal products	32	17	14
Chemical manufacturing	56	30	26
Plastics and rubber products	42	20	16
Nonmetallic minerals products	16	11	7
Primary metal manufacturing	51	23	21
Fabricated metal products	21	8	6
Machinery manufacturing	47	22	19
Computer and electronics products	65	40	37
Electrical equipment and appliances	58	35	30
Transportation equipment	40	22	18
Furniture and related products	13	8	5
Miscellaneous manufacturing	31	19	15
All manufacturing	27	14	11

Note: The table includes only those firms that appear in both the Census of Manufactures and the Linked-Longitudinal Firm Trade Transaction Database (LFTTD).

Source: Bernard, Jensen, Redding, and Schott (2007) using data from the Census of Manufactures and the LFTTD.

reports regression results from that study summarizing differences in characteristics between US manufacturing firms that export goods and firms that import goods compared with firms that do not. For each characteristic (employment, shipments, and so forth), the table reports the "premium" for a group of firms (proceeding from left to right, those that export and those that import) over firms that neither export nor import. The premium is the proportion by which the indicated group outperforms the nonexporting, nonimporting group: For example, exporters on average pay 29 percent higher wages than firms that do not export.

Table 6.2 Trading premiums in US manufacturing, 1997 (percent)

Characteristic	Exporter premium	Importer premium
Employment	150	140
Shipments	29	26
Value added per worker	23	23
Total factor productivity[a]	7	12
Wages	29	23
Capital per worker	17	13
Skill per worker[b]	4	6

a. Total factor productivity is computed as in Caves, Christensen, and Diewert (1982).
b. Measured as nonproduction workers divided by total employment.

Note: The table reports the percent by which the average goods-exporting or goods-importing US manufacturing firm exceeds the average nonexporting, nonimporting firm on the indicated characteristic. Results are from regressions of the indicated firm characteristic on a dummy variable set equal to 1 if the firm is an exporter or an importer. The sample includes only those firms that appear in both the Census of Manufactures and the LFTTD. The regression controls for industry fixed effects and, except in the regressions estimating the employment premium, for firm employment. All results are statistically significant at the 1 percent level.

Source: Bernard, Jensen, Redding, and Schott (2007) using data from the Census of Manufactures and the LFTTD.

The table reveals that goods-exporting manufacturing firms share a variety of positive attributes with manufacturing firms that are importers of goods. On average, they have bigger payrolls, are more productive, pay higher wages, and are more skill and capital intensive than firms that neither export nor import. Again, these results suggest that these firm characteristics are systematically related to participation in international trade, whether importing or exporting. Reductions in trade costs are therefore likely to benefit the largest, most productive, most skill- and capital-intensive firms in any given sector, both because they export more and because they import more.

The fact that the share of firms that import is small in most manufacturing industries suggests that there are impediments to or additional costs associated with importing. For goods, it is well understood that tariffs and transportation costs can make importing more expensive than domestic production, even when the goods in question are cheaper in the producing country. It is also easy to imagine that it is more difficult to identify and set up business relationships with foreign supplies than with domestic suppliers. The fact that importers tend to be larger and more productive than nonimporters, even within narrowly defined industries, is further evidence that in manufacturing at least, importing has significant costs and only the most productive firms are likely to engage in direct importing.

Service Importers

I look next at some more-detailed (but still very limited) information on the prevalence of US firms that import services and compare the results with those reported above, to try to obtain a sense of the relative size of the impediments to trade in goods and services. Data on firm-level service imports are quite rare. However, in 2006, at the request of the Bureau of Economic Analysis, the Census Bureau added a question to its Company Organization Survey (COS, a large survey mailed to about 60,000 firms representing about half of US private-sector employment) asking whether the firm imported services.

Table 6.3 reports, using data from the COS, the share of firms in the business service sector and its major subsectors and in the personal service sector that report importing services. For comparison, data for the manufacturing sector and the wholesale and retail trade sectors are also included, as well as the shares of firms in each sector and subsector that import goods.[1] The manufacturing data provide an interesting point of reference: Whereas 52 percent of manufacturing firms in the survey reported importing goods, only 18 percent reported importing services. Yet even this small share of services-importing manufacturers exceeds the 10 percent of firms in the business service sector that report importing services. Within business services, there is considerable variation, but only firms classified in the professional, scientific, and technical service sector are as likely as the average manufacturing firm to import services. Firms in the information sector are the next most likely to import services, at 16 percent. Perhaps surprisingly, only 5 percent of firms in the finance and insurance sector report importing services.

In addition to being relatively rare, service importers are systematically different from service nonimporters. As table 6.4 shows, service importers tend to be larger and to pay higher wages: The average service importer is 45 percent larger and pays wages that are 48 percent higher than the average service nonimporter. When service importers are compared with nonimporters within the same industry, the size differential actually increases slightly, to 51 percent, but the wage differential decreases, to 27 percent.

The low prevalence of service importing among both manufacturing and service firms, and the fact that, in both sectors, importers tend to be larger than nonimporters, could be due to large fixed costs to importing services. It could also be due to the fact that the United States has comparative advantage in service production, resulting in (relatively) fewer profitable opportunities to import services than to import goods.

---

1. Firms are classified into sectors using establishment-level employment information from the Census Bureau's business register. When a firm operates in more than one sector, it is classified as belonging to the two-digit NAICS sector that accounts for the largest share of the firm's employment. Firms are classified as importing goods if they reported a merchandise import transaction in 2005.

Table 6.3 Shares of US firms importing services and goods, by sector, 2006 (percent)

Sector or industry	Share of firms importing	
	Services	Goods
Manufacturing	18	52
Business services	10	9
Information	16	n.a.
Finance and insurance	5	n.a.
Real estate and leasing	2	n.a.
Professional, scientific, and technical	18	n.a.
Management	15	n.a.
Administrative support and waste remediation	6	n.a.
Personal services	3	4
Wholesale and retail trade	8	29
Other	7	15

n.a. = not available.

Source: Author's calculations using data from the 2006 Company Organization Survey.

Table 6.4 Importer premiums in US services, 2006 (percent)

Characteristic	Without controlling for industry	Controlling for industry
Employment	45	51
Average wage	48	27

Note: The table reports the percentage by which the average importing firm exceeds the average nonimporting firm on the indicated characteristic.

Source: Author's calculations using data from the 2006 Company Organization Survey and the 2006 Business Register.

Service Exporters

Chapter 4 demonstrated that exporters are relatively rare, at least among US manufacturers, and described how theoretical models attribute that rarity to the presence of additional costs to exporting—either sunk costs of entering a new market or additional costs from tariffs and transportation expenses. Here I examine the prevalence of service exporters to try to infer whether the costs associated with exporting services are greater than those in manufacturing.

Table 6.5, adapted from Jensen (2008), reports the shares of manufacturing establishments and of service establishments (in NAICS 51, 54, and 56) that export. (The Census Bureau asks the export question of firms in these three categories, all within business services, because these are the ones considered most likely to export.) The table reports that 27 percent of manufacturing establishments export, and that an even smaller share of service producers (about 5 percent) export.

Table 6.6 shows that the prevalence of exporters varies significantly across the three business service categories reported in table 6.5. The information sector (which includes prepackaged software, movies, and sound recordings) has the highest share of exporters, followed by professional, technical, and scientific industries. Administrative support and waste remediation industries have a very low prevalence of exporters. These differences are likely driven by the inherent tradability or nontradability of these activities.

To control for this effect, table 6.7 reports results of regressions estimating the difference in the probability of exporting between business service producers (in the same three categories as above) and manufacturing plants. The first column shows the raw differences, without controlling for other characteristics. The business service producers are 22 percent less likely than manufacturing plants to export. When locational Gini coefficients (a measure of geographic concentration; see chapter 2) are included to control for whether the service appears tradable within the United States, the difference decreases but remains relatively large: Business service producers are still 15 percent less likely to export. Even when the analysis controls for the firm characteristics previously shown to correlate with trading (the last column), business service establishments are still less likely than manufacturing plants to export.

If services in general were highly tradable, as some digitized services clearly are, one would expect exports-to-sales ratios for these business service industries to be higher than for manufacturing, where transportation costs are still very real. But this is not the case. Table 6.8 reports the results of regressions estimating differences in exports-to-sales ratios between manufacturing plants and business service establishments that export. In a regression that does not control for geographic concentration, exports-to-sales ratios are lower among business service exporters. When geographic concentration is controlled for, the ratios are statistically indistinguishable.

In the case of service imports, it was plausible that US firms do not import more because the United States has comparative advantage in service production. But it is difficult to explain on comparative advantage grounds why US service firms do not export more. The United States *should* be exporting services, because that is where its comparative advantage seems to lie. The statistics on firm participation in export markets thus suggest that there remain significant impediments to trade in services, possibly including culture and language differences, technological barriers, or policy impediments. The next section examines the nature and prevalence of these impediments.

Table 6.5   Prevalence of exporting in US manufacturing and business services, 2002

Industry and characteristic	Mean	Standard deviation	Coworker mean
Manufacturing (N = 146,986)			
Percent exporting	27.0	44.4	55.1
Export shipments (thousands of dollars)	2,150	58,737	82,482
Sales (thousands of dollars)	22,571	169,651	388,486
Exports-to-sales ratio	0.040	0.127	0.084
Business services[a] (N = 390,377)			
Percent exporting	5.3	22.4	8.2
Export shipments (thousands of dollars)	93	10,340	9,685
Sales (thousands of dollars)	4,098	44,126	115,838
Exports-to-sales ratio	0.007	0.061	0.009

a. Firms in NAICS categories 51, 54, and 56 only.

Source: Author's calculations using data from the 2002 Economic Census.

Table 6.6   Prevalence of exporting in selected US business service categories, 2002

Characteristic	Information services	Professional, scientific, and technical services	Administrative support and waste remediation services
Percent exporting	11.4	4.9	0.8
Export shipments (thousands of dollars)	239	66	10
Sales (thousands of dollars)	7,324	3,206	2,750
Exports-to-sales ratio	0.01	0.008	0.002

Source: Author's calculations using data from the 2002 Economic Census.

Impediments to Trade in Services

The variety of service activities, the intangible nature of some services, and the sometimes complex interactions between producers and consumers in service delivery make identifying and quantifying impediments to trade in services quite difficult.[2] In addition, because service transactions are not subject to

---

2. The Organization for Economic Cooperation and Development (OECD) is currently making an effort to develop a Services Trade Restrictiveness Index. See the OECD's website for more information. This section draws on these efforts.

Table 6.7 Regressions estimating the effects of firm characteristics on the probability of exporting

Characteristic	Regression			
	1	2	3	4
Firm is in business service sector	−0.2170	−0.1453	−0.0982	−0.0849
	(0.0012)	(0.0012)	(0.0012)	(0.0011)
Geographic concentration (Gini)		0.2387	0.2192	0.1675
		(0.0019)	(0.0019)	(0.0018)
Log(employment)			0.0286	0.0259
			(0.0003)	(0.0003)
Log(average wage)				0.0503
				(0.001)
Log(labor productivity)				−0.0340
				(0.0021)
Log(other inputs per worker)				0.0466
				(0.0014)

Note: The sample is a pooled sample of manufacturing and business service establishments. Standard errors are in parentheses.

Source: Author's calculations using data from the 2002 Economic Census.

Table 6.8 Regressions estimating differences in exports-to-sales ratios between manufacturing and business service firms

Characteristic	Regression	
	1	2
Firm is in business service sector	−0.0186	−0.0001
	(0.0019)	(0.0021)
Geographic concentration (Gini)		0.0911
		(0.0045)

Note: Sample is a pooled sample of manufacturing and business service establishments. Standard errors are in parentheses.

Source: Author's calculations using data from the 2002 Economic Census.

tariffs to the same extent as traded goods, no tariff schedules exist to use as a measure of impediments to service trade. Instead, the barriers to service trade are more diffuse and sometimes more subtle than those to merchandise trade.

There are legitimate reasons for some of the restrictions that countries impose on service trade. An important one is consumer protection. Many services, particularly the types of business services on which this book focuses, present important information asymmetries between producers and consumers. For example, consumers often find it difficult to judge the quality of the service being provided by a lawyer or a doctor. Lawyers know the law, and doctors know medicine, far better than the average consumer—that is precisely why consumers consult them. For activities where these information asymmetries are important, countries have developed regulations to try to mitigate the problems that they can cause.

Education and licensing requirements are examples of this type of regulation. Aaditya Mattoo and Deepak Mishra (2008) describe the process of obtaining a license in a variety of professions within the United States. Although this process tends to be more open in the United States than in many other countries, it is still time consuming, and the requirements vary because licensing is typically mandated at the state rather than the federal level. Thus, there are state medical boards, state boards of architecture, state engineering boards, state accounting boards, state bars, and so on.

In general, the process of obtaining a license involves several steps. A typical first step is verification of educational credentials, training, and experience. Since university and training programs in some countries are not formally accredited, verification can be time consuming and unpredictable. Sometimes remedial training is required.

The next step is often a professional examination, which may duplicate examinations taken in the applicant's home country. There are often other requirements. Mattoo and Mishra report, for example, that several US states require accountants to be residents of the state as a condition for licensing. This, of course, discriminates not only against foreign professionals but also against out-of-state US professionals. Work experience in the profession may also be required. In medicine, for example, a foreign medical graduate on a J1 visa must work for three years in an underserved area in order to become licensed in the United States.

Frequently, states have different requirements for those who have qualified from within the state, from other states, and from foreign countries. As Mattoo and Mishra (2008) report,

> For example California requires four years of experience for licensure if an engineer is educated from a non-accredited program, whereas Pennsylvania requires a minimum of 12 years of experience. Similarly, international medical graduates (IMGs) are required to complete 3 years of postgraduate training in states such as Alaska, Colorado, Delaware, Washington DC and Missouri whereas the requirement is only 2 years of post graduate training in states such as California, Florida and Illinois. Architecture is an exception in that it has a centralized and strong national body, the National Council for Architectural Registration Boards (NCARB), which works with State Boards to establish qualification, registration and licensing policies.

Despite this heterogeneity in licensing requirements across states, the United States has relatively low impediments to service trade. Other countries impose licensing and accreditation procedures and requirements that make it more difficult for foreign professionals to practice in their country.

Classifying Impediments to Service Trade

An exhaustive list of impediments to service trade would be beyond the scope of this book. However, it is possible to provide a flavor of the types and range of these impediments. Box 6.1 spells out the many policy barriers to a single service industry (architectural services) in just one country.

Several groups have made concerted efforts to develop measures of impediments to service trade. For example, in the late 1990s and early 2000s, the Australian Government Productivity Commission produced a number of studies that constructed indices of these impediments across a variety of countries (see Findlay and Warren 2000). The following list of some of the most significant restrictions to professional service trade is from one of those studies:

– Requirements on the form of establishment—restrictions on incorporation and other business structures. For example, professionals may be prohibited from incorporating, and hence may only practice in partnership or sole proprietorship. Restrictions on the legal form of businesses apply equally to both foreign and domestic service providers, but can limit the ability of foreign firms to establish branches and subsidiaries. In general, they can have the effect of preventing the development of large-scale professional firms.

– Foreign partnership restrictions—limitations on foreign firms and professionals seeking to enter into partnership or joint venture with local professionals. As partnership is a common mode of professional practice, prohibition on foreign partnership can be an important barrier to foreign entry and establishment in the domestic market. Partnership with local professionals also represents a way to enter the domestic market without the need to obtain a local licence. In certain cases, economies may require establishment through local partnership or joint venture.

– Ownership and investment restrictions—limitations on ownership and control of local firms by *foreign* professionals, and limitations on ownership and control of local firms by *non-professional* investors. The latter category applies to both domestic and foreign providers and usually requires owners of professional firms to be locally licensed or qualified.

– Nationality requirements—conditions to practice on the basis of nationality or citizenship. Nationality requirements differ in scope—ranging from restrictions on the use of a professional title but with practice being relatively free, to comprehensive requirements to exclude foreign professionals from local practice. Nationality requirements may be applied with reciprocity or exemptions for certain economies.

– Residency and local presence requirements—obligations to be established or resident in the market where the service is provided. Residency requirements apply to individual professionals, while local presence requirements apply to professional firms. These requirements raise the costs of establishment and tend to have the effect of excluding cross-border trade in professional services.

– Licensing and accreditation of foreign professionals—licensing and qualification conditions that exclude foreign professionals by not recognizing their foreign licence and qualifications. Foreign qualified professionals may be

Box 6.1 An example of policy impediments to architectural service trade

The Organization for Economic Cooperation and Development provides a useful example of the types of policy impediments firms can face in the architecture industry in one (unnamed) country (see chapter 1 for definitions of the "modes" of service trade).

Mode 1: Commercial presence is required for the cross-border supply of architectural services.

Mode 3: The amount of foreign investment must be over a minimum threshold. Foreign investors must notify the host government of their proposed investments; if the activity appears on the "negative list" or is related to areas deemed sensitive such as public health and safety, it may be rejected. … Quotas exist for collection and treatment services of industrial wastewater. The provision of collection, transport and disposal of industrial refuse services, cleaning services of exhaust gases and noise abatement services, purity testing and analysis services are subject to an economic means test. Some construction services, such as those for long distance and local pipelines, installation and assembly, are subject to limits on contract values and a compulsory sub-contracting system; new licenses are issued each year.

Mode 4: Stays of "executives," "senior managers," and "specialists" are limited to three years, but can be extended if deemed necessary; they may also be limited to 90 days, depending on their function; for representatives of foreign suppliers not making direct sales of services to the public, stay limited to 90 days.

Other measures: Licenses are issued annually in the construction and engineering sectors; to qualify for public projects, foreign firms must obtain a license for either construction, construction supervision or design. This may be costly (USD 800,000 per license) and time-consuming, and few of the related laws or application forms are translated into other languages. Registration is required for foreign engineering firms.

Source: Excerpted from OECD (2001, 23).

required to undertake full local retraining or pass stringent tests to practice. Recognition of foreign qualifications may involve a case-by-case assessment process in which discretion is exercised, or mutual recognition of qualifications between economies based on objective and technical criteria.

— Limitations on the scope of activities—regulations that reserve certain activities to the exclusive exercise of the profession or some groups within the profession. For example, regulations may provide accountants the exclusive right to perform audit services. Similarly, domestic lawyers may have sole rights to provide services relating to domestic law, while foreign lawyers may be limited to the practice of home country or international law. These regulations can have the effect of providing a monopoly position to the profession.

– Multi-disciplinary practices restrictions—regulations that restrict partnership or association between different professions or between particular groups within the profession.

– Fee and advertising restrictions—regulations that set limits or prohibit fee setting and advertising among professionals. These regulations typically reduce competition on the basis of price. (Nguyen-Hong 2000, 7–8, italics in original)

Besides these various types of regulation, service firms can face other forms of impediments. Mattoo and Mishra (2008) note that *"quotas and fiscal discrimination*, in the form of restrictive visa regimes, prohibitions and economic needs tests on foreign providers, as well as discriminatory treatment in taxes and government procurement" are possible additional barriers. Discriminatory government procurement practices are a potentially important impediment and are likely to become even more important. Chapter 9 returns to this issue.

Quantifying Impediments to Service Trade

An ongoing World Bank project, described in Gootiiz and Mattoo (2009) and Borchert, Gootiiz, and Mattoo (2011), seeks to measure impediments to trade in services in countries around the world. To date, the project has collected survey information on actual policies that impede service trade from 32 developing and transition economies and 24 developed countries.

The sectors included in the project are financial services (retail banking, life and automobile insurance, and reinsurance), telecommunications (fixed and mobile), retail distribution, transportation (air passenger, road and rail freight, maritime international shipping, and maritime auxiliary services), and selected professional services. In each sector the project covers the most relevant modes of supplying the service: cross-border trade (in financial, transportation, and professional services), commercial presence or foreign direct investment (in all sectors), and the presence of individuals (in professional services).

For the 32 developing and transition countries, surveys were sent to local law firms familiar with the policy regime in the various sectors. For the 24 developed countries, comparable policy information was collected from various publicly available sources, including documents detailing countries' commitments under the General Agreement on Trade in Services and sector-specific databases, and summarized for each country. The survey information and the policy summaries were confirmed by government trade officials during 2008.

The World Bank researchers used the data to calculate an index of the overall restrictiveness of service trade policies for each country. Figure 6.1, reproduced from Gootiiz and Mattoo (2009), plots this restrictiveness index

Figure 6.1 Restrictiveness of service trade policies by GDP per capita in 56 countries, 2005

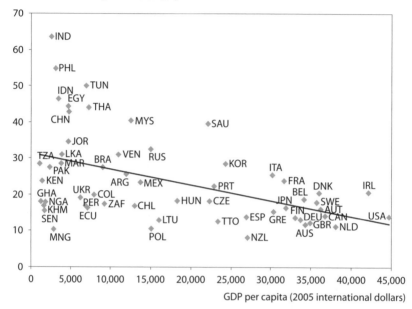

restrictiveness index (100 = maximum)

AUS = Australia; AUT = Austria; ARG = Argentina; BRA = Brazil; BEL = Belgium; CAN = Canada; CHL = Chile; CHN = China; COL = Colombia; CZE = Czech Republic; DEU = Germany; DNK = Denmark; ECU = Ecuador; EGY = Egypt; ESP = Spain; FRA = France; FIN = Finland; GBR = United Kingdom; GHA = Ghana; GRE = Greece; HUN = Hungary; IDN = Indonesia; IND = India; IRL = Ireland; ITA = Italy; JOR = Jordan; JPN = Japan; KEN = Kenya; KHM = Cambodia; KOR = Korea; LKA = Sri Lanka; LTU = Lithuania; MAR = Morocco; MEX = Mexico; MNG = Mongolia; MYS = Malaysia; NLD = Netherlands; NGA = Nigeria; NZL = New Zealand; PAK = Pakistan; PER = Peru; PHL = Philippines; POL = Poland; PRT = Portugal; RUS = Russia; SAU = Saudi Arabia; SEN = Senegal; SWE = Sweden; THA = Thailand; TTO = Trinidad and Tobago; TUN = Tunisia; TZA = Tanzania; UKR = Ukraine; USA = United States; VEN = Venezuela; ZAF = South Africa

Note: The sample includes 32 developing and 24 developed countries. The trade restrictiveness index covers restrictions in the following industries: financial, telecommunications, retailing, maritime, air passenger transport, and professional services. International dollars adjust for differences in the purchasing power of the dollar.

Source: Gootiiz and Mattoo (2009).

against GDP per capita for a large sample of countries. The resulting scatterplot shows a fairly strong negative correlation: Countries with higher income per capita tend to have less restrictive barriers to service trade, whereas some countries with low incomes per capita have some of the highest levels of service trade restrictions. But not all. Some relatively poor countries, like Cambodia, Ghana, Mongolia, Nigeria, and Senegal, have relatively low levels of service trade restrictions—possibly the result of reform programs under World Bank and International Monetary Fund auspices, as well as aspirations toward World Trade Organization accession. Gootiiz and Mattoo note that some of the most

Box 6.2   Limits on foreign participation in China's booming real estate development market

Because land [in China] is owned by the government, public projects are awarded by government sponsored competition. Private development projects entail a "scheme gathering" solicitation of design firms to prepare concepts. These are submitted to "expert" panels who evaluate and rank design concepts for creativity, relationship to context and constructability. Top finalists receive stipends; winning design firms have an opportunity to negotiate to provide further design services.

While the process is generally open and transparent, as with everything in China, relationships can be important. Foreign architects are currently limited to presenting preliminary designs, providing aesthetic, structural, materials, energy-efficiency, spatial use and other expertise to "local design institutes" (LDIs) of architects, construction engineers and building code compliance specialists. Requested drawings may be only 50–75% complete, compared to detailed plans submitted in the U.S., allowing flexibility for the LDIs to lock in a final design. A developer may continue to retain a representative of the foreign firm through the construction phase to work with the LDI, or may terminate its relationship once drawings are submitted. Likewise, foreign construction firms can serve as general contractors, but the actual construction work is subcontracted to local firms.

At times the process has produced creative tensions as the original design concept is dramatically changed to lower costs, address code issues or put the developer's or LDI's creative stamp on a project. Still, partnerships between foreign architects and LDIs are being institutionalized, and China is becoming an increasingly important market for many Bay Area design firms.

Sources: Excerpted from Bay Area Council Economic Institute (2006, 86–87).

restrictive policies are in large or fast-growing economies like China, Egypt, India, Indonesia, Malaysia, the Philippines, Saudi Arabia, and Thailand. Box 6.2 reports on the policy barriers facing foreign architectural and construction firms seeking to do business in China.

Gary Hufbauer, Jeffrey Schott, and Woan Foong Wong (2010) review a number of methodologies for quantifying impediments to service trade and provide new estimates of tariff equivalents of these barriers. Their estimates, shown in figure 6.2, again indicate that developed countries tend to have the lowest barriers to service trade (tariff equivalents ranging between 0 and 7 percent), whereas several large, fast-growing economies have much higher barriers.

Figure 6.2 Tariff equivalents of service barriers in 21 countries

percent ad valorem

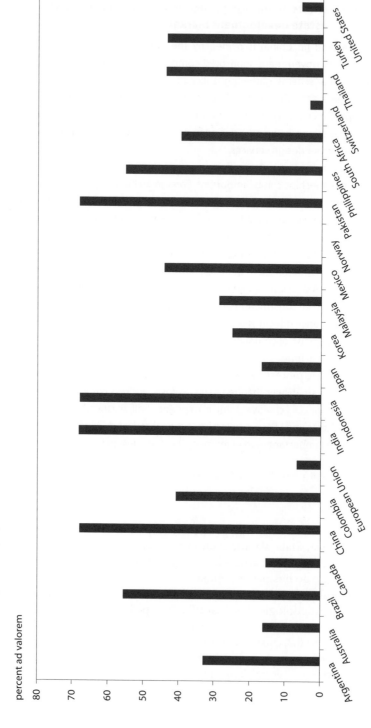

Source: Hufbauer, Schott, and Wong (2010).

Conclusion

The United States is a relatively open economy for trade in services, although not the most open. A number of the world's large, fast-growing economies are significantly less open to trade in services, as measured by the World Bank study. The United States has comparative advantage in many tradable services and it makes sense for it to pursue increased liberalization of service trade.

What would happen if the impediments to service trade were reduced significantly? The history of trade in the manufacturing sector indicates how that process is likely to play out. Reallocation according to comparative advantage would be expected to occur: Skill-abundant countries, for example, would specialize in skill-intensive service activities. Because many tradable business services are skill-intensive activities, the United States would be likely to reallocate economic activity toward these services. Reallocation would occur both across industries and within industries, as described in chapter 4. This reallocation away from low-productivity activities and firms toward high-productivity activities and firms would tend to increase productivity in the business service sector.

Service trade liberalization would also benefit the large, fast-growing economies that today impose high barriers to trade in services. Increased availability of low-cost, world-class services that are intermediate inputs to the industries in which these countries specialize would lower the costs to firms in those industries, making them even more productive. Francois and Hoekman (2010) review a range of studies that demonstrate that service trade liberalization increases productivity in the manufacturing sector. Increased service trade would improve the level of service in telecommunications, finance, and other business services in developing countries for businesses and consumers.

Increased trade in services has the potential to contribute significantly to productivity growth in the US service sector, just as increased trade has contributed to productivity growth in the manufacturing sector. But increased trade in services has probably even more potential to improve productivity in the service sector in developing countries, where service productivity is not as high. Thus, increased trade in services offers significant potential to improve living standards both in the United States and around the world.

Service trade liberalization is not going to be easy, however, and would not be easy even if there were a domestic consensus in its favor. Unfortunately, there is no such consensus. Rather, the debate on trade in services is overshadowed by fear of domestic job losses to low-wage, labor-abundant countries. Chapter 7 examines whether this fear of potential job losses from increased trade in services has any merit.

7

Labor Market Impact of Increased Service Trade

The big concern with regard to increased US trade in services is that it will have an effect on workers in tradable services similar to what is perceived to have happened to US manufacturing workers when trade in that sector expanded. Some observers, like Alan Blinder in the *Foreign Affairs* article quoted in chapter 4, argue that the US labor force should prepare for wrenching adjustment in response to increased service imports from unskilled-labor-abundant, low-wage countries.

Should US workers fear an increase in offshoring from continued liberalization of service trade? I argue that there is considerable room for service trade liberalization, particularly in large developing markets like China, India, and Indonesia. Such liberalization—both there and in the United States—has the potential to increase productivity on both sides, benefiting firms, consumers, and many workers in all countries that participate. I have presented evidence on how increased trade in goods has increased productivity in the US manufacturing sector. Higher productivity has increased profits and often wages in many companies, while lowering the cost to consumers of many goods. It is reasonable to expect the same kind of gains from increased trade in services.

But there are also sure to be some costs from liberalization. Chapter 4 showed that the productivity gains in manufacturing from increased trade were due in part to a reallocation of economic activity and employment within the manufacturing sector. Competition with imports from low-wage, unskilled-labor-abundant countries such as China caused a shift in activity in the United States toward manufactured products more consistent with US comparative advantage, and a shift away from those that are not. The former tend to be produced more efficiently than the latter, with fewer workers per unit of output, and the shift in their favor thus contributed to net job losses in manufacturing—this is a large part of the story behind the decline in US manufacturing employment. The United States today imports large quantities of unskilled-labor-intensive products that compete with a reduced number of low-wage, low-skill products "made in the USA," while importing relatively small shares of high-skill, high-wage products from low-wage countries. At the same time, however, the United States continues to produce and export high-wage, high-skill products, to the benefit of workers in those industries. Trade in manufacturing thus has driven a reallocation of economic activity toward the United States' comparative advantage.

Chapters 3 and 5 showed that tradable services tend to be relatively high-wage, high-skill activities and cited several pieces of evidence indicating that the United States has comparative advantage in these activities. One is that the United States has for many years run a trade surplus in services overall. Another is that relatively high-skill, high-wage industries within the US tradable service sector tend to have relatively high exports. Yet another is that the services that the United States does import tend to come from other high-wage, skill-abundant countries, not from low-wage, unskilled-labor-abundant countries. Even the US multinationals that establish affiliates overseas to export services back to the parent tend to be located in high-income countries (and pay relatively high wages). All this suggests that the United States as a whole would benefit from increased service trade and should neither fear nor discourage it, but rather encourage steps to increase it. But in doing so, US policymakers should bear in mind that increased service trade is likely to impose costs on some US firms and workers.

This chapter takes a closer look at the prospects for employment dislocation in the tradable service sector. I examine whether tradable service workers are more or less vulnerable to dislocation than manufacturing workers and analyze recent trends in net employment growth and worker dislocation in both manufacturing and tradable services. The discussion draws on the analysis of previous chapters that suggested that it is low-wage service industries in the United States that are likely to face import competition from low-wage, unskilled-labor-abundant countries. I start by trying to quantify the share of the workforce in the tradable service sector that is likely to face import competition from low-wage countries and compare it with the corresponding share in the manufacturing sector.

Prospects for Employment Dislocation

Having seen how imports from low-wage countries have affected the US manufacturing sector in recent decades, one can expect that some share of tradable service activities in the United States will also move to other countries whose workforces earn lower wages than the average US worker. But one can also expect that the activities that move to developing countries will largely be relatively lower-wage, lower-skilled activities (albeit sometimes in higher-end service industries, like business services). Higher-wage, higher-skilled service activities will tend to remain in the United States and provide a source of potential exports.

On average, workers in tradable service activities are better educated and have higher earnings than workers in similar but nontradable service activities, and higher earnings and more education than manufacturing workers. Tradable services also tend to require greater skill than these other activities, which suggests that they are consistent with US comparative advantage. Indeed, US service establishments that export tend to be in high-wage industries and, within those industries, to pay higher wages on average, again consistent with the notion that the United States has comparative advantage in tradable service production. Because the United States has comparative advantage in high-skill, high-wage production, it is these activities, both in the manufacturing sector and within the tradable service sector, that the United States is likely to retain and, indeed, increase as trade barriers diminish.

The evidence presented in chapters 4 and 5 suggests that there is no sharp dividing line between activities where low-wage, unskilled-labor-abundant countries have comparative advantage and those where the advantage lies with high-wage, high-skill countries. However, if one had to pick such a threshold, the same evidence suggests that it would be at an average annual wage of around $40,000. Industries in the United States that pay average wages above that threshold seem to be mostly ones in which the United States has comparative advantage, whereas those that pay lower wages do not. As trade in services increases, service activities below the threshold are likely to face competitive pressure from service imports (and offshoring) from low-wage, unskilled-labor-abundant countries, while those above the threshold are likely to expand. It seems likely, then, that relatively low wage service activities will experience increased levels of job dislocation. However, this does not mean that there will be widespread dislocation throughout the tradable service sector. Because most tradable services are relatively skill intensive, relatively high wage activities in which the United States has comparative advantage, the dislocation is likely to be much lower in most tradable service industries.

This line of argument focuses on one key dimension on which services do differ from manufacturing, namely, the share of total employment in the sector that is likely to suffer from import competition from low-wage countries. An important difference between tradable services and tradable manufacturing is that the share of employment in industries paying below the notional wage threshold cited above is much smaller in tradable services. Figure 7.1 shows that about 23 percent of employment in the tradable service sector, but almost 40 percent of employment in tradable manufacturing, is in industries with average annual wages below $40,000. If the threshold is set at $50,000, the difference is even greater: Fewer than a third (31 percent) of tradable business service workers, but over two-thirds of tradable manufacturing workers (69 percent, more than double the share for tradable business services) are in industries with average annual wages below $50,000. And the pattern still holds when the threshold is raised to $60,000 or above.

It is certainly true that the United States has seen growth in service imports from India. Is India an exception to the above generalization that

Figure 7.1   Cumulative wage distribution of employment in tradable manufacturing and business service industries in the United States, 2007

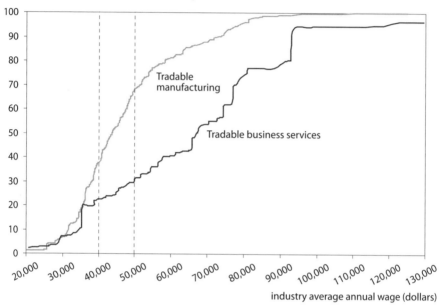

percent of employment below indicated wage

Tradable manufacturing

Tradable business services

industry average annual wage (dollars)

Note: The figure shows the share of employment in tradable manufacturing industries and the share in tradable business services industries where the average annual wage in the industry is below the indicated level on the horizontal axis.

Source: Author's calculation using 2007 County Business Patterns data from the US Census Bureau, www.census.gov.

the United States will not lose its high-wage, high-skill service jobs to developing countries? Chapter 5 discussed the apparent anomaly of India exporting services. As a low-wage, unskilled-labor-abundant country, India should have comparative advantage in manufacturing, not in services. Why, then, is it today a leading exporter of services? The apparent explanation is the heavy regulatory burden imposed on India's manufacturing sector, which makes India's manufactured goods relatively expensive (see box 5.2 in chapter 5). Conversely, because India's service industries largely escape regulation, they are relatively inexpensive, given India's low average wages. In other words, India has an artificial comparative advantage in service production.

This surely cannot last. Although India does have a large number of highly skilled and highly educated people, it is not a skill-abundant country in the sense that matters for comparative advantage, namely, the *share* of workers who are highly skilled. India's vast population of illiterate or poorly educated workers far outnumbers its cadre of well-educated, highly skilled workers. When one looks at the skill composition of the Indian workforce as a whole, it is hard to conclude anything other than that India is a low-skilled-labor-abundant country that should be producing low-wage, labor-intensive products and services. Moreover, as India's development proceeds, demand will grow for the skilled workers now exporting services to undertake other activities that require skill and education, such as managing manufacturing firms and providing services to the growing Indian middle class. This will drive wages for these workers upward, reducing the price advantage of Indian services in world markets.

Further evidence consistent with the notion that relatively high wage service activities will stay in the United States is that the supply of educated workers with the appropriate productivity—even in large countries like India— is not limitless. Work by the McKinsey Global Institute (2005) suggests that the number of engineers and computer programmers in the developing world that are "multinational company ready" is less than 20 percent of the total, and that other factors, like accessibility and domestic competition for this talent, will further reduce the pool available for offshoring. Indeed, as reported in the *Wall Street Journal*, salaries for highly skilled computer programmers in India are now approaching those in the United States, leading some US firms to close their Bangalore offices and bring the work back onshore.[1]

A more sensationalist news story that made the rounds, and may have resonated with people's fears, was the risk of Indian radiologists displacing radiologists in the United States. Although medical tourism does happen, the risk of significant displacement among US medical professionals has been overstated in the popular media. This phenomenon is examined in a more thorough (and level-headed) manner in box 7.1.

These facts suggest that the bulk of US workers in tradable services are not likely to face significant competition from imports from low-wage countries. But that is not to say that there will not be any dislocation of workers from increased service trade. Indeed, it is likely that US service workers in relatively low wage activities will face increased competitive pressure from low-wage countries, just as workers in low-wage manufacturing industries have for decades. Increased trade in services with the emerging economies of the world is likely to pose significant challenges for these low-wage, low-skill (often less educated) workers—some of whom, ironically, entered service employment after being displaced from manufacturing jobs. Worse yet, if the manufacturing sector continues to shed low-skill jobs under growing trade pressures, the competition for the shrinking number of these jobs throughout the US economy will be all the greater.

To summarize: The share of tradable business service workers in industries likely to face increasing competition from low-wage imports is smaller than the share in tradable manufacturing. The reason is that, compared with tradable manufacturing, tradable service industries generally employ workers with higher educational attainment and higher wages, who do not face direct

---

1. "Second Thoughts: Some in Silicon Valley Begin to Sour on India," *Wall Street Journal*, July 3, 2007.

Box 7.1   The limits to offshoring radiology

Frank Levy and Kyoung-Hee Yu (2010) describe how regulatory processes and business practices act to limit international trade in services in one high-skill-intensive industry, namely, teleradiology, or the interpretation of radiographic images taken in one country and transmitted electronically to a trained radiologist in another:

> There are enough isolated facts for a good news story. An Indian radiologist in Mumbai or Bangalore likely earns less than the equivalent of $35,000 a year, about one-eighth of a US radiologist's income. US medical images are read in Bangalore and other offshore locations. Indian teleradiology firms are developing new markets in the United Kingdom and Singapore. Beyond reading images per se, Indian firms are also doing 3D image reconstruction for US hospitals, work done in the United States by trained medical technicians.
>
> But an examination of all the facts suggests that teleradiology is not garden variety offshoring. About fifteen (15) Indian radiologists currently read US images. This number is unlikely to expand much in the near future. When US images are offshored to other countries, the typical reader is a US radiologist living abroad.
>
> Indian radiologists are developing a stronger presence in the United Kingdom and Singapore. But even in these countries potential expansion is limited in the short run and uncertain in the long run. And no client country, including the United States, shows evidence of radiologist or technologist displacement. Many of these outcomes reflect the characteristics of radiology including its extensive training requirements and its heavy government regulation. But significant training and regulation characterize many professional services and so the teleradiology story provides a useful caution about just how flat the world is....
>
> To demonstrate competence—to be allowed to legally read images generated in the United States—a radiologist must have completed his/her medical residency in a US program, passed US medical board examinations, be licensed in the state where the image was taken and have privileges in the hospital where the image was taken. A radiologist who does not fulfill these requirements cannot obtain malpractice insurance and a doctor who refers an image to an uncertified radiologist risks his or her own malpractice insurance.

Thus, regulation and insurance practices effectively limit the amount of radiology performed offshore. But Levy and Yu (2010) also trace out a larger impediment to the offshoring of radiology to low-wage, labor-abundant locations like India, namely, supply and demand (and by implication comparative advantage):

> Truth wins out in the end and the story of US-radiology-to-India will soon lose its luster. But before dismissing the story, it is worth considering why the story was wrong—why the world is not as flat for radiologists as it is for textile workers.
>
> Most of the answer lies in supply and demand. "The world is flat" is a story about large numbers of developing country workers who can do industrialized country jobs at much lower wages. In today's economy, there are three reasons why this story has particular force for back office services and manufacturing jobs:

(continued on next page)

Box 7.1   The limits to offshoring radiology *(continued)*

1. Much of the work in these jobs involves rules-based tasks that can be easily taught. This makes the assumption about large numbers of developing country workers realistic.

2. The rules-based nature of the work makes output quality easy to determine and so markets for back office services and manufactured goods are typically lightly regulated. The lack of regulation eliminates a possible barrier to offshoring the work.

3. Because much of the work is rules-based, workers in both developed and developing countries face competition from computerized work. Domestic and offshore workers are competing with each other in a declining market for labor.

For the moment, diagnostic radiology satisfies none of these conditions. Because the work rests on pattern recognition and extensive tacit knowledge, it requires expensive, multi-year training in every country. As a result, relatively few people worldwide are capable of doing the work and the supply is not increasing very fast. Because tacit knowledge (i.e., unarticulated rules) is so important, radiologists currently face no computer substitution and, in fact, the opposite is true: radiologists are an indispensable complement to computerized medical imaging, and rapid advances in imaging expand demand for radiologists' services. The result is a tight labor market for radiologists—expanding demand and restricted supply—that is the mirror image of the global labor market for factory and back office workers.

Within this tight labor market, wages do differ significantly across countries. Because most radiologists are concentrated in high wage countries and supplies in any country can change only slowly, an unregulated global radiology market would increase Indian wages more than it would lower US and EU wages. But full convergence is purely hypothetical since, again unlike factory or back office work, the radiology market is heavily regulated.

In other words, although regulation (in this case on the developed-country side, unlike in box 6.1 in chapter 6) is an important part of the story explaining why teleradiology performed by developing-country practitioners has yet to catch on globally, another important part is, once again, comparative advantage. Radiology is, as this case study demonstrates, a highly technical discipline requiring an extreme level of skill. Regulation merely ensures that no one attempts to short-cut that requirement. And skill is what the United States has in relative abundance—in the case of radiology and other medical fields, thanks to decades-long US investment in medical education. Although India and other developing countries are rapidly adding to their ranks of skilled medical practitioners, their relative scarcity within India will also tend to raise their wages rapidly, thus making it less likely that India will become a source of low-wage competition for high-wage jobs in this field.

competition from low-wage workers abroad. This strongly indicates that the United States will *not* see the widespread dislocation of service workers predicted by some. However, workers in low-skill, low-wage industries within tradable services do face competition from workers in low-wage countries and are likely to experience some degree of job dislocation.

Labor Market Impact to Date: Aggregates

The previous section discussed the predictions of economic theory, based on the experience of US manufacturing workers, about the future impact of increased service trade on employment in the US service sector. But what is the actual evidence on that impact to date? Unfortunately, the same data limitations I encountered in chapter 5 make it difficult to pursue the type of detailed, plant-level analysis described in chapter 4 for manufacturing. Instead this section examines differences in net job creation in tradable and nontradable activities, in the aggregate and at the industry and occupation level, both across and within sectors.

Table 7.1, which reports data on employment and the change in employment for broad US sectors for 1998 and 2007,[2] reveals that the manufacturing sector in general did indeed shed a significant number of workers over that period. Low-wage industries (defined here as those paying average annual wages under $40,000) in the tradable manufacturing sector suffered job losses of 2.3 million. High-wage tradable manufacturing industries also lost jobs, but far fewer: Employment in these industries fell by about 1.2 million workers.

In contrast, the tradable business service sector increased its employment over the period, adding almost 5 million jobs and accounting for over 40 percent of total net employment growth in the private workforce over these years. High-wage and low-wage industries contributed about equally to this growth. Nontradable business services, in contrast, contributed far less to total net employment growth. One reason is that tradable business services employed more workers at the beginning of the period: More than 17 million compared with fewer than 10 million in nontradable business services. But net employment in tradable business services also grew faster than net employment in nontradable business services.

The available data also allow me to examine net employment growth by occupation category, as I did in chapter 3. Table 7.2 presents aggregate employment growth data for occupation groups for the period from 1999 to 2009 and shows a pattern similar to that just described for industries.[3] Employment

---

2. The choice of years is driven by the availability of data on an NAICS industry basis: 1998 is the first year for which the Census Bureau reported employment data on an NAICS basis, and 2007 is the most recent year for which such data are available as of this writing.

3. The choice of years is again driven by the availability of data: 1999 is the first year for which Occupational Employment Survey data using the 2000 occupation classification system are avail-

Table 7.1 Changes in US employment by industry tradability and wages, 1999–2009

Industry group and wage category[a]	Employment		Change in employment		
	1998	2007	Number of workers	Percent	As percent of total change in employment
Business services	27,260,982	33,420,035	6,159,053	23	53
Nontradable industries, low wages	9,088,235	10,360,958	1,272,723	14	11
Nontradable industries, high wages	608,152	688,141	79,989	13	1
Tradable industries, low wages	6,178,829	8,521,935	2,343,106	38	20
Tradable industries, high wages	11,385,766	13,849,001	2,463,235	22	21
Manufacturing	16,945,834	13,260,427	-3,685,407	-22	-32
Nontradable industries, low wages	1,637,696	1,480,485	-157,211	-10	-1
Nontradable industries, high wages	106,468	74,585	-31,883	-30	0
Tradable industries, low wages	10,422,185	8,123,733	-2,298,452	-22	-20
Tradable industries, high wages	4,779,485	3,581,624	-1,197,861	-25	-10
Personal services	32,169,477	38,930,236	6,760,759	21	58
Other	30,728,341	33,168,027	2,439,686	8	21

a. Tradable industries are defined as those with a locational Gini coefficient of 0.1 or greater. The cutoff between low- and high-wage industries is at an annual wage of $40,000.

Source: Author's calculations using County Business Patterns data from the US Census Bureau, www.census.gov.

Table 7.2 Changes in US employment by occupation tradability and wages, 1999–2009

Occupation group and wage category[a]	Employment		Change in employment		
	1999	2009	Number of workers	Percent	As percent of total change in employment
High-end business services[b]	16,705,890	20,203,840	3,497,950	21	28
Nontradable occupations, low wages	1,261,560	2,905,180	1,643,620	130	13
Nontradable occupations, high wages	4,873,910	4,538,950	−334,960	−7	−3
Tradable occupations, low wages	1,144,150	2,164,610	1,020,460	89	8
Tradable occupations, high wages	9,426,270	10,595,100	1,168,830	12	9
Production-related occupations[b]	17,348,560	15,097,930	−2,250,630	−13	−18
Nontradable occupations, low wages	8,479,870	7,834,880	−644,990	−8	−5
Nontradable occupations, high wages	1,905,310	1,772,490	−132,820	−7	−1
Tradable ocupations, low wages	6,822,940	5,361,090	−1,461,850	−21	−12
Tradable occupations, high wages	140,440	129,470	−10,970	−9	0
Sales and administration occupations	33,984,260	36,051,460	2,067,200	6	17
Nontradable occupations, low wages	29,060,830	30,508,950	1,448,120	5	12
Nontradable occupations, high wages	687,430	739,330	51,900	8	0
Tradable occupations, low wages	2,100,450	2,444,020	343,570	16	3
Tradable occupations, high wages	2,135,550	2,359,160	223,610	10	2
Social services and health occupations	9,636,250	12,978,960	3,342,710	35	27
Other occupations	40,578,440	46,315,460	5,737,030	14	46

a. Tradable occupations are defined as those with a locational Gini coefficient of 0.1 or greater. The cutoff between low- and high-wage occupations is at an annual wage of $40,000.

b. Defined as in figure 7.3.

Source: Author's calculations using 1999 and 2009 Occupational Employment Statistics data from the Bureau of Labor Statistics, www.bls.gov.

in high-end business services—occupations in the Standard Occupational Classification (SOC) major groups 11 (management), 13 (business and financial operations), 15 (computer and mathematical), 17 (architecture and engineering), 19 (life, physical, and social sciences), and 23 (legal)—increased by over 20 percent and accounted for more than a quarter of the aggregate growth in employment. Tradable occupations within high-end business service occupations contributed 17 percent of aggregate employment growth, split fairly evenly between high-wage and low-wage occupations. Table 7.2 also shows a significant decline in employment in production-related activities.

Labor Market Impact to Date: Industries and Occupations

Having gleaned information from the broad aggregate data, I look next at the level of individual industries and occupations. In Jensen and Kletzer (2006, 2008) we reported net employment growth rates in tradable and nontradable service activities at this more detailed level and found little difference between them. This section updates that analysis with the most recent available data for tradable and nontradable industries. This analysis uses data from the County Business Patterns program, an establishment-based data collection program of the US Census Bureau that uses primarily administrative data and thus has nearly universal coverage of establishments within its range.[4] It appears that tradable and nontradable service activities, whether analyzed by industry or by occupation, continue to have similar net employment growth rates. These findings suggest that neither offshoring nor exporting of services has yet had a significant impact on the US labor market.

Figure 7.2 shows the average net change in industry employment for 1998–2007 by sector (business services and manufacturing) and by whether the industry is tradable or nontradable.[5] The figure reveals that tradable manufacturing industries suffered job losses on average (as did nontradable manufacturing industries), but that service industries of both types experienced employment *increases*, which were modestly higher for the tradable service industries.

Figure 7.3 shows corresponding employment growth rates for occupation categories for 1999–2009.[6] Here, too, tradable production-oriented occupations experienced employment losses while tradable service occupations

---

4. For more information on the County Business Patterns program, see www.census.gov/econ/cbp/index.html.

5. I am constrained to use 1998 as the starting year because it is the first year that County Business Patterns data were produced on an NAICS basis.

6. The Occupational Employment Statistics program, conducted by the Bureau of Labor Statistics, is also an establishment-based program but is collected through a survey instrument. For more information on this program, see www.bls.gov/oes/home.htm. I am constrained to use 1999 as the starting year because it is the first year that Occupational Employment Survey data were produced on an SOC basis.

Figure 7.2   Changes in US net employment in tradable and nontradable business service and manufacturing industries, 1998–2007

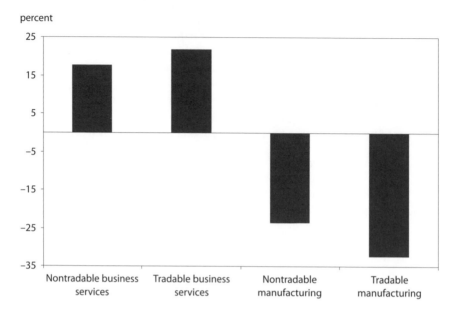

percent

Note: The vertical axis shows unweighted average net employment change in the industries in the sector.

Source: Author's calculations using 1998 and 2007 County Business Patterns data from the US Census Bureau, www.census.gov.

enjoyed gains similar to—or slightly higher than—those in nontradable service occupations. Again, it appears that trade in services did not have a significant impact on net employment growth in these occupations over this period.

Trade in Services and Job Displacement

The above analysis examined net employment changes, but it is also possible to track individual job displacements. Jensen and Kletzer (2008), using data from the Displaced Worker Survey (DWS), reported on the incidence, scope, and characteristics of job displacement associated with potential services tradability.[7]

---

7. The Displaced Worker Survey (DWS), conducted by the Bureau of Labor Statistics as a supplement to the monthly Current Population Survey, provides basic information on the scope and cost of involuntary job loss. The DWSs offer large sample sizes, are nationally representative, and allow several key elements to be investigated, including the incidence of job loss, the characteristics of workers affected, the likelihood of reemployment, industry and occupation of reemployment, and earnings changes. These surveys have been used extensively to study manufacturing job loss (see Kletzer 2001).

Figure 7.3   Changes in average US net employment in tradable and nontradable high-end business service and production occupations, 1999–2009

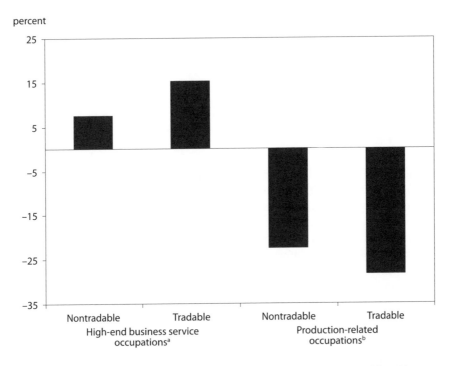

a. Standard Occupational Classification (SOC) major groups 11 (management), 13 (business and financial operations), 15 (computer and mathematical), 17 (architecture and engineering), 19 (life, physical, and social sciences), and 23 (legal).

b. Agricultural, production, extractive, and construction occupations.

Source: Author's calculations using 1999 and 2009 Occupational Employment Statistics data from the Bureau of Labor Statistics, www.bls.gov.

Table 7.3, from Jensen and Kletzer (2008), reports job loss rates over the period 2003–05 in manufacturing and in three service subsectors: information, financial services, and professional and business services.[8] Job losses are reported as the share of workers who were involuntarily displaced from their jobs at some point over the period. In total, about 4 percent of workers lost their jobs over this period; the risk of job loss was lower in the three service subsectors than in manufacturing. Tradable industries overall had a somewhat

8. The classification used in most of this book treats information, financial, and professional services as subcategories within business services, whereas the DWS includes in "professional and business services" only two subcategories—professional and technical services, and management, administrative, and waste services—and treats information and financial services as separate categories.

Table 7.3   Job loss rates in US manufacturing and services, 2003–05
(percent of initial employment)

Sector	All industries	Tradable industries	Nontradable industries
Manufacturing	12	12	17
Services			
Information	4	4	15
Financial services	4	3	12
Professional and business services	4	5	2
All sectors	4	6	3

Source: Jensen and Kletzer (2008).

higher risk of job loss than nontradable industries (6 percent versus 3 percent). Within manufacturing, however, nontradable industries had a higher rate of job loss (17 percent) than did tradable industries (about 12 percent).[9] In information and in financial services, the job loss rate for nontradable industries was notably higher than that for tradable industries. In professional and business services, however, the reverse held. Most notable about this subsector is its overall low rate of job loss, even in tradable activities, compared with manufacturing.

Parallel to the discussion of worker characteristics in previous chapters, table 7.4 reports selected demographic and educational characteristics of workers displaced from tradable and nontradable nonmanufacturing industries for the period 2003–05; the table also reports data for tradable manufacturing industries for comparison. Kletzer (2001) noted that workers displaced from service industries are slightly younger, less tenured, less likely to be male, and considerably more educated than workers displaced from manufacturing. These patterns still held in 2003–05. Just under 75 percent of workers displaced from jobs in tradable service industries had at least some college experience. The comparable share for displaced manufacturing workers was about 45 percent.

Also evident in table 7.4 is that workers displaced from jobs in tradable service industries are more educated, more likely to have health insurance, more likely to have lost a full-time job, and had higher earnings in the job they lost than workers displaced from nontradable industries. The educational attainment differences are stark: 41 percent of workers displaced from nontradable service industries had no college experience, compared with 26 percent of workers displaced from tradable service industries. The educational differences are consistent with workers' predisplacement weekly earnings and with

---

9. Analysis of the period 2001–03 reveals a much larger difference in job loss: 15 percent for tradable compared with about 8 percent for nontradable.

Table 7.4 Characteristics of displaced workers by sector, 2003–05

Characteristic	Tradable manufacturing	Nonmanufacturing Tradable	Nonmanufacturing Nontradable
All displaced workers			
Highest educational attainment (percent of total)[a]			
Did not complete high school	15	4	10
Completed high school	40	22	31
Some college	25	35	34
College degree or more	20	38	25
Percent with health insurance at predisplacement job	69	58	42
Percent full-time at predisplacement job	95	85	76
Weekly earnings of predisplacement full-time workers (dollars)			
Mean	723.21	855.38	605.10
Standard deviation	520.50	573.17	465.65
Reemployed workers			
Percent of all displaced workers in sector	67	74	66
Percent working full-time	85	67	66
Change in earnings at new job (percent)			
Mean	−17	−8.2	−7.3
Standard deviation	51	61	68
Median	−5.4	−2.8	0
Percent with no earnings loss at new job	37	43	48

a. Percentages may not sum to 100 because of rounding.

Note: Workers in agriculture, mining, forestry, and construction are omitted.

Source: Jensen and Kletzer (2008).

the United States having comparative advantage in skill-intensive activities, as noted above.

Outcomes for workers after displacement also differ across groups: Reemployment rates were higher for workers displaced from jobs in tradable service jobs than for those displaced from nontradable service jobs. The median loss in weekly earnings for the manufacturing workers was about 5 percent for 2003–05 (and 15 percent for 2001–03). Median earnings losses are smaller for both service groups, and a larger share of service workers than of manufacturing workers experienced no earnings loss. Workers displaced from nontradable service industries experienced smaller earnings losses than workers displaced from tradable service industries, in part because their predisplacement earnings were lower.

Conclusion

To date, there is little evidence of a labor market impact from trade in services—either for good or for bad. To the extent that displacement rates for tradable service workers are slightly higher than for other workers, this seems mitigated by the higher reemployment rates for these workers. Looking forward, it appears that a smaller share of tradable service jobs is at risk from competition from low-wage countries than within the manufacturing sector. As a result, the prospects for broad dislocation are smaller in the tradable service sector than in manufacturing.

8

Tradable Services across US Regions: Opportunities and Vulnerabilities

In chapter 7 I argued that increased trade in services is not likely to pose inordinate adjustment problems for the United States, because most tradable service activities seem consistent with US comparative advantage. Indeed, most US tradable service industries, especially those paying high wages, should see increased opportunities for exports if impediments to trade in services continue to diminish. But other, mostly low-wage industries will face challenges. As chapter 2 demonstrated, the geographic distribution of service industries is not uniform. Rather, some industries are concentrated in particular cities or regions. This uneven distribution, combined with differing prospects for high-wage and low-wage tradable service industries, raises the concern that some regions of the United States will benefit from increased service trade while others will be hurt.

Manufacturing, too, is unevenly distributed geographically, and the same process of increased trade and reallocation in that sector, starting several decades ago, led to economic hardship in some regions, including much of the industrial Midwest (the Rust Belt) and the South (textile mills in the Carolinas, for example). Restructuring within these highly geographically concentrated industries posed significant challenges for many communities in those regions, which some have yet to overcome.

Would an increase in service trade present similar challenges? This chapter looks at the geographic distribution of service industries and occupations across US metropolitan areas and regions and explores their exposure to increased trade in services. If service trade continues to grow, whether because of significant liberalization or because further advances in technology facilitate such trade, are some regions especially likely to benefit? Are others likely to face serious dislocations?

I find that, yes, some regions do have disproportionately large shares of tradable service workers, but these are also regions where most such workers are in activities that tend to be highly paid. These tend to be highly skill-intensive activities and as such are less likely to face strong import competition and more likely to experience gains from increased trade. The regions in which these activities are located are likely to benefit as well. But the converse is not true: There appear to be no US regions with large concentrations of low-wage tradable service activities; rather, these activities tend to be more widely dispersed across the country. Hence there appear to be no regions likely to suffer disproportionately from growth in service trade.

Tradable Services across Regions

I begin by looking at regions in the United States where a large share of employment is either in tradable business service industries or in tradable business service occupations. The first map shows the Bureau of Economic Analysis-defined Labor Market Areas within the United States that have disproportionate shares of workers in tradable business service industries. The second map does the same for tradable business service occupations.[1] The highlighted Labor Market Areas in each figure are those whose share of employment in tradable business service industries or occupations is above 15 percent (the sector's share of total US employment). Table 8.1 ranks the top 25 Labor Market Areas by share of employment in tradable business service industries (left panel) and occupations (right panel).

Several facts are immediately evident from the maps and table 8.1. One is that both tradable service industries and tradable service occupations tend to be concentrated in the very largest Labor Market Areas by population. A number of these populous regions appear in both lists (usually near the top), including Boston, Dallas-Fort Worth, New York, the San Francisco Bay Area, and Washington. All of the 10 largest US metropolitan areas are on either or both lists; the largest on neither list is Phoenix (number 12).

These results suggest a high positive correlation between population and the share of employment in tradable business services. To test for this correlation, figure 8.1 plots the relationship between the size of a Labor Market Area's workforce (in logarithms) and the share of its employment in either tradable business service industries (top panel) or occupations (bottom panel). The positive correlations (0.76 for industries, 0.68 for occupations) are quite evident visually.

---

1. Labor Market Areas typically include a major city and a group of surrounding counties identified as tied to the city on the basis of commuting patterns. Tradable business service industries are defined here as industries within the NAICS 50s that are classified as tradable. The tradable business service occupations are those classified as tradable within the following major occupation groups: management occupations, business and financial operations occupations, computer and mathematical occupations, architecture and engineering occupations, life, physical, and social science occupations, and legal occupations.

US regions with high shares of tradable business service industries

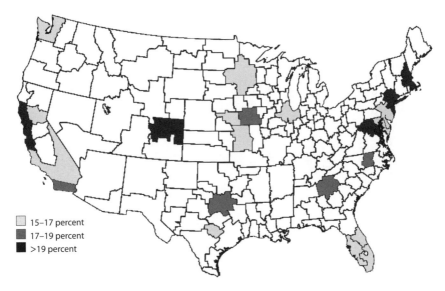

15–17 percent
17–19 percent
>19 percent

Source: Author's calculations using 2007 American Community Survey data.

US regions with high shares of tradable business service occupations

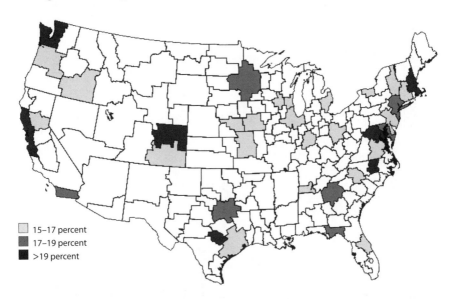

15–17 percent
17–19 percent
>19 percent

Source: Author's calculations using 2007 American Community Survey data.

Table 8.1 US Labor Market Areas ranked by share of employment in tradable services

a. Ranked by share in tradable service industries			b. Ranked by share in tradable service occupations		
Labor Market Area	**Percent**	**Workforce (thousands)**	**Labor Market Area**	**Percent**	**Workforce (thousands)**
Washington, DC	23.6	3,065	Washington, DC	28.9	3,065
New York, NY	19.7	9,211	San Francisco-Oakland-San Jose, CA	23.0	3,670
San Francisco-Oakland-San Jose, CA	19.1	3,670	Boston, MA	20.8	3,194
Denver, CO	19.1	1,758	Seattle, WA	20.2	2,134
Boston, MA	19.1	3,194	Austin, TX	20.0	878
Dallas-Fort Worth, TX	18.0	3,002	Raleigh-Durham, NC	19.9	837
San Diego, CA	17.9	1,404	Denver, CO	19.7	1,758
Des Moines, IA	17.4	441	San Diego, CA	19.0	1,404
Raleigh-Durham, NC	17.1	837	Baltimore, MD	18.3	1,301
Atlanta, GA	17.1	2,846	Tallahassee, FL	18.1	194
Kansas City, MO	16.5	1,142	New York, NY	18.1	9,211
Omaha, NE	16.4	445	Minneapolis-St. Paul, MN	17.9	2,130
Chicago, IL	16.3	4,438	Atlanta, GA	17.8	2,846
Miami-Fort Lauderdale, FL	16.3	2,606	Dallas-Fort Worth, TX	17.4	3,002
Seattle, WA	16.3	2,134	Chicago, IL	16.9	4,438
Los Angeles, CA	16.2	7,856	Boise, ID	16.9	296
Baltimore, MD	16.0	1,301	Philadelphia, PA	16.7	3,627
Austin, TX	15.9	878	Omaha, NE	16.6	445

Philadelphia, PA	15.5	3,627	Richmond-Petersburg, VA	16.6	757
Orlando-Melbourne-Daytona Beach, FL	15.3	1,376	Sacramento, CA	16.5	1,107
Minneapolis-St. Paul, MN	15.3	2,130	Columbus, OH	16.5	1,043
Sacramento, CA	15.2	1,107	Huntsville-Florence, AL	16.5	304
Tampa-St. Petersburg, FL	15.1	2,166	Detroit, MI	16.2	2,250
Albuquerque, NM	14.8	564	Houston, TX	16.0	2,778
Columbus, OH	14.6	1,043	Madison, WI	16.0	427

Source: Author's calculations using data from the 2007 American Community Survey.

Figure 8.1   Region workforce size and share of the workforce in tradable business service activities

a. Industries

percent of workforce in tradable industries

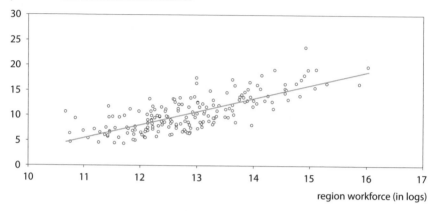

region workforce (in logs)

b. Occupations

percent of workforce in tradable occupations

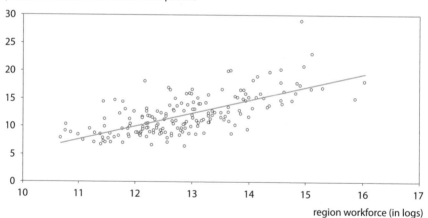

region workforce (in logs)

Note: Each dot represents a region or Labor Market Area.

Source: Author's calculations using 2007 American Community Survey data.

While there is a strong correlation between population and the share of employment in tradable service activities, service exporters are located in small cities and towns, too. Box 8.1 highlights a well-known, but often overlooked, geographically dispersed service exporter: higher education.

Several factors could explain the correlations between city size and share of tradable service activities. There could be agglomeration economies that attract tradable business service activities to large metropolitan areas: For example, businesses in such areas can draw on a larger pool of workers with

Box 8.1 Exporting education

While most tradable service jobs are located in major metropolitan areas like New York, Los Angeles, Chicago, and Washington, these are not the only homes to tradable service activities. Many small and medium-sized cities and towns host service exporters.

For example, Kalamazoo College, located in Kalamazoo, Michigan, is a small, selective, liberal arts college. Like many institutions of higher education, Kalamazoo College is an exporter of services. In a September 19, 2010 article in the *Kalamazoo Gazette*, Paula M. Davis[1] wrote:

> Looking for the academic exploration she felt would elude her in Bangkok, Anya Khongthavornpipat said she long aspired to study in the United States.
>
> In Thailand, "once you go into your major, you're locked in.... You can't explore any other interests at all, and if you want to change your major, you have to start all over," the 18-year-old said.
>
> With fall classes beginning Monday, Khongthavornpipat's dream to study abroad is being realized at Kalamazoo College, where she plans to explore physics, computer science, economics and geopolitics.

Ms. Khongthavornpipat is not alone. This year, 12 percent, or 41 of the 343-member freshman class, is composed of international students seeking a "K College" bachelor's degree. While Kalamazoo College's freshman class is more international than US higher education overall (which has about 3.5 percent international students), the United States hosted more than 690,000 international students in the academic year 2009–10, according to the Institute of International Education. All these students represent exports of US services.

American institutions of higher education are consistently ranked as global leaders—and students from around the world go there to study. Higher education exemplifies many of the characteristics of trade in services: It is high-skill intensive, the United States has comparative advantage and exports these services around the world, and both the United States and the recipients of these service exports benefit. Higher education shows the possibilities of trade in services both in large metropolitan areas like Boston or New York and in small cities and towns like Grinnell, Oberlin, and Kalamazoo.

-----

1. Paula M. Davis, "Reaching out around the globe: Kalamazoo College starts year with record international enrollment," *Kalamazoo Gazette*, September 19, 2010.

Source: Institute of International Education, Open Doors Fact Sheet, 2010, www.iie.org/en/Research-and-Publications/Open-Doors.

the skills they need, and workers may value the greater ease of moving from employer to employer within their profession. In addition, tradable service activities are often knowledge and information intensive, and it is possible that being colocated with other firms and workers in similar businesses or industries increases the sharing of information, giving firms an advantage over firms in other regions. It could also be that the amenities of large urban areas attract well-educated service workers to large metropolitan areas, who in turn attract service businesses willing to employ them. In any case, the fact that service activities are concentrated in large metropolitan areas may matter less than the fact that they are typically concentrated in metropolitan areas that are diverse, both socially and economically, and often economically dynamic. In addition to the fact that these tradable service industries pay high wages and are thus not likely to face low-wage import competition, the concentration of these activities in large, diverse urban areas is likely to further mitigate the risk of dislocation for the regions that host them. This would be in stark contrast to the challenges that restructuring in the manufacturing sector has presented in the Rust Belt, where many communities are single-company or single-industry towns.

Geographic Concentration of Low-Wage Tradable Services

Although tradable business services tend to be relatively high-wage, high-skill activities, some pay relatively low wages. Do these activities also tend to be concentrated in large metropolitan areas, where the risks of concentrated dislocation seem less acute, or in smaller regions, where dislocation might present more of a policy challenge? Or in neither?

Figure 8.2 plots the share of employment in low-wage tradable business service industries and occupations against total workforce size for all US Labor Market Areas. As in previous chapters, "low-wage" is defined as an average wage in the industry or occupation below $40,000 per year, consistent with the notional cutoff for US comparative advantage. It is also roughly the average wage in the median industry and median occupation in the United States. For ease of comparison with figure 8.1, the scale on the vertical axis is the same as in that figure.

What figure 8.2 reveals is that no region has a share of employment in low-wage tradable business service industries greater than 2 percent. Rather, these activities are distributed fairly evenly across regions. A similar plot of tradable business service occupations is not shown, for the simple reason that none of these occupations have average wages below the $40,000 threshold; consequently, all regions have zero percent employment in low-wage tradable business service occupations. This fact, together with the finding of a low concentration of low-wage tradable business service industries, suggests that the risk to any individual US community of significant dislocation from increased trade in business services is quite small.

Also, because low-wage tradable business service activities are fairly evenly distributed, their distribution does not introduce a difference between the concentration of high-wage tradable business service activities and that of tradable business services overall (shown in the maps). Thus, it seems likely

Figure 8.2   Region workforce size and share of the workforce in low-wage tradable business service industries

percent of workforce in low-wage tradable industries

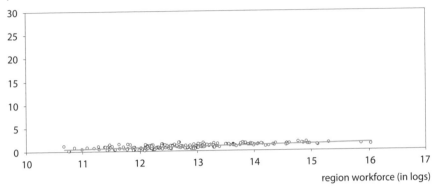

region workforce (in logs)

Note: Each dot represents a region or Labor Market Area.

Source: Author's calculations using 2007 American Community Survey data.

that the regions that currently have high shares of these activities will benefit from increased trade in services—nothing about the distribution of low-wage service activities indicates that their losses would offset the gains to the high-wage activities in the communities that host them. That low-wage tradable service activities are broadly dispersed and not concentrated in any particular region suggests that communities will be in a better position to adjust than if these activities were concentrated in a few regions.

In summary, the opportunities for increased service exports in most of the nation's major metropolitan areas mean that these areas are likely to gain jobs from increased service trade, and the jobs gained are likely to pay high wages. Even if some reallocation does result from increased trade, these regions are large, diverse, and dynamic, and thus likely to absorb the shock without too much difficulty. Meanwhile there is little evidence that any region is at risk from a high concentration of low-wage tradable service activities. Rather, these activities account for a small share of employment and are spread evenly across the country.

9

Conclusions and Policy Implications

The service sector is a large and growing contributor to the US economy. Even by the narrowest definition, it employs the majority of American workers, and many industries and subsectors within services pay average wages above the average wage in manufacturing.

Trade in services, both imports and exports, is also growing, and within the sector the share of employment in tradable activities is large. This means that a large share of the US workforce beyond the manufacturing sector is potentially exposed to the risks and opportunities of the global economy. Among that large share of tradable service jobs are many high-skill, high-wage jobs.

Few of these high-wage jobs are likely to be lost to low-wage countries. Indeed, precisely because they require a high degree of skill, they are jobs that the United States is likely to retain—and that can support exports. This book has cited numerous examples of the types of service activities that are tradable and in which the United States is likely to enjoy comparative advantage. These include engineering services like those offered by the two Siemens facilities in Wisconsin (box 1.2), advanced satellite imaging services like those marketed by GeoEye (box 5.1), and architectural services like those described in the Bay Area profiles (box 2.2), not to mention traditional services in which the United States has excelled, such as computer software.

Should the United States push for increased liberalization of trade in services? Increased trade in services would undoubtedly dislocate some US workers. But only a relatively small share of employment in tradable services is in the low-wage, low-skill activities that are likely to face competition from low-wage, unskilled-labor-abundant countries. Further, the jobs that might be affected by low-wage competition are fairly evenly distributed around the country. As a result, any dislocation associated with increased trade in these

181

activities would likely be spread broadly, often over large metropolitan areas, avoiding the type of concentrated dislocation that has been seen in the manufacturing sector. Most employment in tradable services, meanwhile, is in the high-skill, high-wage activities in which the United States enjoys comparative advantage. Yet participation by US service firms in the international economy lags that of manufacturing firms, in part because services have not yet been fully liberalized in countries around the world. Increased liberalization of service trade thus seems to offer considerable opportunity for these firms and their workers.

The analysis in this book yields the following conclusion: The United States should not fear increased trade in services. Instead, it should be aggressively seeking to liberalize the policy impediments to service trade wherever and whenever possible—whether in multilateral forums like the World Trade Organization, regional agreements like the North American Free Trade Agreement (NAFTA), or bilateral agreements like the recent US-Canada government procurement agreement. Indeed, the opportunities for increasing service trade are many. What, then, should be the nation's priorities in realizing these opportunities?

Reasonable people—researchers, policymakers, and other interested participants, above all those whose living derives from the production of services—will undoubtedly have different recommendations for how to proceed. This concluding chapter presents some general observations regarding trade policy that follow naturally from the analysis presented in this book. These observations are not exhaustive, nor will they be particularly sensitive to the subtleties of the negotiations surrounding individual agreements. Instead, they are focused on the long-run, big-picture objectives that seem to flow quite logically from the analysis thus far.

Some Observations on Service Trade—and Their Policy Implications

Observation 1: The United States is relatively open to service trade; a number of large and fast-growing economies are less so.

Research by the World Bank, described in chapter 6, suggests that the United States is already relatively open to trade in services. In contrast, a number of large and fast-growing countries, notably China, India, Indonesia, and Russia, have relatively high barriers to trade in services. Other increasingly important economies, notably Brazil and Korea, maintain lower but still high barriers to service trade. These economies benefit from the open world trading regime in goods, and some of them benefit from the relatively open access that the US market provides to foreign service producers.

Service trade liberalization in these countries would allow US firms with comparative advantage in service provision to start exporting, or to increase their exports, to these countries. The US economy would benefit from increased productivity through the resulting increase in specialization. So would the economies of other developed countries, like Canada, Japan, and many EU countries, all of which are similar in comparative advantage to the United States and would likely see their service exports grow as well. The countries that liberalize would also benefit from the increased productivity that comes from being able to import, as inputs to their own production, the world's best services at the best price.

Implication 1: The United States should be pushing aggressively, in cooperation with other developed countries, to open these large and fast-growing markets to service trade.

Observation 2: Intellectual property is important in a number of the United States' most important service-exporting industries.

Figure 5.3 in chapter 5 showed that US service industries differ widely in their participation in exporting, where participation is measured by their exports per worker. It is also easy to see from this figure that many of the most export intensive service industries are those with important holdings of intellectual property—copyrighted creative works, patented innovations, and so forth—and thus are heavily reliant on intellectual property protections. Motion picture and video production and distribution, sound recordings, and software all depend on these protections to remain viable in export markets.

Yet several large and fast-growing economies make perennial appearances in US government reports on countries with weak intellectual property protections. The 2010 Special 301 Report, issued by the US Trade Representative, appraises intellectual property protections in countries around the world and lists China, India, Indonesia, and Russia on its "priority watch list."

Implication 2: The United States needs to continue to stress to its trading partners the importance of intellectual property protections for US service export industries and push for improved intellectual property protections internationally.

Observation 3: The world, led by a number of fast-growing developing countries, is about to undergo an infrastructure boom of historic proportions. Many US service firms are competitive in the types of services that will be needed for these projects.

It is estimated that over $40 trillion could be spent on infrastructure of all types worldwide over the next 25 years, more than 80 percent of it outside the United States.[1] China and India alone have infrastructure needs valued at $10 trillion over that period, and even many developed countries are facing huge expenditures to replace and refurbish their decaying infrastructure systems. All this represents a potential bonanza for construction and engineering firms and for international banks and financial service providers (see box 9.1). More than half of the sum would be spent for water and sewer treatment systems, requiring just the type of services that the Siemens divisions

---

1. Nicholas Timmins, "In the Global Rush for the New, Don't Neglect the Old," *Financial Times,* June 7, 2010, www.ft.com; Leonora Walters, "Build an Income with Infrastructure," *Investors Chronicle,* July 15, 2010, www.investorschronicle.co.uk.

Box 9.1 A glimpse into the globally competitive engineering service arena

Engineering services are essential for the planning, design, and management of large infrastructure projects—and are tradable. They are also big business in the United States. The US engineering service industry employed almost 1 million workers in 2007 (well over 1 million when combined with architectural services and other closely related industries), more than the automobile industry and twice as many as the aerospace industry (see table B9.1.1). And with average annual wages of about $73,000, engineering service firms pay more on average than either of those manufacturing industries. US engineering and construction companies have valuable expertise that could be—and is being—exported to developing countries in the building of water and sewer treatment systems, roads, bridges, airports, seaports, railroads, and other types of projects.

Table B9.1.1 Employment and average annual wages in selected US service and manufacturing industries, 2007

NAICS code	Industry[a]	Employment	Average annual wage (dollars)
541330	Engineering services	977,031	73,000
541310	Architectural services	205,883	67,000
5413	Total engineering, architectural, and related services	1,423,209	68,000
3361, 3362, 3363	Motor vehicles	909,665	52,000
3364	Aerospace	441,418	68,000

NAICS = North American Industry Classification System

a. Figures for motor vehicles and aerospace include employment in parts manufacturing.

Source: 2007 Economic Census.

The stereotypical image of engineering service firms as small partnerships, employing a handful of professionals to serve a limited base of mostly local or regional clients, is increasingly outdated. Indeed, at least 10 such firms are in the Fortune 500. The third-largest of these (behind Fluor and KBR), and an important exporter of engineering, construction, and other services, is Jacobs Engineering Group. The company's 2010 SEC 10-K filing describes its activities:

> Our business focuses exclusively on providing a broad range of technical, professional, and construction services to a large number of industrial, commercial,

(continued on next page)

Box 9.1   A glimpse into the globally competitive engineering service arena *(continued)*

and governmental clients around the world. We provide four broad categories of services:

- Project Services (which includes engineering, design, architectural, and similar services);
- Process, Scientific, and Systems Consulting services (which includes services performed in connection with a wide variety of scientific testing, analysis, and consulting activities);
- Construction services (which encompasses traditional field construction services as well as modular construction activities, and includes direct hire construction and construction management services); and
- Operations and Maintenance services (which includes services performed in connection with operating large, complex facilities on behalf of clients as well as services involving process plant maintenance).

Headquartered in Pasadena, California, Jacobs Engineering employed about 38,500 full-time employees (including contract staff) in 2010 at offices and subsidiaries in Europe, the Middle East, Asia, and Australia as well as elsewhere in North America. That same year, Jacobs earned approximately 30 percent of its revenue from clients outside the United States.

The activities in which Jacobs Engineering operates are intensely competitive, with firms of all sizes vying for an increasingly global business. Some, like Jacobs, are publicly traded companies, whereas others, like Bechtel, are privately held. Although large, internationally well-known companies like Jacobs have an advantage in bidding for large construction and operations-and-maintenance projects, low barriers to entry in other activities such as engineering, design, and consulting give rise to myriad opportunities for smaller competitors, including new entrants. The following, also from the company's 10-K, gives a sense of the array of competitors Jacobs faces and how that competition varies by type of service, geographic market, and project:

> Our larger competitors for engineering, construction, and maintenance services for process plants include Bechtel, Fluor, Foster Wheeler, KBR, Aker Kvaerner, Technip, WorleyParsons, the Shaw Group, and AMEC. In the area of buildings, our competitors include several of the competitors previously mentioned as well as HDR, HOK, AECOM, and Turner. In the area of infrastructure, our competitors include several of the competitors previously mentioned as well as URS, Parsons Brinckerhoff, HNTB, Tetra Tech, Parsons, and W.S. Atkins. In the area of national government programs, our principal competitors include several of the competitors listed above as well as SAIC, CH2M Hill, Weston, Lockheed Martin, and Computer Sciences Corporation.

One way that Jacobs meets the competitive challenge is by actively acquiring other firms that possess key technological expertise. The firm's 10-K also

(continued on next page)

10-K also describes some of its recent acquisitions, giving a further sense of the breadth of services Jacobs provides and the employment associated with these services—and of the extent to which the relevant skills remain relatively abundant across the United States:

- In April 2007, we acquired Edwards and Kelcey, Inc....a nationally recognized engineering, design, planning, and construction management firm serving public and private clients in the fields of transportation, planning/environmental, communications technology, buildings/facilities, and land development. Headquartered in Morristown, New Jersey, Edwards and Kelcey employed approximately 1,000 people in offices located primarily in the Northeastern region of the United States.

- In November 2007, we acquired Carter & Burgess, Inc. Headquartered in Fort Worth, Texas, Carter & Burgess was an approximately 3,200-person professional services firm providing architecture, engineering, design, and planning services to public and private sector clients operating in the fields of transportation, water, infrastructure programs, building programs, land development, and planning.

- In December 2009, we acquired TYBRIN Corporation, a 1,500-person professional services firm headquartered in Fort Walton Beach, Florida. Founded in 1972, TYBRIN is a leading supplier of mission planning solutions, systems engineering, software development, modeling and combat environment simulation, engineering and testing, range safety, and other services to the U.S. Department of Defense, the National Aeronautics and Space Administration, and other government clients.

- In February 2010, we acquired Jordan, Jones and Goulding, Inc., a 500-person professional services firm headquartered in Atlanta, Georgia. Founded in 1958, JJG provides engineering, planning, and consulting services for water, wastewater, environmental and other clients....

Source: Jacobs Engineering Group Inc., 10-K, Annual report pursuant to section 13 and 15(d), filed on 11/23/2010, filed period 10/01/2010, available at http://phx.corporate-ir.net (accessed on May 5, 2011).

---

based in Wisconsin (profiled in chapter 1) provide. Box 9.2 describes the role of US service firms in an ambitious development project to build an entire city in South Korea.

The opportunity presented by this infrastructure boom is clear, as is the need to ensure that US firms have equal access to compete for the financing, architecture, engineering, project management, and construction work associated with this boom. What is less clear is exactly how to proceed. As chapter 6 described, trade in services is subject to a complex suite of impediments that are more difficult to negotiate down than tariffs. For example, licensing and accreditation are often issues for individual professional service providers,

Box 9.2 Songdo International Business District, South Korea

The scale of the coming global infrastructure boom—and the opportunities it presents—is hard to fathom. Take the Songdo International Business District in South Korea as an example. The district is a planned city being built from scratch not far from the international airport outside Seoul. The city is rising on reclaimed land and is ultimately planned to be on 1,500 acres with 45 million square feet of office space, 30 million square feet for residential use, and 10 million square feet for retail. The district eventually will be home to 65,000 citizens and host approximately 300,000 commuters daily.

The cost of the development is estimated to be $35 billion, possibly the largest private development project ever. What distinguishes Songdo is not just the scale but the vision of a sustainable, environment-friendly city. The layout includes specially designed waste, water, and transportation systems and dozens of LEED-certified buildings.

Given the scale and innovative nature of the project, it is not surprising that US firms are well represented in the team building Songdo. The lead developer is New York–based Gale International. The lead architect and master planner is New York–based Kohn Pederson Fox. A number of US multinationals—large and small service firms and manufactures—are partners in the development, including Microsoft, Parsons Brinckerhoff, Cisco, United Technologies, and some not-so-household names, the Whitman Strategy Group (environmental consultants), Kitson and Partners (golf course design), and Taubman (retail developer).

and many countries require foreign service firms to establish a commercial presence or take on local partners. But the difficulties involved in negotiating access are not an excuse for not pushing hard for improvements.

Indeed, the United States has already made progress in negotiating access for service providers, both in regional agreements like NAFTA and in bilateral agreements like the Korea-US Free Trade Agreement. Yet such agreements are lacking with other large, fast-growing economies, and it is precisely these countries where most of the growth is going to be and where US comparative advantage in the relevant services is most pronounced. Other developed economies also have comparative advantage in services and would be natural partners in persuading the large, fast-growing countries with high service barriers to liberalize.

Implication 3: The United States, working through the General Agreement on Trade in Services (GATS), should join with other developed countries in pushing for further liberalization of business services, to ensure that US service firms and workers have the opportunity to compete in the coming infrastructure boom.

Observation 4: The WTO's government procurement agreement is likely to prove an important framework for enabling US firms to compete for infrastructure projects—but a number of large, fast-growing economies are not signatories to the agreement.

Much of the spending for infrastructure in the coming boom is likely to be controlled or financed, at least in part, by governments—national, regional, and local. Those governments are sure to be subject to domestic political pressure to favor domestic producers in granting contracts for this work. This makes guaranteeing equal treatment in government procurement a crucial issue for foreign service providers. The WTO's Agreement on Government Procurement was negotiated during the Tokyo Round of GATT negotiations in the early 1980s with the intention of reducing preferences to domestic firms in public procurement and opening public works spending to international trade. Its coverage was extended tenfold in the subsequent Uruguay Round and now extends to government purchases totaling several hundred billion dollars annually. However, this large sum obscures the fact that to date only a relative handful of countries have signed the agreement, virtually all of them in the developed world. In particular, none of the large developing countries expected to account for the bulk of infrastructure spending in coming decades—Brazil, China, India, and Russia—are participants in the agreement.

Nor is the lack of developing country participation the only problem: Even the current signatories sometimes find it difficult to adhere to their obligations under the agreement. The issue was highlighted by the "Buy American" provisions in the 2009 American Recovery and Reinvestment Act, the main US stimulus legislation in response to the 2007–09 recession. The act's provisions gave US producers preferential access to government contracts financed by stimulus funds, creating difficulties not only for would-be foreign suppliers but even for US firms with Canadian subsidiaries that provide inputs to their products: Under the law, if too much Canadian content was included in a product, the product was ineligible for stimulus money.

The United States and Canada recently signed an agreement to prevent this type of distortion, but the episode shows how political considerations can bias government procurement decisions even when the countries involved are developed economies, close neighbors, and signatories to the WTO agreement. The pressures are naturally much more acute and harder to overcome when the countries are half a world apart and have very different business systems and cultures. This emphasizes the need for stronger protections in the area of government procurement. Getting all the large, fast-growing economies of the world to sign on to the WTO agreement will not solve all problems, but it would be a move in the right direction.

Implication 4: The United States, again in cooperation with other developed countries, should strongly encourage large and fast-growing countries to sign on to the WTO government procurement agreement.

Observation 5: Education matters.

Some observers contend that service offshoring negates the benefits of education, claiming that having an education does not prevent one's job from being outsourced. But this is far from true.

It *is* true that having an education does not prevent one's job from being *tradable*. Indeed, as previous chapters show, tradability and education are positively correlated: Workers in tradable jobs, in both manufacturing and services, tend to have more skills and more education than workers in nontradable jobs. But to argue that because a job is tradable it will therefore be traded away, and that therefore education confers no protection, is a counsel of despair—and unwarranted. In fact, high-skill, high-wage service jobs are precisely the types of jobs that are likely to stay in the United States. That is the lesson of comparative advantage—and of the US experience in manufacturing. Also, better-educated workers have lower displacement rates and higher reemployment rates. Education remains a good investment for individual workers.

Education is a good collective investment as well. The farsighted investments that the United States made in primary, secondary, and college education during the latter part of the 19th century and throughout the 20th century created the comparative advantage in skilled production that the nation enjoys today. The United States has historically been well out in front of the rest of the world in the share of its workforce that is college educated. Unfortunately, this is less true today than it has been in the past.

Figure 9.1 shows, for a number of developed and developing countries worldwide, average educational attainment for the population aged 25 to 29 and for the population aged 60 to 64; the size of each bubble represents the population of the indicated cohort in the indicated country. The developed economies have historically been relatively skill abundant countries, with the United States in the lead. This is reflected in the height of the bubbles for the 60-to-64 cohorts in these countries. The bubbles for the 25-to-29 cohorts show, however, that the rest of the world has learned the lesson that higher levels of educational attainment are strongly associated with higher living standards. A number of important countries in the world economy, including Brazil, China, Indonesia, Japan, Korea, and Mexico, have made dramatic increases in average education levels. India's average improvement is smaller but noteworthy for the sheer number of people whose education has increased. As a result, the United States is no longer an outlier—indeed, average educational attainment actually falls in the United States as one moves from the older to the younger cohort. The failure of the United States to maintain its lead in educational attainment is likely to alter the country's skill abundance relative to other countries, with sobering implications for the nation's comparative advantage and living standards.

Implication 5: The United States should make access to good primary, secondary, and postsecondary education a high national priority.

Figure 9.1   Average years of schooling by age cohort in selected countries, 2010

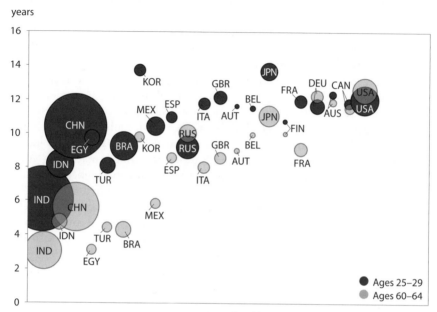

years

countries ordered by per capita GDP (international dollars)

IND = India; IDN = Indonesia; CHN = China; EGY = Egypt; TUR = Turkey; BRA = Brazil; KOR = Korea; MEX = Mexico; ESP = Spain; RUS = Russia; ITA = Italy; GBR = United Kingdom; AUT = Austria; BEL = Belgium; JPN = Japan; FIN = Finland; FRA = France; DEU = Germany; AUS = Australia; CAN = Canada; USA = United States

Note: Bubble sizes are proportional to cohort population.

Source: Author's calculations using data from Barro and Lee (2010).

Observation 6: There will continue to be dislocation of workers at the low end of the skill and income distribution, both in the manufacturing sector and increasingly in the service sector. Some of this will be driven by trade, some by automation, and it will be difficult to discern how much is due to each.

As a condition for further service trade liberalization in the GATS, the United States may find it necessary to change its regulatory practices and policies in a way that actually increases the competitive pressure on low-wage, low-skill US workers. For example, in return for concessions that favor US service producers, other countries may demand that the United States allow more temporary construction workers or nursing aides to enter the country. High-skill, high-wage US firms and workers—and consumers—would likely be the beneficiaries of such a bargain, but workers at the low end of the distribution are likely to bear a disproportionate share of the adjustment costs. In such a scenario, it would make sense to reinforce the social safety net for workers in general, but particularly for the lowest paid and least skilled, to mitigate the downside risks they face from a dynamic economy. The extension of trade adjustment assistance benefits to service workers in 2009 was a useful start, though this modest extension of benefits has since expired. More can be done.

Implication 6: The United States should strengthen the social safety net for workers dislocated by trade and technological advancement.

The Need for Better Data on Services

The policy agenda with respect to services and service trade is challenging. As such, it will succeed only if those charged with implementing it are well informed. To make sound decisions about the service economy at home and to represent their countries effectively in negotiations on service trade, all policymakers need detailed and timely information about a range of service-related topics, including what services are currently being traded, on what scale, and with which other countries. They also need a solid basis for estimating how this trade will evolve in the future, and in particular what services might be traded tomorrow that are not yet being traded today. For that, information is needed about the intensities of the different factors used in service production, as well as about the relative abundance of those factors in different regions. Detailed information about the producers and traders of services, actual and potential, is needed as well, including information about firm size, the productive factors used and their compensation, productivity, and the extent to which firms in different industries, of different sizes, and in different locations are already engaged in trade. Perhaps most daunting of all, policymakers need reliable information not only about the services produced within their jurisdictions, but also about the services produced in other countries with which their own country might trade, now or in the foreseeable future.

The simple truth is that information about services and service trade of the necessary depth and breadth is lacking for every country in the world—not excepting the United States, although the data produced by the US official statistical agencies are far better than what is available for most countries. Appendix A presents a detailed analysis and specific recommendations for expanding and improving the collection and presentation of US data on services, drawing on the report of an MIT working group of which I was a member. However, two overarching needs can be signaled here as high priorities for any such effort:

1. *Increased industry and geographic detail on trade in services:* Current statistics on trade in services are not detailed enough to support robust empirical analysis. Increasing this detail will require the collection of information from a larger sample of firms, improved access to an adequate sampling frame to support representative sampling, and lower reporting thresholds.

2. *More-detailed information on the inputs used in domestic service production:* Current data on service production do not provide enough information

on the factor inputs used. More information should be collected on skill intensity, capital intensity, and services purchased as inputs. These data should be collected at the establishment level to the extent possible to increase the industry and geographic detail available.

Obviously, the improvements recommended here and in appendix A will require that increased resources be allocated to the official statistical agencies, at a time when the need to tighten rather than expand the federal budget over the long run is universally recognized. However, as appendix A also shows, there are at present some unnecessary inefficiencies in how the tasks of data collection and analysis are apportioned across agencies. Although no one would suggest that removing these inefficiencies would allow the recommendations presented here to pay for themselves in full, one can be almost certain that it would go some way toward reducing the net cost. One thing that is certain is that the improved understanding of the nation's service sector that would result from improved data collection would eventually repay the effort many times over.

Conclusion

Services in the United States have long gotten too little respect. It is no exaggeration to say that the service sector has often been treated like a poor stepchild, deemed capable of performing only menial, supportive tasks while her more favored stepsisters, manufacturing in particular, capture the limelight. Championed by pundits and courted by policymakers, the stepsister sectors remain the center of attention in both domestic economic policy deliberations and international trade negotiations.

Services' turn as the star of the ball may be coming, however. Awareness is growing not only that the service sector is the largest and the fastest growing sector in the US economy by virtually any measure, but also that many service industries—employing in the aggregate more workers than the whole manufacturing sector—pay good wages, indeed better than the manufacturing average. Service firms employ many of the United States' best-educated and most creative workers in activities that typically pose few health and safety risks and that leave a small environmental footprint.

In short, many if not most US service jobs are jobs well worth keeping in the United States, not because they are a last resort for otherwise unemployable ex-manufacturing workers, but because they are good, high-paying, "clean" jobs. Today, however, falling costs of travel and telecommunications are exposing this formerly stay-at-home sector to international competition, leading to fears that a wide swath of service firms and workers will suffer as output and jobs are lost to foreign countries where average wages are often much lower.

These fears are understandable—every debutante is nervous on the eve of the big gala. But as this book hopes to have shown, they are also unwarranted. The US service sector is globally competitive, as evidenced most concretely by the fact that the nation's balance of trade in services, in sharp contrast to the merchandise balance, has been consistently positive for decades. This suggests—and the analysis in this book provides ample evidence to confirm—that the United States has comparative advantage in many, perhaps most, of the services that technology is now opening to trade. In particular, the high-skilled, high-wage jobs typical of the business service sector—a large sector that includes engineering, finance, design, computer programming, and many other activities—are precisely the kind that low-wage developing countries will find difficult to match and that therefore the United States should be able to retain. Increasing trade in services will allow the best, most efficient US service firms to expand, thus increasing overall US productivity, while US consumers and businesses gain greater access to the best services that the rest of the world has to offer.

To be sure, there are risks. Some low-skill, low-wage service workers almost certainly will be displaced by imports from other countries that have comparative advantage in those industries, just as US manufacturing lost many such jobs in the recent past. Another risk is that some of the countries to which those activities migrate will fail to reciprocate by lowering their own barriers to service trade, thereby placing an artificial handicap on US service exporters.

However, it is unlikely that the globalization gala will end with America's fast-growing service exporters turning into pumpkins. The risks of growing service trade seem manageable, and in any case the technologies driving that carriage are almost impossible for the usual government-imposed barriers to halt or even restrain. But as I have argued, there is much that US policymakers, working with their counterparts in other developed countries through the existing WTO framework, can do to keep the carriage from veering off the road:

- They can encourage developing countries to lower their barriers to service trade, to the benefit of those countries themselves as well as that of developed country exporters.

- They can push for enhanced enforcement of intellectual property rights of all kinds, so that service exporters worldwide can realize a return that gives them an incentive to continue investing in innovation.

- They can advocate, within the context of the GATS, for a faster pace of liberalization of trade, particularly in the services needed to support the coming worldwide infrastructure boom.

- They can pressure developing countries, especially the largest and fastest-growing ones, to sign the WTO's government procurement agreement—and set an example themselves by adhering to its letter and its spirit.

- They can reaffirm their commitment to public support for education at all levels, as education is the very basis of comparative advantage in high-skilled services.

- They can work to strengthen the social safety net for workers dislocated by trade, whatever their sector or occupation, not just because those workers deserve no less, but also as a way of enlisting them as willing social partners in liberalizing service trade.

The globalization clock may not be counting down to midnight, but there is nonetheless reason for urgency in liberalizing world trade in services. The imminent global infrastructure boom is a huge opportunity that US and other developed country firms can avail themselves of only if they are able to compete for the vast array of services that will support that undertaking. Most of that infrastructure will be built in developing countries, and it is precisely they that have the furthest to go in opening their procurement practices, safeguarding the intellectual property rights of foreign innovators, harmonizing their entry and licensing requirements with global standards, and clearing away the other entanglements that now impede service trade. Developing countries should do these things not for the sake of boosting the profits of US (and other developed country) firms and the wages of US workers—although such measures it will do that. Rather, they should do them because they will thereby gain access to the world's best talent and know-how, allowing them to meet their infrastructure needs more quickly and cheaply and with the best practices and methods. Thus, service trade liberalization is as much in their interest as it is in the interest of US service providers and the US economy more broadly. For their part, the United States and the other developed countries should be encouraging and supporting this liberalization while ensuring that their own policies toward the service sector are in harmony with each other and supportive of beneficial trade for all.

Appendices

Appendix A
Data Needs for Analyzing Trade in the Service Sector

To understand how increased trade in services might affect the US economy, both theory and previous empirical work stress some key considerations:

- the prevalence (how many activities?), scale (how much is being traded?), and direction (who is trading with whom?) of trade in services,
- how trade in services has evolved over time,
- the intensities of the factors used in service provision,
- the factor intensities across locations, and
- firm-level heterogeneity (differences in size, factor intensities, productivity, trade activity, and in other respects) within and across industries and countries.[1]

Investigation into any of these requires timely and reliable data of sufficient depth and breadth to allow statistical analysis to elicit robust results. Although the economic data collected by the various statistical agencies of the US government are unsurpassed in their comprehensiveness, reliability, and level of detail, the available datasets are not without some serious shortcomings, especially with respect to data on the service sector. This appendix briefly describes some of the areas where the data on services and the methods used in their collection are in greatest need of improvement.

---

1. Although not exactly a data need, researchers examining producer heterogeneity need access to producer-level information, called microdata, which are often collected under a pledge of confidentiality.

Measuring Trade in Services

The Bureau of Economic Analysis (BEA), an agency within the US Department of Commerce, collects information on trade in services and reports aggregate data on international service transactions through three publication programs: on cross-border trade in services in the international transactions accounts; on sales of services through affiliates of multinationals, some portion of which represent cross-border trade; and the benchmark input-output tables.

The program on cross-border trade in services provides the basis for all of the BEA's service trade data. As a result, this program provides the best sense of the trade data the BEA collects. As the BEA itself explains:

> The estimates of cross-border transactions cover both affiliated and unaffiliated transactions between US residents and foreign residents. Affiliated transactions consist of intra-firm trade within multinational companies—specifically, the trade between US parent companies and their foreign affiliates and between US affiliates and their foreign parent groups. Unaffiliated transactions are with foreigners that neither own, nor are owned by, the US party to the transaction.
>
> Cross-border trade in private services is classified into the same five, broad categories that are used in the US international transactions accounts—travel, passenger fares, "other transportation," royalties and license fees, and "other private services." (*Survey of Current Business,* November 2001)

Data on transactions between international affiliates are collected through the second program, the BEA's US Direct Investment Abroad and Foreign Direct Investment in the United States. Comprehensive benchmark surveys are collected every five years, and less comprehensive collections are conducted annually.

The BEA collects data on US international transactions in private services with unaffiliated foreigners through 11 surveys. These surveys fall into three broad categories: the surveys of "selected" services, which cover mainly business, professional, and technical services; the specialized surveys of services, which cover construction, engineering, architectural, and mining services, insurance services, financial services, and royalties and license fees; and the surveys of transportation services. These data collection programs are the principal source of the BEA's estimates of trade in services, but the estimates of some services are based on data from a variety of other sources, including US Customs and Border Protection and surveys conducted by other federal government agencies, private sources, and partner countries.

Needed: Increased Detail by Industry and Country

Detailed data on international service transactions for cross-border trade are currently available from 1986 through 2006. Service imports and exports are reported for approximately 30 (1986–91) to 35 (1992–2006) types of services; for some types, additional detail is available on whether the transactions are between affiliated or unaffiliated parties. These data are available for approximately 35 countries and country groupings for 1986–2006.

Table A.1 shows how the categorization of trade in services (both affiliated and unaffiliated) data published by the BEA has increased significantly in detail over the past decade. However, when one compares this categorization with the over 8,000 export categories and over 10,000 import categories available for the manufacturing sector, it becomes clear how large the gap in detail is between the two sectors. The detail for services is moving in the right direction, but clearly it has much further to go. Sturgeon et al. (2006) comment on what is lost by the current lack of detailed information:

> What is most troubling for us is that the seventeen industry categories listed ...exhaust the detail on services trade collected by United States government statistical agencies. What is going on in the other service product categories that have been mentioned as moving offshore, such as the wide variety of back-office functions like accounting, customer support, and software programming? What about the interpretation of radiology images, market and legal research, and research to support financial services? Are customized software services staying onshore while only basic software coding is moving offshore, or is higher-skilled work and work related to innovation and new product creation also being imported? Because very few questions are asked, very little detail is collected, leaving us with extremely thin data on services trade, even if steps are taken to improve data quality. Contrast the seventeen descriptive categories for traded services products ... with the more than 16,000 detailed product codes for goods collected by the United States Department of Commerce and the magnitude of the data gap becomes clear. It is clearly infeasible to collect as much product detail on services trade as is generated by the customs forms filled out when goods are shipped across borders. But much more detail could and should be collected. (Sturgeon et al. 2006, 26)

The BEA has taken some steps to improve the level of detail in its service trade statistics. For example, it has resolved the inconsistency between the survey formats for affiliated and unaffiliated trade, allowing greater detail in reporting the types of services traded. Although this represents progress, it does not resolve the issue of the need for greater detail.

Needed: Lower Reporting Thresholds

Sturgeon et al. (2006) also note:

> While the BEA surveys that ask firms to quantify their trade in services are mandatory, firms are exempted from reporting categories of services in which they have import transactions of less than $6M [million] per year and export transactions of less than $8M per year. In the case of services, in particular, because firms tend to be smaller than firms engaged in goods trade, the current thresholds very likely exclude many transactions. Because of this, we believe that the thresholds for mandatory reporting of international services transactions should be lowered. (Sturgeon et al. 2006, 25)

Table A.1 Categories of services reported by the Bureau of Economic Analysis, 1992–2006

1992	1997	2001	2006
Travel	Travel	Travel	Travel
Passenger fares	Passenger fares	Passenger fares	Passenger fares
Other transportation	Other transportation	Other transportation	Other transportation
Royalties and license fees	Royalties and license fees	Royalties and license fees	Royalties and license fees
Other private services	Other private services	Other private services	Other private services
Education	Education	Education	Education
Financial services	Financial services	Financial services	Financial services
Insurance services	Insurance services	Insurance services	Insurance services
Telecommunications	Telecommunications	Telecommunications	Telecommunications
Business, professional, and technical services	Business, professional, and technical services	Business, professional, and technical services	Business, professional, and technical services
	Computer and information services	Computer and information services	Computer and information services
		Management and consulting services	Management and consulting services
		Research and development and testing services	Research and development and testing services
Operational leasing	Operational leasing	Operational leasing	Operational leasing

			Other business, professional, and technical services
			Accounting, auditing, bookkeeping services
			Advertising
			Architectural, engineering, and other technical services
			Construction
			Industrial engineering
			Installation, maintenance, and repair of equipment
			Legal services
			Medical services
			Mining
			Sports and performing arts
			Trade-related services
			Training
			Other
		Other business, professional, and technical services	Other services
			Film and television tape rentals
			Other
	Other business, professional, and technical services	Medical services	
		Other services	
		Film and television tape rentals	
		Other	
Other business, professional, and technical services	Medical services		
	Other services		
	Film and television tape rentals		
	Other		
Medical services			
Other services			
Film and television tape rentals			
Other			

Source: Bureau of Economic Analysis, www.bea.gov.

Needed: Larger Samples and an Improved Sampling Frame

Related to the issue of lowering reporting thresholds is the need to improve the BEA's capacity to develop sampling frames for their surveys. A sampling frame is the list of all possible respondents (in this case, companies) to whom surveys could be sent. The sample to be surveyed is then drawn from this list. To ensure that the sample is statistically representative, a good sampling frame is essential. Sturgeon et al. (2006) comment:

> Another explanation for the apparent undercounting of services trade is that the BEA is not collecting data from the right companies, or is sending inappropriate surveys to the companies on its mailing lists. To test for potential undercounting of US services imports, the Government Accountability Office (GAO) provided the BEA with a list of 104 firms identified from press and company reports as likely to be importing services from India. The BEA was asked to compare this list with the survey responses it had received from firms on its mailing lists. The BEA had 87 (84%) of the firms identified by the GAO on its mailing lists. The BEA stated that it had dropped some of the missing companies from its mailing lists because they had not previously met the reporting thresholds for services trade.

> Furthermore, only 54 (52%) of the firms identified by the GAO had received appropriate surveys from the BEA (e.g., firms with offshore affiliates were not sent the survey on affiliated trade). Finally, only 15 (14%) of the 104 firms identified by the GAO as likely to be importing services from India reported such imports.... One explanation for the low level of reporting of services trade with India is that firms that had transactions valued beneath the thresholds mentioned above, while not required to do so, nevertheless filled out the BEA surveys but did not provide detail on the source or destination countries associated with their international transactions because they were not required to do so.

> Still, the BEA believes that its data on services trade is of good quality. When the BEA contacted the companies on the GAO list that were missing from its mailing lists, it did not identify any company with substantial imports of services that were not already being reported. Nevertheless, the BEA recognizes that more resources need to be allocated toward maintaining lists of survey respondents since the identity of transactors may change from year to year. The BEA has a variety of initiatives underway to improve its mailing lists and improve survey compliance.... The BEA also plans to merge the collection of its data on affiliated international services transactions with its data on unaffiliated international services transactions, so that a given type of service is covered in exactly the same detail, whether it is imported or exported, and whether it is with an affiliated or an unaffiliated foreign party. We believe that these efforts are significant and very helpful, especially if combined with lower thresholds for mandatory survey compliance. (Sturgeon et al. 2006, 25–26)

The BEA has undertaken efforts to improve its sampling frame. It commissioned the Census Bureau to add a question to its 2006 Company Organization Survey to ask whether firms imported services. But in this area, too, much remains to be done, as discussed in Chapter 9.

Measuring the Impact of Service Trade on the US Economy

Understanding how increased trade in services has affected or is likely to affect the US economy requires both the detailed information on trade flows described above and the ability to link it to detailed information on domestic producers. Specifically, it requires detailed information on the inputs that service firms use (labor, capital, land, buildings, accounting services, intellectual property, etc.) and the outputs they produce (computer programs, lawsuits, advertising campaigns, medical procedures, etc.). These data would help researchers explore the relationship between growth in demand for particular services and the demand for inputs to those services. The data would also contribute to an understanding of whether service sector productivity is increasing over time, and whether this growth is in response to particular changes in the economic environment. To understand how the service sector affects employment outcomes across US regions, one would want these data on as detailed a geographic basis as possible. One would also need to be able to link these data to detailed information on international trade in services (the type of information discussed above).[2]

Needed: More-Detailed Industry Classification

The data covering the US service sector are not as robust as the data for the manufacturing sector in a number of dimensions. The information collected from the service sector, for both inputs and outputs, is less detailed. One can see this simply by looking at the NAICS codes for the different sectors and observing the number of workers in each coded industry.[3] There are about 470 NAICS industrial codes for the manufacturing sector (NAICS 31-33), compared with about 325 for the service sector (NAICS 51-81). But whereas the manufacturing sector employed about 13 million people in 2007, the service sector employed about 68 million, more than five times as many. As a result, there were about 28,000 workers per NAICS code in manufacturing in 2007 and about 208,000 workers per code in services. By this admittedly crude metric, the service sector is substantially underclassified (by more than sevenfold). One can easily imagine the difficulty that researchers have in analyzing the labor market impacts of service trade using data at this coarse a level.

---

2. As described above, this type of data is already available for the manufacturing sector. The Census Bureau makes such data available publicly in aggregated form, and in disaggregated form to approved researchers at the Center for Economic Studies. The research community has learned a great deal about the manufacturing sector across a wide range of topics—productivity dynamics, job creation and destruction, impact of environmental regulation, impact of trade, just to name a few—through access to producer-level information at the Census Bureau.

3. Although this is not necessarily the only (or the best) way to think about classification, if one is interested in labor market impacts it is instructive to note the significant difference in the industry detail available across sectors.

Here, too, work is being done to improve the data. The implementation of a new classification system, the North American Product Classification System (NAPCS), is improving the level of detail for the output of establishments in the service sector. The 2007 Economic Census forms for the service sector have considerable detail for output product categories within service industries.[4]

Needed: More-Detailed Information on Production Inputs

Another way in which the service sector data are less robust than the manufacturing sector data is with regard to the collection of data on inputs into the production process. Again from Sturgeon et al. (2006):

> The Census Bureau has developed detailed classification schemes for material inputs and manufactured products that it uses to collect information on what individual manufacturing establishments buy and sell. These product categories have been developed with a great deal of care, and government surveys have been tuned to specific sectors. For example, establishments in the plastics industry are required to provide detailed information about the consumption of chemical feedstock and the production of various kinds of plastics while establishments producing furniture are required to provide detail about the consumption of wood, metal, hardware, glue, and fabric and the production of various kinds of furniture. This pattern holds true across the manufacturing sector. The US Census Bureau's Numerical List of Manufactured and Mineral Products contains hierarchically organized descriptions of the principal products and services of the manufacturing and mining industries in the United States. These codes are used to collect data for the Economic Census and are used by the Bureau of Economic Analysis for the input-output matrix that underlies the national accounts. But as in international trade in services, far less detail is collected on the services products that are consumed and produced domestically. Again, there are more than 6,000 codes for physical products but fewer than 100 for services.
>
> The lack of detail on domestic trade in services means that the Bureau of Economic Analysis largely estimates the contribution of services to the national accounts. While resulting estimation cannot claim precision, BEA analysts believe that their techniques capture the magnitude and direction of change in services accurately enough to support policy. While this may be true today, we think the view of the US Census Bureau... bears repeating, "If [the information gap between manufacturing and services goes] unaddressed, economic policymakers will be increasingly misinformed and misdirected about changes in the real economy, related to rates and sources of growth in output, prices, productivity, and trade." Clearly, an accelerated and sustained effort to collect more detail on domestic trade in services is required. Our second recommendation, therefore, is for the US Census Bureau to accel-

---

4. Although this is helpful, an issue with classifying establishments into broad industries and collecting detailed product information is that it is difficult to allocate inputs across outputs. Additional refinement of the service sector industry codes would improve the ability to measure things like productivity.

erate the completion of the North American Product Classification System (NAPCS), and fully and rapidly deploy it in the Economic Census, at the establishment level, for both inputs and outputs. (Sturgeon et al. 2006, 27)

Action on this recommendation would lead to important improvements and would be beneficial toward understanding how the service sector functions.

In addition to increased information on purchased services, two other improvements would be worthwhile. The literature on the impact of trade on the manufacturing sector (chapter 4) showed that factor intensities (of both capital and skilled labor) are important determinants of how establishments behave in response to international competition. Currently, however, the economic censuses do not consistently collect information on labor inputs other than total employment and salaries and wages.[5] It would be useful if, in addition, the Census Bureau collected information on workers' level of skill. Although detailed information on skills or educational attainment would be costly to collect and burdensome to provide, research along these lines in the manufacturing sector demonstrates that it is possible to collect data using very crude classifications (distinguishing, for example, production from nonproduction workers) that still provide important information about the skill intensity of firms' production processes.

For services, the classification of production versus nonproduction workers might not make sense, but an analogous classification might distinguish employees exempt from the requirement to be paid overtime (under the Fair Labor Standards Act) from nonexempt employees. This distinction is based on salary and job duties and thus approximates the distinction between managerial and nonmanagerial workers. Hence, although not an ideal measure of skill, this classification is likely to capture meaningful variation in skill intensity across producers and industries. These data would be relatively easy to collect and probably relatively straightforward for firms to report.

Another input that has proved to be an important determinant in plant survival in the manufacturing sector is capital intensity. Currently, the economic censuses do not consistently collect information on firms' capital. Although such data might not be particularly meaningful for some service industries, for others it is not difficult to imagine that capital intensity would have something to do with firm performance. (For example, one can imagine that the capital intensity of hospitals would be systematically related to outcomes and, perhaps, to their likelihood of participating in international trade.)

Needed: Information on a Geographic Basis

The Census Bureau does collect information on capital expenditure in the Annual Capital Expenditure Survey (ACES); however, ACES is an enterprise-level survey. Because many large firms (as measured by employment and

---

5. For some industries the censuses collect information on the type of worker (by training or activity).

output) operate in multiple industries and multiple geographic markets, deriving industry and geographic information on capital expenditure from this enterprise-level information requires that capital service inputs be allocated across the locations and industries in which the enterprise operates, which can be difficult. This highlights another important dimension where information on the service sector needs improvement, namely, geographical information.

To understand how international trade is affecting regions within the United States, it is important to be able to examine whether and how producers in different regions vary in factor intensity and productivity. This need highlights the importance of collecting as much information as possible at the establishment level. Such information enables researchers to link economic phenomena with particular regions and allows a much tighter alignment of inputs and outputs. Collecting information at the enterprise rather than the establishment level seriously reduces the product and geographical specificity of the data. For some purchased inputs (such as advertising), it may be difficult to collect the information at the establishment level, but for inputs like physical capital it does seem feasible to collect capital stock and flow data at this level. (Capital stock information is collected in the Census of Manufactures.)

Needed: Ability to Access and Link Microdata

As described above, research using microdata provides a better understanding of how globalization affects the US economy. Researchers need access to microdata to conduct this type of research. Sturgeon et al. (2006) offer the following recommendation:

> Steps should be taken to extract as much information as possible from the data that is currently collected by government programs. An inventory of current and potential microdata resources should be made, and as many "micro-data" sets as possible should be archived, maintained, and made available to both government and academic researchers.

> Micro-data are the data that support government administrative programs and underlies published statistics. In general, quantitative research based on micro-data can provide a better and more detailed view of services offshoring and its effects than research based on published statistics. (Sturgeon et al. 2006, 40)

A minor issue related to microdata access is the desirability of permitting researchers to combine data that have already been collected by different agencies to answer important questions. As Sturgeon et al. (2006) argue, this is a cost-effective way of increasing the usefulness of data that have already been purchased:

> Finally, it is important to encourage research that links various sets of micro-data. While there can be legislative and institutional barriers to sharing micro-data across agencies, reducing these barriers could enable some extremely

powerful research. For example if the outbound foreign affiliate investment collected by the Bureau of Economic Analysis in its surveys of multinational firms were to be combined with the firm, establishment, and trade data collected by the US Census Bureau, it would help researchers create a more comprehensive picture of the operations of US firms—both at home and abroad. The combined data could reveal domestic activity at the establishment level (with product level information, geographic information, and export information), the relationship between the establishments within the firm, the amount of trading the firm does (using the matched transaction and firm data), and the nature of the firm's foreign affiliate operations (employment, wage bill, location, local sales, trade with parent, etc). This would allow researchers to examine the relationship between domestic activity, trade, and foreign direct investment. (Sturgeon et al. 2006, 32)

Combining information from different agencies in this way does raise concern that the identity of specific firms could inadvertently be revealed. It is important to protect the confidentiality (and the perception of confidentiality) of respondent-level information—among other things to ensure that respondents have no incentive to withhold, or to misreport, information. It is the author's strong sense that the necessary protocols and infrastructure are in place at the Census Bureau, the BEA, and the Bureau of Labor Statistics (BLS) to restrict access to approved uses and thus to protect the confidentiality and the perception of confidentiality—but also that bureaucratic impediments continue to hinder researchers' ability to combine and link datasets from different statistical agencies.

Impediments to Improvement

This section describes what appear to be impediments to improving the quality of data needed to properly evaluate the impact of trade in services on the US economy.

Resources

Despite the growing importance of the service sector, the infrastructure for collecting information on services is not as robust as that for other sectors, such as manufacturing. A primary reason for this disparity is that Congress does not allocate resources for that task proportional to the sector's size. Therefore, it should not come as a surprise that one impediment to improving statistics on trade in services and domestic service activity is lack of sufficient resources.

As a simple metric of the disparity in resources devoted to the various sectors, table A.2 shows the fiscal 2009 budget for the Economic Census by sector. The table also shows the number of employees and the number of establishments in each sector and calculates budgeted dollars per employee and per establishment across sectors. The table reveals that by both of the last two measures, the resources devoted to the service sector are significantly lower than those devoted to manufacturing or mining. On a per establishment basis, Congress allocates more than six times more money for data collection in the manufacturing sector than in the service sector. On a per employee basis, the disparity is smaller but still more than twofold. The disparities between services and mining are even greater. This simple (maybe simplistic) calculation makes the point that service sector data collection is relatively resource poor. To bring the data available for the (domestic) service sector to a level similar to that for the manufacturing sector will require a commensurate investment of resources.

One would also like to have information on trade in services that is comparable to the information available on trade in goods. However, this does not seem feasible because, unlike goods, services do not pass through ports of entry, and their "shippers" are not required to file customs forms or export declarations. These administrative systems for trade in goods provide a relatively inexpensive means of collecting very detailed information on that trade. It is not obvious how such a low-cost data collection system could be devised for services. Instead, it seems likely that collecting information on service trade will require firm surveys, which are obviously more expensive than piggybacking off administrative systems that are already collecting the data. Thus, collecting better information on service trade will at a minimum require a significantly increased investment of resources. The next sections describe additional prerequisites for collecting better service trade data.

Sampling Frame

An issue identified by Sturgeon et al. (see box A.1) is that the BEA does not have access to an adequate sampling frame for conducting its surveys of international service transactions. The BEA recognizes the need to improve its sampling frame and is taking steps to do so, as described above. Yet it remains an open question whether these modest steps are sufficient. What the BEA needs is access to a sampling frame similar to that maintained by the Census Bureau.

Data-sharing legislation already provides authorization for the statistical agencies to share confidential data, but the situation is complicated by the fact that the Census Bureau's business sampling frame contains federal tax information provided by the Internal Revenue Service. For the Census Bureau to share its sampling frame with the BEA or the BLS, companion legislation would have to be passed amending Title 26, section 6103(j), which governs the use of federal tax information. This companion "j-bill" has been introduced from time to time but never passed, and evidence to date leaves one less than optimistic about its passage. However, if the Census Bureau could provide sampling frame information to the BEA, it would be a significant improvement in the BEA's capacity to conduct surveys.

Table A.2 Budget for the Economic Census by program component, fiscal 2009

Program component	Budget (millions of dollars)	US employment, 2007	US establishments, 2007	Budget per US employee (dollars)	Budget per US establishment (dollars)
Services	39.9	68,026,666	4,382,720	0.59	9.10
Retail trade	23.7	15,610,710	1,122,703	1.52	21.11
Manufactures	17.8	13,333,390	293,919	1.33	60.56
Wholesale trade	12.6	6,295,109	432,094	2.00	29.16
Construction	6.8	7,399,047	725,101	0.92	9.38
Transportation, communication, utilities	3.1	5,068,192	234,805	0.61	13.20
Minerals	1.7	703,129	21,169	2.42	80.31

Note: Not all periodic census activity associated with the Economic Census occurred in fiscal 2009. However, because the timing of the processing for the various sectors within the Economic Census is similar, it is assumed that the relative size of the budgets is representative of the total costs associated with each sector.

Source: US Census Bureau, Periodic Censuses and Programs Budget Amendment FY 2009, as presented to Congress, June 2008, Exhibit 12.

Box A.1   MIT offshoring working group recommendations

The report cited in this appendix as Sturgeon et al. (2006) is the report of a working group on data needs relating to offshoring; the work was sponsored by the Industrial Performance Center of the Massachusetts Institute of Technology. The working group, which included myself, had two purposes: first, to evaluate the data available for characterizing and measuring service offshoring and its effects on the US economy, and second, to make recommendations for improvements in data collection, dissemination, and analysis. The group's main recommendations were as follows:

> We see three broad solutions to this problem, each of which should be aggressively pursued: 1) more and better data on services trade should be collected, 2) more information should be extracted and published from existing data resources, and 3) quantitative research methods should be combined with qualitative methods to provide a better view of the context and character of services offshoring....

1) Collect more detail on international trade in services.

> The BEA should collect more detail on services products that are traded internationally (affiliated and unaffiliated services imports and exports). It currently collects data on only 17 categories of traded services products. In contrast, import and export statistics for the United States are currently available for more than 16,000 categories of goods. Without a more detailed view of which services are traded internationally, it will remain impossible to determine which sectors experience pressure from import competition. As a result, we cannot know where in the economy to look for the effects of services offshoring with any precision. This in turn renders other data on services less useful.

2) Collect more detail on domestic trade in services.

> The US Census Bureau should accelerate its efforts to collect more detailed statistics on services traded within the United States (services inputs and outputs). These more detailed statistics will help to provide a better view of the role that services play in the economy of the United States. Services account for more than 85 percent of US private sector GDP, but we have very little information on the services that are bought and sold by companies.

3) Collect more detail and publish time series data on employment by occupation.

> Because service work plays a role in all industries, adequate data on employment by occupation is necessary to determine the employment and wage effects of services offshoring. Data should be collected at the establishment level to enable links to data on domestic and international trade. We recommend two concrete steps in this regard:

>> 1) The BLS should publish consistent time series on employment by occupation from the Occupational Employment Statistics (OES) program. If possible these data should be published by industry at the national, state, and metropolitan levels. Time-series data will allow policymakers to track employment trends in the occupations most vulnerable to job loss from services offshoring.

(continued on next page)

2) The BEA should collect data on more occupational categories in its surveys on the activities of US-based multinational firms. More detail on the occupations created by multinational firms, at home and abroad, will provide a clearer picture of the employment effects of services offshoring.

4) Archive and provide access to more microdata resources.

Steps should be taken to extract as much information as possible from the data that is currently collected by government programs. An inventory of current and potential microdata resources should be made, and as many microdata sets as possible should be archived, maintained, and made available to both government and academic researchers.

Microdata are the data that supports government administrative programs and underlies published statistics. In general, quantitative research based on microdata can provide a better and more detailed view of services offshoring and its effects than research based on published statistics.

5) Accelerate research that combines quantitative and qualitative research methods.

No single approach or dataset can hope to bring the complex and dynamic phenomena of services offshoring into complete focus. An interdisciplinary, collaborative approach is needed to combine insights from data collected by government programs with insights from researcher-generated surveys and field interviews. Quantitative methods allow researchers to estimate the magnitude and speed of economic change and to implement causality tests, while qualitative methods can provide can provide a rich and nuanced picture of the complexity, context, and dynamics of services offshoring.

Source: Sturgeon et al. (2006, iv-vi).

Given the lack of an adequate sampling frame, the resource constraints mentioned above, and the fact that the principal mission of the BEA is to produce aggregate economic accounts, the BEA focuses its data collection efforts on large organizations that it deems likely to trade in services. Given the constraints, it seems unlikely that the samples used in the international transaction surveys are statistically representative across service sector industries, firm size classes, or geography. To improve the level of detail available for trade in services, the BEA will need to increase the number of organizations it surveys and, presumably, increase the statistical representativeness of the sample. These steps will require access to an adequate sampling frame.

Organizational Structure

Some organizational changes at the statistical agencies might facilitate improvements in service sector data. If one takes a step back and looks at the existing allocation of responsibilities for the collection of service trade data, the logic of its organization is less than clear. The BEA is a recipient of large amounts of data collected by other statistical agencies (including the BLS and the Census Bureau). It is also a data collection agency itself. This leads naturally to the question, Why does the BEA collect information on some types (such as multi-national enterprises and international service transactions) and not others?

This author's impression, which is not based on any systematic historical research, is that service trade statistics have historically been collected largely to fulfill the needs of national income and product accounts (NIPA) construction. Perhaps this feature of the data made it logical for the BEA to collect the service trade data. Other types of production and international trade data are collected for a broad range of uses (including, importantly, for the NIPAs). Historically, however, there has not been great demand for detailed service trade statistics beyond the need to complete the NIPAs.

This is beginning to change, however. As the service sector's share of the US economy increases and trade in services grows, there will be an increasing need to analyze the impact of a broader range of phenomena associated with increased trade in services (for example, the regional implications within the United States and the impact of the service components of trade agreements).

Understanding the impact of trade in services from a variety of perspectives, including the impact on local and regional economies, as well as the impact of such things as trade agreements on trade in services, will require much more detailed data regarding that trade. Researchers and policymakers need comprehensive data across detailed industry classifications and geographical regions of the United States—ideally not only on which firms participate in global service trade but also on which do not. The data should be consistent with other production-related data and easily linked to those data.

Collecting detailed, statistically representative information on trade in services across detailed industries, countries, and regions within the United States would be a major undertaking. An open question is whether the BEA is the most appropriate agency for that task. There may be reasons for having a dedicated statistical agency within the BEA collect this type of information. But such a fragmented collection system would also have significant drawbacks.

The first drawback is that data collection has fairly significant fixed costs, especially with regard to developing and maintaining a sampling frame. As described above, the BEA's inability to access an adequate sampling frame is a significant impediment to improved data collection on service trade. Other examples of fixed costs might include the design of forms and capacity for survey processing and follow-up.

Another drawback involves data consistency and potential problems with data integration. As an example, when the BEA and the Census Bureau were directed to produce statistics at the establishment level on foreign direct investment in the United States, the data comparability and matching issues were not insignificant. If the foreign direct investment surveys and international service transactions surveys were instead conducted by the Census Bureau using the bureau's sampling frame and industrial and geographic coding systems, it would significantly increase the ease with which the data could be used in conjunction with other production data.

There may be advantages to having the BEA conduct the survey that I am not aware of. However, the BEA and the Census Bureau already work closely together on other aspects of data collection for the NIPAs, and the Census Bureau has the existing infrastructure to collect detailed, statistically representative statistics on trade in services. For example, it has arguably the best sampling frame for this type of application within the statistical agency system. The Census Bureau already surveys all the relevant firms and establishments. It appears that the efficiencies in data collection and improvements in comparability from having these data collection activities housed within the Census Bureau are potentially significant. This argues for looking further into the costs and benefits of moving the foreign direct investment and international service transactions data collection programs to the Census Bureau.

Appendix B
Data Used in the Book

Worker Microdata

The data used for this book include worker microdata (individual survey responses for which the worker is the unit of observation) from the sources described below.

2000 Decennial Census of Population and Households, Public Use Micro Sample

The 2000 Decennial Census of Population and Households collected information about 115.9 million housing units and 281.4 million people across the United States. As it does every 10 years, the Census collected detailed information on individuals' age, race, sex, occupation, industry, income, and other socioeconomic measures (using the "long form" questionnaire) from a sample of approximately one-sixth of the US population. The Census Bureau provides information from the Decennial Census long form in a variety of formats. One of the most useful of these for social science researchers is the Public Use Micro Sample (PUMS) format.

The PUMS data contain information collected about persons and housing units individually, in a manner that avoids disclosure of information about households or individuals. The Census Bureau uses confidential survey responses to produce the summary data that go into its reports, summary files, and special tabulations. The PUMS data are extracts from these confidential microdata that are modified to further protect confidentiality.

The PUMS files essentially allow "do-it-yourself" special tabulations. The Census 2000 files furnish nearly all of the detail recorded on the long form questionnaire, subject to the limitations of sample size, geographic identification, and confidentiality protection. Researchers can construct a wide variety of tabulations interrelating any desired set of variables.

The advantages of the PUMS data include the following:

- The sample is very large (approximately 8 million working-age adults).
- The data contain detailed industry and occupation information.
- The data also contain information on educational attainment and other socioeconomic characteristics as well as age, sex, and race.
- The data are available at a more refined level of geographic detail than other files.

Disadvantages include the following:

- The survey is conducted only every 10 years and is being replaced by the American Community Survey.
- The 2000 Decennial Census used different industry and occupation classification schemes from the 1990 Decennial Census, making it difficult to compare changes over time.

2007 American Community Survey, PUMS

The American Community Survey (ACS) is an ongoing survey that collects and provides data similar to those from the Decennial Census long form every year. The Census Bureau makes a PUMS version of the ACS available. Its main advantage is that it is very similar to the 2000 decennial PUMS but more recent. Its main disadvantage is that the sample is smaller than that in the 2000 decennial.

Firm Microdata

This book also uses three sources of microdata in which the individual firm or establishment is the unit of analysis.

2002 Economic Census

The Economic Census collects information on economic activity from business establishments with employees across a broad range of sectors in the United States. This information includes data on a range of operating characteristics from establishments in a wide range of industries. The information collected typically includes such things as employment, payroll, sales, location, and primary industry, but the exact set of data collected varies across industries.

Business establishments in the Economic Census are grouped into industries based on the similarity of their production processes. These industries are coded according to the North American Industry Classification System (NAICS).

The main advantages of the Economic Census microdata are as follows:

- Access to individual establishment data allows custom cross-tabulations not available from Census Bureau publication programs.
- Information is available at a detailed industry classification level.
- Information is available at the establishment level on employment, wages, and output.

The principal disadvantage is that the data are available only with a relatively long lag (the most recent microdata available are for 2002).

2006 Company Organization Survey

All companies with payroll and their establishments, except companies engaged exclusively in agricultural production, are covered in the Census Bureau's annual Company Organization Survey. This is a mail-out, mail-back survey of selected companies, with larger sample sizes in years preceding an Economic Census. Smaller companies are selected where separate administrative data indicate a probable organizational change, and by a probability sampling procedure. Both larger and smaller companies are identified from those maintained on the Business Register.

The fact that this survey collects information on service imports is its main advantage to researchers interested in this sector. Among its disadvantages are its limited sample size (approximately 60,000 firms, representing more than half of private sector employment), the fact that the sample is skewed toward larger firms, and the fact that the data are at the firm level, making classification difficult for large, multisector firms.

2004 Benchmark Survey of US Direct Investment Abroad

The Benchmark Survey of US Direct Investment Abroad, conducted every five years, is the BEA's most comprehensive survey of foreign direct investment by US firms in terms of both the coverage of companies and the amount of information collected. The most recent Benchmark Survey for which data are publicly available is that of 2004.

The Benchmark Survey collects three related types of data from all known US multinational companies: financial and operating data of their foreign affiliates, financial and operating data of the US multinationals themselves (the parent), and the direct investment position and balance of payments data for the parent.

The financial and operating data include a variety of indicators of the overall operations of US parent companies and their foreign affiliates, including balance sheets and income statements; property, plant, and equipment; employment and compensation of employees; US trade in goods; sales of goods and services; value added; research and development activities; taxes; and external financial position.

The advantage of these data is that they provide detailed information on trade in services between US parents and their foreign affiliates. Disadvantages include the long lag time until data are publicly available and the infrequent collection.

Aggregate Data by Firm or Establishment

In addition to the microdata sources described above, this book draws on a number of sources of conventional aggregate data.

1997, 2002, and 2007 Economic Censuses

This book uses publicly available aggregate data from the 1997, 2002, and 2007 Economic Censuses. The 2007 Economic Census covers nearly all of the US economy in its basic collection of establishment statistics. Besides the advantage of broad coverage at a detailed industry classification, it also provides information on a rich array of establishment characteristics such as employment, wages, and sales. A disadvantage is that the census is conducted only every five years.

1998–2007 County Business Patterns

This book uses data at the six-digit NAICS industry level from the 1998–2007 County Business Patterns survey, conducted annually by the Census Bureau. This series, which provides subnational economic data by industry, is useful for studying the economic activity of small geographic areas, for analyzing economic changes over time, and as a benchmark for statistical series, surveys, and databases between Economic Censuses.

County Business Patterns covers most of the country's economic activity. The series excludes data on self-employed individuals, employees of private households, railroad employees, agricultural production employees, and most government employees.

This series has been published annually since 1964 and at irregular intervals dating back to 1946. The comparability of the data over time may, however, be affected by definitional changes in establishments, activity status, and industrial classifications.

Basic data items in County Business Patterns are extracted from the Business Register, a file of all known single- and multi-establishment employer companies that is maintained and updated by the Census Bureau. The annual Company Organization Survey (see above) provides individual establishment data for multi-establishment companies. Data for single-establishment companies are obtained from various Census Bureau programs, such as the

Annual Survey of Manufactures and Current Business Surveys, as well as from administrative record sources.

The main advantages of County Business Patterns are its detailed industry classification and broad coverage, as well as the fact that the data are reported annually. A disadvantage is that it reports data on establishments' employment and wages only and not output.

International Service Transactions

The Bureau of Economic Analysis collects information on trade in services and reports aggregate data on international service transactions through three publication programs: on cross-border trade in services in the international transactions accounts; on sales of services through affiliates of multinationals, some portion of which represent cross-border trade; and the benchmark input-output tables.

The cross-border trade in services program provides the basis for all of the BEA's service trade data. The advantages of these data are that they provide official estimates of trade in services for a number of categories and a number of important countries and regions. The disadvantages are described in detail in appendix A and include inadequate detail on service categories and incomplete detailed geographic coverage.

Appendix C
NAICS Major Sectors and SOC Major Occupation Groups

NAICS Major Sectors[1]

Sector 11—Agriculture, Forestry, Fishing, and Hunting

The Agriculture, Forestry, Fishing, and Hunting sector comprises establishments primarily engaged in growing crops, raising animals, harvesting timber, and harvesting fish and other animals from a farm, ranch, or their natural habitats. The establishments in this sector are often described as farms, ranches, dairies, greenhouses, nurseries, orchards, or hatcheries.

Sector 21—Mining

The Mining sector comprises establishments that extract naturally occurring mineral solids, such as coal and ores; liquid minerals, such as crude petroleum; and gases, such as natural gas. The term mining is used in the broad sense to include quarrying, well operations, beneficiating (e.g., crushing, screening, washing, and flotation), and other preparation customarily performed at the mine site, or as a part of mining activity.

Sector 22—Utilities

The Utilities sector comprises establishments engaged in the provision of the following utility services: electric power, natural gas, steam supply, water

---

1. US Census Bureau, North American Industry Classification System (NAICS), available at www.census.gov/eos/www/naics.

221

supply, and sewage removal. Within this sector, the specific activities associated with the utility services provided vary by utility: electric power includes generation, transmission, and distribution; natural gas includes distribution; steam supply includes provision and/or distribution; water supply includes treatment and distribution; and sewage removal includes collection, treatment, and disposal of waste through sewer systems and sewage treatment facilities.

Sector 23—Construction

The construction sector comprises establishments primarily engaged in the construction of buildings or in engineering projects (e.g., highways and utility systems). Establishments primarily engaged in the preparation of sites for new construction and in subdividing land for sale as building sites also are included in this sector. Construction work may include new work, additions, alterations, or maintenance and repairs.

Sectors 31–33—Manufacturing

The Manufacturing sector comprises establishments engaged in the mechanical, physical, or chemical transformation of materials, substances, or components into new products. The assembling of component parts of manufactured products is considered manufacturing, except in cases where the activity is appropriately classified in Sector 23, Construction.

Establishments in the Manufacturing sector are often described as plants, factories, or mills and characteristically use power-driven machines and materials-handling equipment. However, establishments that transform materials or substances into new products by hand or in the worker's home and those engaged in selling to the general public products made on the same premises from which they are sold, such as bakeries, candy stores, and custom tailors, may also be included in this sector. Manufacturing establishments may process materials or may contract with other establishments to process their materials for them. Both types of establishments are included in manufacturing.

The materials, substances, or components transformed by manufacturing establishments are raw materials that are products of agriculture, forestry, fishing, mining, or quarrying as well as products of other manufacturing establishments. The materials used may be purchased directly from producers, obtained through customary trade channels, or secured without recourse to the market by transferring the product from one establishment to another, under the same ownership.

The new product of a manufacturing establishment may be finished in the sense that it is ready for use or consumption, or it may be semifinished to become an input for an establishment engaged in further manufacturing. For example, the product of the alumina refinery is the input used in the primary production of aluminum; primary aluminum is the input to an aluminum wire drawing plant; and aluminum wire is the input for a fabricated wire product manufacturing establishment.

Manufacturing establishments often perform one or more activities that are classified outside the Manufacturing sector of NAICS. For instance, almost all manufacturing has some captive research and development or administrative operations, such as accounting, payroll, or management. These captive services are treated the same as captive manufacturing activities. When the services are provided by separate establishments, they are classified to the NAICS sector where such services are primary, not in manufacturing.

Sector 42—Wholesale Trade

The Wholesale Trade sector comprises establishments engaged in wholesaling merchandise, generally without transformation, and rendering services incidental to the sale of merchandise. The merchandise described in this sector includes the outputs of agriculture, mining, manufacturing, and certain information industries, such as publishing.

The wholesaling process is an intermediate step in the distribution of merchandise. Wholesalers are organized to sell or arrange the purchase or sale of (a) goods for resale (i.e., goods sold to other wholesalers or retailers), (b) capital or durable nonconsumer goods, and (c) raw and intermediate materials and supplies used in production.

Sectors 44–45—Retail Trade

The Retail Trade sector comprises establishments engaged in retailing merchandise, generally without transformation, and rendering services incidental to the sale of merchandise.

The retailing process is the final step in the distribution of merchandise; retailers are, therefore, organized to sell merchandise in small quantities to the general public. This sector comprises two main types of retailers: store and nonstore retailers.

1. Store retailers operate fixed point-of-sale locations, located and designed to attract a high volume of walk-in customers. In general, retail stores have extensive displays of merchandise and use mass-media advertising to attract customers. They typically sell merchandise to the general public for personal or household consumption, but some also serve business and institutional clients. These include establishments such as office supply stores, computer and software stores, building materials dealers, plumbing supply stores, and electrical supply stores. Catalog showrooms, gasoline service stations, automotive dealers, and mobile home dealers are treated as store retailers.

2. Nonstore retailers, like store retailers, are organized to serve the general public, but their retailing methods differ. The establishments of this

subsector reach customers and market merchandise with methods such as the broadcasting of "infomercials," the broadcasting and publishing of direct-response advertising, the publishing of paper and electronic catalogs, door-to-door solicitation, in-home demonstration, selling from portable stalls (e.g., street vendors, except food), and distribution through vending machines. Establishments engaged in the direct (nonstore) sale of products, such as home heating oil and newspaper delivery, are included here.

Sectors 48–49—Transportation and Warehousing

The Transportation and Warehousing sector includes industries providing transportation of passengers and cargo, warehousing and storage for goods, scenic and sightseeing transportation, and support activities related to modes of transportation. Establishments in these industries use transportation equipment or transportation-related facilities as a productive asset. The type of equipment depends on the mode of transportation. The modes of transportation are air, rail, water, road, and pipeline.

Sector 51—Information

The Information sector comprises establishments engaged in the following processes: (a) producing and distributing information and cultural products, (b) providing the means to transmit or distribute these products as well as data or communications, and/or (c) processing data.

The main components of this sector are the publishing industries, including software publishing, and both traditional publishing and publishing exclusively on the internet; the motion picture and sound recording industries; the broadcasting industries, including traditional broadcasting and those broadcasting exclusively over the internet; the telecommunications industries; the industries known as internet service providers and web search portals, data processing industries, and the information services industries.

Sector 52—Finance and Insurance

The Finance and Insurance sector comprises establishments primarily engaged in financial transactions (transactions involving the creation, liquidation, or change in ownership of financial assets) and/or in facilitating financial transactions. Three principal types of activities are identified:

1. Raising funds by taking deposits and/or issuing securities and, in the process, incurring liabilities. Establishments engaged in this activity use raised funds to acquire financial assets by making loans and/or purchasing securities. Putting themselves at risk, they channel funds from lenders to borrowers and transform or repackage the funds with respect to maturity, scale, and risk. This activity is known as financial intermediation.

2. Pooling of risk by underwriting insurance and annuities. Establishments engaged in this activity collect fees, insurance premiums, or annuity considerations; build up reserves; invest those reserves; and make contractual payments. Fees are based on the expected incidence of the insured risk and the expected return on investment.

3. Providing specialized services facilitating or supporting financial intermediation, insurance, and employee benefit programs.

In addition, monetary authorities charged with monetary control are included in this sector.

Sector 53—Real Estate and Rental and Leasing

The Real Estate and Rental and Leasing sector comprises establishments primarily engaged in renting, leasing, or otherwise allowing the use of tangible or intangible assets, and establishments providing related services. The major portion of this sector comprises establishments that rent, lease, or otherwise allow the use of their own assets by others. The assets may be tangible, as is the case with real estate and equipment, or intangible, as is the case with patents and trademarks.

This sector also includes establishments primarily engaged in managing real estate for others, selling, renting, and/or buying real estate for others, and appraising real estate. These activities are closely related to this sector's main activity, and it was felt that from a production basis they would best be included here. In addition, a substantial proportion of property management is self-performed by lessors.

Sector 54—Professional, Scientific, and Technical Services

The Professional, Scientific, and Technical Services sector comprises establishments that specialize in performing professional, scientific, and technical activities for others. These activities require a high degree of expertise and training. The establishments in this sector specialize according to expertise and provide these services to clients in a variety of industries and, in some cases, to households. Activities performed include: legal advice and representation; accounting, bookkeeping, and payroll services; architectural, engineering, and specialized design services; computer services; consulting services; research services; advertising services; photographic services; translation and interpretation services; veterinary services; and other professional, scientific, and technical services.

This sector excludes establishments primarily engaged in providing a range of day-to-day office administrative services, such as financial planning, billing and recordkeeping, personnel, and physical distribution and logistics. These establishments are classified in Sector 56, Administrative and Support and Waste Management and Remediation Services.

Sector 55—Management of Companies and Enterprises

The Management of Companies and Enterprises sector comprises (1) establishments that hold the securities of (or other equity interests in) companies and enterprises for the purpose of owning a controlling interest or influencing management decisions or (2) establishments (except government establishments) that administer, oversee, and manage the company or enterprise and that normally undertake the strategic or organizational planning and decision-making role of the company or enterprise. Establishments that administer, oversee, and manage may hold the securities of the company or enterprise.

Sector 56—Administrative and Support and Waste Management and Remediation Services

The Administrative and Support and Waste Management and Remediation Services sector comprises establishments performing routine support activities for the day-to-day operations of other organizations. These essential activities are often undertaken in-house by establishments in many sectors of the economy. The establishments in this sector specialize in one or more of these support activities and provide these services to clients in a variety of industries and, in some cases, to households. Activities performed include office administration, hiring and placing of personnel, document preparation and similar clerical services, solicitation, collection, security and surveillance services, cleaning, and waste disposal services.

Sector 61—Educational Services

The Educational Services sector comprises establishments that provide instruction and training in a wide variety of subjects. This instruction and training is provided by specialized establishments, such as schools, colleges, universities, and training centers. These establishments may be privately owned and operated for profit or not for profit, or they may be publicly owned and operated. They may also offer food and accommodation services to their students.

Educational services are usually delivered by teachers or instructors who explain, tell, demonstrate, supervise, and direct learning. Instruction is imparted in diverse settings, such as educational institutions, the workplace, or the home through correspondence, television, or other means. It can be adapted to the particular needs of the students, for example, sign language can replace verbal language for teaching students with hearing impairments. All industries in the sector share this commonality of process, namely, labor inputs of instructors with the requisite subject matter expertise and teaching ability.

Sector 62—Health Care and Social Assistance

The Health Care and Social Assistance sector comprises establishments providing health care and social assistance for individuals. The sector includes both health care and social assistance because it is sometimes difficult to distinguish between the boundaries of these two activities. The industries in this sector are arranged on a continuum starting with those establishments providing medical care exclusively, continuing with those providing health care and social assistance, and finally finishing with those providing only social assistance. The services provided by establishments in this sector are delivered by trained professionals. All industries in the sector share this commonality of process, namely, labor inputs of health practitioners or social workers with the requisite expertise. Many of the industries in the sector are defined based on the educational degree held by the practitioners included in the industry.

Sector 71—Arts, Entertainment, and Recreation

The Arts, Entertainment, and Recreation sector includes a wide range of establishments that operate facilities or provide services to meet varied cultural, entertainment, and recreational interests of their patrons. This sector comprises (1) establishments that are involved in producing, promoting, or participating in live performances, events, or exhibits intended for public viewing; (2) establishments that preserve and exhibit objects and sites of historical, cultural, or educational interest; and (3) establishments that operate facilities or provide services that enable patrons to participate in recreational activities or pursue amusement, hobby, and leisure-time interests.

Some establishments that provide cultural, entertainment, or recreational facilities and services are classified in other sectors.

Sector 72—Accommodation and Food Services

The Accommodation and Food Services sector comprises establishments providing customers with lodging and/or preparing meals, snacks, and beverages for immediate consumption. The sector includes both accommodation and food services establishments because the two activities are often combined at the same establishment.

Sector 81—Other Services (except Public Administration)

The Other Services (except Public Administration) sector comprises establishments engaged in providing services not specifically included elsewhere in the classification system. Establishments in this sector are primarily engaged in activities such as equipment and machinery repair, promoting or administering religious activities grant making, advocacy, and providing drycleaning and laundry services, personal care services, death care services, pet care services, photofinishing services, temporary parking services, and dating services.

Sector 92—Public Administration

The Public Administration sector consists of establishments of federal, state, and local government agencies that administer, oversee, and manage public programs and have executive, legislative, or judicial authority over other institutions within a given area. These agencies also set policy, create laws, adjudicate civil and criminal legal cases, and provide for public safety and for national defense. In general, government establishments in the Public Administration sector oversee governmental programs and activities that are not performed by private establishments. Establishments in this sector typically are engaged in the organization and financing of the production of public goods and services, most of which are provided for free or at prices that are not economically significant.

Major Occupational Groups[2]

Occupations are classified based upon work performed, skills, education, training, and credentials of the people employed in the occupation.

Each occupation in the Standard Occupational Classification (SOC) is placed within one of these 23 major groups:

11-0000 Management Occupations
13-0000 Business and Financial Operations Occupations
15-0000 Computer and Mathematical Occupations
17-0000 Architecture and Engineering Occupations
19-0000 Life, Physical, and Social Science Occupations
21-0000 Community and Social Services Occupations
23-0000 Legal Occupations
25-0000 Education, Training, and Library Occupations
27-0000 Arts, Design, Entertainment, Sports, and Media Occupations
29-0000 Health Care Practitioners and Technical Occupations
31-0000 Health Care Support Occupations
33-0000 Protective Service Occupations
35-0000 Food Preparation and Serving Related Occupations
37-0000 Building and Grounds Cleaning and Maintenance Occupations
39-0000 Personal Care and Service Occupations
41-0000 Sales and Related Occupations
43-0000 Office and Administrative Support Occupations
45-0000 Farming, Fishing, and Forestry Occupations

---

2. Bureau of Labor Statistics, Standard Occupational Classification, SOC Major Groups, available at www.bls.gov/soc/2000/soc_majo.htm.

47-0000 Construction and Extraction Occupations
49-0000 Installation, Maintenance, and Repair Occupations
51-0000 Production Occupations
53-0000 Transportation and Material Moving Occupations
55-0000 Military Specific Occupations

Appendix D
Correction for Demand-Based Agglomeration

To correct for the possibility that some activities are geographically concentrated because of demand for their output as intermediate inputs in concentrated industries, Lori Kletzer and I (2006) constructed region-specific measures of demand for each industry using the national input-output use tables produced by the Bureau of Economic Analysis.[1] This measure of industry demand share $(IDS_{i,p})$ represents how much geographic concentration there is in demand for a good or service i in a particular region p. We constructed the demand for industry i in Place of Work Metro Area p as

$$IDS_{i,p} = \sum_j (Y_{i,j}/Y_i \times InEMP_{j,p}/InEMP_j), \tag{D.1}$$

where

$Y_{i,j}$ = the output of industry i used by industry j (counting government and private households as "industries");
Y_i = total output of industry i;
$InEMP_{j,p}$ = industry j employment in region p;
$InEMP_j$ = total employment in industry j.

We included in Y both direct use of industry i output and investment in the "use" of industry i output by industry j.

---

1. We used the 1999 input-output use tables published by the BEA. (For more information, see www.bea.doc.gov/bea/dn2/i-o.htm.) We aggregated some BEA industries to a level consistent with the Census industry classification in the 2000 decennial PUMS.

To construct the occupation-region-specific demand measures, we weighted the industry-region-specific demand measures described above by the share of an occupation's employment in an industry:

$$\text{ODS}_{o,p} = \Sigma_j \, (\text{IDS}_{j,p} \times \text{OcEMP}_{o,j}/\text{OcEMP}_o), \tag{D.2}$$

where

$\text{IDS}_{j,p}$ = industry demand share for industry j in region p;
$\text{OcEMP}_{o,j}$ = occupation o employment in industry j;
OcEMP_o = total employment in occupation o.

These adjustments take account of the concentration of downstream industry and adjust the "denominator" in the geographic concentration measures that follow.

The measure of geographic concentration we use is the Gini coefficient. The Gini coefficient (G) for the concentration of industry activity is given by:

$$G_i = |\, 1 - \Sigma_p \, (\sigma Y_{i,p-1} + \sigma Y_{i,p}) \times (\sigma X_p - \sigma X_{p-1}) \,|, \tag{D.3}$$

where the ps index regions (sorted by the region's share of industry employment), $\sigma Y_{i,p}$ is the cumulative share of industry i employment in region p, $\sigma Y_{i,p-1}$ is the cumulative share of industry i employment in the region $(p-1)$ with the next-lowest share of industry employment, σX_p is the cumulative share of total employment in region p, and σX_{p-1} is the cumulative share of total employment in region $(p-1)$. We modified the Gini measure to

$$G_i = |\, 1 - \Sigma_p \, (\sigma Y_{i,p-1} + \sigma Y_{i,p}) \times (\sigma \text{IDS}_{i,p} - \sigma \text{IDS}_{i,p-1}) \,|, \tag{D.4}$$

where $\text{IDS}_{i,p}$ is the region's share of demand for industry i.

References

Autodesk, Inc. 2009. *Annual Report*. Available at http://investors.autodesk.com.

Baldwin, Robert E., Robert E. Lipsey, and J. David Richardson. 1998. *Geography and Ownership as Bases for Economic Accounting*. Chicago: University of Chicago Press.

Barro, Robert J., and Jong-Wha Lee. 1993. International Comparisons of Educational Attainment. *Journal of Monetary Economics* 32, no. 3 (December): 363–94. Data revised in January 1994.

Barro, Robert, and Jong-Wha Lee. 2010. *A New Data Set of Educational Attainment in the World, 1950-2010*. NBER Working Paper 15902. Cambridge, MA: National Bureau of Economic Research.

Bay Area Council Economic Institute. 2006. *Ties That Bind: The San Francisco Bay Area's Economic Links to Greater China*. San Francisco, CA. Available at www.bayeconfor.org.

Bernard, Andrew B., and J. Bradford Jensen. 1995. Exporters, Jobs, and Wages in U.S. Manufacturing: 1976-87. *Brookings Papers on Economic Activity: Microeconomics* 1995: 67–119.

Bernard, Andrew B., and J. Bradford Jensen. 1999. Exceptional Exporter Performance: Cause, Effect, or Both? *Journal of International Economics* 47, no. 1: 1–25.

Bernard, Andrew B., and J. Bradford Jensen. 2004. Exporting and Productivity in the US. *Oxford Review of Economic Policy* 20, no. 3: 343–57.

Bernard, Andrew B., and J. Bradford Jensen. 2007. Firm Structure, Multinationals, and Manufacturing Plant Deaths. *Review of Economics and Statistics* 89, no. 2: 193–204.

Bernard, Andrew B., J. Bradford Jensen, and Peter K. Schott. 2002. *Survival of the Best Fit: Competition from Low Wage Countries and the (Uneven) Growth of U.S. Manufacturing Plants*. NBER Working Paper 9170. Cambridge, MA: National Bureau of Economic Research.

Bernard, Andrew B., J. Bradford Jensen, and Peter K. Schott. 2005. Facing the Dragon. Manuscript.

Bernard, Andrew B., J. Bradford Jensen, and Peter K. Schott. 2006a. Survival of the Best Fit: Exposure to Low-Wage Countries and the (Uneven) Growth of US Manufacturing Plants. *Journal of International Economics* 68, no. 1: 219–37.

Bernard, Andrew B., J. Bradford Jensen, and Peter K. Schott. 2006b. Trade Costs, Firms, and Productivity. *Journal of Monetary Economics* 53, no. 5: 917–37.

Bernard, Andrew B., Stephen J. Redding, and Peter K. Schott. 2007. Comparative Advantage and Heterogeneous Firms. *Review of Economic Studies* 74, no. 1: 31–66.

Bernard, Andrew B., Jonathan Eaton, J. Bradford Jensen, and Samuel Kortum. 2003. Plants and Productivity in International Trade. *American Economic Review* 93, no. 4: 1268–90.

Bernard, Andrew B., J. Bradford Jensen, Stephen J. Redding, and Peter K. Schott. 2007. Firms in International Trade. *Journal of Economic Perspectives* 21, no. 3: 105–30.

Blinder, Alan S. 2006. Offshoring: The Next Industrial Revolution? *Foreign Affairs* 85, no. 2: 113–28.

Borchert, Ingo, Batshur Gootiiz, and Aaditya Mattoo. 2011. *Policy Barriers to International Trade in Services: New Empirical Evidence*. Washington: World Bank (forthcoming).

Borga, Maria. 2009. Improved Measures of U.S. International Services: The Cases of Insurance, Wholesale and Retail Trade, and Financial Services. In *International Trade in Services and Intangibles in the Era of Globalization*, eds. Marshall Reinsdorf and Matthew J. Slaughter. Chicago and London: University of Chicago Press.

Caves, Douglas W., Laurits R. Christensen, and W. Erwin Diewert. 1982. The Economic Theory of Index Numbers and the Measurement of Input, Output and Productivity. *Econometrica* 50, no. 6: 1393–1414.

Clark, Colin. 1940. *The Conditions of Economic Progress*. London: Macmillan & Co.

Cohen, Stephen S., and John Zysman. 1987. *Manufacturing Matters: The Myth of the Post-Industrial Economy*. New York: Basic Books.

Davis, Steven J., John C. Haltiwanger, and Scott Schuh. 1996. *Job Creation and Destruction*. Cambridge, MA: MIT Press.

Eichengreen, Barry, and Poonam Gupta. 2009. *The Two Waves of Service Sector Growth*. NBER Working Paper 14968. Cambridge, MA: National Bureau of Economic Research.

Ethier, William J. 1982. National and International Returns to Scale in the Modem Theory of International Trade. *American Economic Review* 72, no. 3: 389–405.

Feketekuty, Geza. 1988. *International Trade in Services: An Overview and Blueprint for Negotiations*. Cambridge, MA: Ballinger for American Enterprise Institute, Washington.

Findlay, Charles, and Tony Warren, eds. 2000. *Impediments to Trade in Services: Measurement and Policy Implications*. New York: Routledge.

Fisher, Allan G. B. 1935. *The Clash of Progress and Security*. London: Macmillan & Co.

Francois, J., and B. Hoekman. 2010. Services Trade and Policy. *Journal of Economic Literature* 48, no. 3: 642–92.

Freund, Caroline, and Diana Weinhold. 2002. The Internet and International Trade in Services. *American Economic Review* 92, no. 2 (May): 236–40.

Fuchs, Victor R. 1965. The Growing Importance of the Service Industries. *Journal of Business* 38, no. 4: 344–73.

Graham, Edward M., and Paul Krugman. 1995. *Foreign Direct Investment in the United States*, 3d ed. Washington: Institute for International Economics.

Gootiiz, Batshur, and Aaditya Mattoo. 2009. Services in Doha: What's on the Table? *Journal of World Trade* 43, no. 5: 1013–30.

Grubel, Herbert G., and Peter J. Lloyd. 1975. Intra-Industry Trade: The Theory and Measurement of International Trade in Differentiated Products. *The Economic Journal* 35, no. 339: 646–48.

Heckscher, Eli. 1919. The Effects of Foreign Trade on the Distribution of Income. *Ekonomisk Tidskrift* 21: 497–512.

Helpman, Elhanan. 1981. International Trade in the Presence of Product Differentiation, Economies of Scale, and Monopolistic Competition: A Chamberlin-Heckscher-Ohlin Model. *Journal of International Economics* 11, no. 3: 305–40.

Helpman, Elhanan, and Paul Krugman. 1985. *Market Structure and Foreign Trade: Increasing Returns, Imperfect Competition and the International Economy*. Cambridge, MA: MIT Press.

Helpman, Elhanan. 2006. Trade, FDI and the Organization of Firms. *Journal of Economic Literature* 44, no. 3: 589–630.

Hufbauer, Gary Clyde, Jeffrey J. Schott, and Woan Foong Wong. 2010. *Figuring Out the Doha Round.* Policy Analyses in International Economics 91. Washington: Peterson Institute for International Economics.

Jensen, J. Bradford. 2008. Trade in High-Tech Services. *Journal of Industry, Competition, and Trade* 8, no. 3-4: 181–97.

Jensen, J. Bradford, and Lori G. Kletzer. 2006. Tradable Services: Understanding the Scope and Impact of Services Offshoring. In *Offshoring White-Collar Work—Issues and Implications*, Brookings Trade Forum 2005, ed. Lael Brainard and Susan M. Collins. Washington: Brookings Institution.

Jensen, J. Bradford, and Lori G. Kletzer. 2008. *"Fear" and Offshoring: The Scope and Potential Impact of Imports and Exports of Services.* Policy Briefs in International Economics 08-1. Washington: Peterson Institute for International Economics

Kletzer, Lori G. 2001. *Job Loss from Imports: Measuring the Costs.* Washington: Institute for International Economics.

Krugman, Paul. 1980. Scale Economies, Product Differentiation, and the Pattern of Trade. *American Economic Review* 70, no. 5: 950–59.

Krugman, Paul R. 1991. *Geography and Trade.* Cambridge, MA: MIT Press.

Krugman, Paul R. 2008. Trade and Wages, Reconsidered. *Brookings Papers on Economic Activity* (Spring): 103–37.

Kuznets, Simon. 1957. Quantitative Aspects of the Economic Growth of Nations II: Industrial Distribution of National Product and Labor Force. *Economic Development and Cultural Change* 5, no. 4 (supplement, July): 1–111.

Levy, Frank, and Kyoung-Hee Yu. 2010. Offshoring Radiology Services to India. Massachusetts Institute of Technology. Unpublished draft. Available at http://web.mit.edu/flevy/www/indian_rad.pdf (accessed on June 1, 2011).

Lewis, Howard, and J. David Richardson. 2001. *Why Global Commitment Really Matters!* Washington: Institute for International Economics.

Lipsey, Robert E. 2009. Measuring International Trade in Services. In *International Trade in Services and Intangibles in the Era of Globalization*, ed. Marshall Reinsdorf and Matthew J. Slaughter. Chicago and London: University of Chicago Press.

Mann, Catherine L., assisted by Jacob Funk Kirkegaard. 2006. *Accelerating the Globalization of America: The Role for Information Technology.* Washington: Institute for International Economics.

Mattoo, Aaditya, and Deepak Mishra. 2008. *Foreign Professionals and Domestic Regulation.* World Bank Policy Research Working Paper 4782. Washington: World Bank.

McKinsey Global Institute. 2005. *The Emerging Global Labor Market.* Report by McKinsey & Company. Available at www.mckinsey.com.

Melitz, Marc J. 2003. The Impact of Trade on Intra-Industry Reallocations and Aggregate Industry Productivity. *Econometrica* 71, no. 6: 1695–1725.

Nguyen-Hong, Duc. 2000. *Restrictions on Trade in Professional Services.* Productivity Commission Discussion Paper no. 1638. Melbourne: Australian Government Productivity Commission.

OECD (Organization for Economic Cooperation and Development). 2001. *Trade in Services: Negotiating Issues and Approaches.* OECD Report. Paris.

OECD (Organization for Economic Cooperation and Development). 2007. *Summary Report of the Study on Globalisation and Innovation in the Business Services Sector.* OECD Report. Paris.

Ohlin, Bertil. 1933. *Interregional and International Trade.* Cambridge, MA: Harvard University Press.

Panagariya, Arvind. 2008. *India: The Emerging Giant.* New York: Oxford University Press.

Randolph, R. Sean, and Neils Erich. 2009. *Global Reach: Emerging Ties Between the San Francisco Bay Area and India*. Bay Area Council Economic Institute Report. San Francisco, CA. Available at www.bayeconfor.org.

Ricardo, David. 1821. *On the Principles of Political Economy and Taxation*, 3d ed. London: John Murray. (First edition published 1817.)

Richardson, J. David, and Karin Rindal. 1995. *Why Exports Really Matter!* Washington: Institute for International Economics and Manufacturing Institute.

Richardson, J. David, and Karin Rindal. 1996. *Why Exports Matter: More!* Washington: Institute for International Economics and Manufacturing Institute.

Sturgeon, Timothy, Frank Levy, Clair Brown, J. Bradford Jensen, and David Weil. 2006. *Services Offshoring Working Group Final Report*. MIT IPC Working Paper Series 06-006. Cambridge, MA: Massachusetts Institute of Technology, Industrial Performance Center. Available at http://web.mit.edu/ipc (accessed on May 20, 2011).

Tybout, James R. 2003. Plant- and Firm-Level Evidence on the "New" Trade Theories. In *Handbook of International Trade*, ed. E. Kwan Choi and James Harrigan. Oxford: Basil Blackwell.

Index

low-wage countries, competition from, 109, 111. *See also* employment dislocation
low-wage tradable services, geographic concentration of, 178–79, 179*f*

Management of Companies and Enterprises sector (NAICS), 16, 17*t*, 226
    employment and wages, 18*t*, 59*t*
    geographic concentration, 56*t*
    imports, 142*t*
    worker characteristics, 72*t*, 77*f*, 79*f*, 114*t*
manufacturing sector
    comparative advantage (*See* comparative advantage)
    employment in, 91–92, 92*f*, 99–100, 100*f* (*See also* employment)
    exporters, 138–41, 139*t*, 140*t*, 144*t* (*See also* export(s))
    geographic concentration, 43, 44*t*, 171
        by export measures, 60, 60*t*
        by industries, 51, 52*f*–53*f*, 54, 58
        by occupations, 61, 62*f*
    job loss rates, 168*t*, 168–69
    multinational affiliates, 131–34, 132*t*–134*t*
    NAICS code, 16, 17*t*, 222–23
    preoccupation with, 11–12
    producer characteristics, 21–23, 22*t*, 23*t*, 119, 120*t*
    trading premiums, 105*f*, 105–106, 139–40, 140*t*
    wages (*See* wages)
    worker characteristics, 71*t*, 75–78, 77*f*
Massachusetts Institute of Technology (MIT), offshoring working group, 210*b*–211*b*
McKinsey Global Institute, 159
Metropolitan Statistical Areas (MSAs), 50
microdata
    accessing and linking, 206–207, 211*b*
    definition of, 103–104
    firm, 216–18 (*See also* firm level)
    worker, 215–16 (*See also* worker characteristics)
Mining sector (NAICS), 16, 17*t*, 221
    employment and wages, 18*t*, 59*t*, 67*t*
    exports, 132*t*
    geographic concentration, 52*f*, 54
    multinational affiliates, 129*t*, 130*t*, 131
MIT (Massachusetts Institute of Technology), offshoring working group, 210*b*–211*b*
MSAs (Metropolitan Statistical Areas), 50
multi-disciplinary practices restrictions, 149
multinational affiliates
    service imports from, 125–31, 129*t*, 130*f*
    vertically integrated, 131–34, 132*t*–134*t*

NAFTA (North American Free Trade Agreement), 182, 187
NAICS codes. *See* North American Industry Classification System codes
NAPCS (North American Product Classification System), 204–205
national income and product accounts (NIPA), 212
nationality requirements, 147
nontradable industries
    employment shares, 66–67, 67*t*
        changes in, 162–65, 163*t*, 166*t*, 167*t*
    tradable occupations in, 67–69, 69*t*
    wages, 5, 5*f*
    worker characteristics, 70–76, 71*t*–75*t*
nontradable occupations
    employment shares, changes in, 163–65, 164*t*, 166*t*, 167*t*
    versus tradable, 5, 5*f*, 67
    worker characteristics, 70–76, 75*t*
        versus tradable occupations, 72–76, 75*t*, 78–80, 79*f*, 80*f*, 81*t*
North American Free Trade Agreement (NAFTA), 182, 187
North American Industry Classification System (NAICS) codes, 16, 17*t*, 217
    data needs, 203–204
    employment, 17, 18*t*–19*t*
        by degree of tradability, 54, 59*t*
        manufacturing industry, 100*f*, 100–101
    exports by, 116–17, 117*f*
    locational coefficients, 51, 52*f*–53*f*, 55*t*–58*t*, 55*t*–59*t*
    major sectors, 221–28
    wages, 18*t*–19*t*, 20
North American Product Classification System (NAPCS), 204–205
Numerical List of Manufactured and Mineral Products (Census Bureau), 204

Occupational Employment Statistics (OES) program, 165*n*, 210*b*
Occupational Employment Survey data, 162*n*
occupations
    classification of (*See* Standard Occupational Classification groups)
    employment growth by, 162–65, 163*t*, 164*t*
    labor market impact by, 165–66, 166*f*
    nontradable (*See* nontradable occupations)
    tradable (*See* tradable occupations)
OECD. *See* Organization for Economic Development
OES (Occupational Employment Statistics) program, 165*n*, 210*b*

size and growth of, 14–15, 15f, 16f, 40, 137
subcategories, 15–17, 36–37 (*See also specific category*)
wages in (*See* wages)
Services Trade Restrictiveness Index (OECD), 145n
service trade. *See also* tradable services
overview of, 2–3
balance, 3, 4, 11, 84, 112, 113f, 156, 193
barriers to, 7
comparative advantage (*See* comparative advantage)
composition of, 36–37, 38f, 39f
data on (*See* data)
definition of, 27–28
economic impact of, measurement of, 203–207
examples of, 28–30, 29b, 31b–33b
exporters, 143–44, 144t, 145t (*See also* export(s))
growth in, 36, 37f, 40, 137
factors contributing to, 30–34
impediments to, 3, 144–53, 182–83
classifying, 147–49
quantifying, 149–53
importance of, 1, 26–27, 192
importers, 141–42, 142t (*See also* import(s))
job loss rates, 168t, 168–69
measuring, 198–202
modes of, 28
openness to, 182–83
prevalence of, 138–44, 144t
service trade liberalization
benefits of, 3, 6, 153, 156, 182–83
labor and (*See* employment dislocation; labor market impact)
policy recommendations, 7–8, 181–94
risks of, 3, 155–56, 193
Siemens, 29–30, 31b–33b, 181, 183
skill abundance, 87. *See also* educational attainment
comparative advantage and, 82, 111–12
employment dislocation threshold and, 158–59
income per capita correlated with, 87, 88f
in manufacturing sector, 94–96, 95t, 96f
in services sector, 113–15, 114t
Small-Scale Industries (SSI) reservation policy, 126b–128b
SOC groups. *See* Standard Occupational Classification groups
social safety net, 190–91, 194
software production, 45, 45n, 46b
Songdo International Business District, 187b

Space Matrix, 47b
Special 301 Report (USTR), 183
SSI (Small-Scale Industries) reservation policy, 126b–128b
Standard Occupational Classification (SOC) groups, 81n
employment growth by, 165
locational Gini coefficients by, 61, 63t
major groups, 228–29
statistics. *See* data
sunk costs, 106, 106b, 138
survival threshold, 106–107, 107f

tariff equivalents, of service barriers, 151–53, 152f
tax discrimination, 149
tax information, sharing of, 208
technological advancement, manufacturing productivity and, 93–94
telecommunications costs, 30–34, 35f
teleradiology services, 160b–161b
temporary movement across borders, 28
Tokyo Round (GATT), 7, 188
tradability
concept of, 41
education correlated with, 8–9, 66, 189
employment and wage changes by, 162–65, 163t, 164t, 166t, 167t
employment dislocation and, 166–69, 168t
at industry versus occupation level, 42, 61, 70, 72–76, 75t
threshold of, 54, 118
tradable industries
employment shares, 66–69, 67t, 69t
changes in, 162–65, 163t, 166t, 167t
geographic concentration, 51–60, 52f–53f, 55t–59t
percent of workforce in, 172–76, 176f
worker characteristics, 70–76, 71t–75t
tradable occupations, 67
employment shares, 67–69, 69t
changes in, 163–65, 164t, 166t, 167t
geographic concentration, 60–61, 62f, 63t
versus nontradable, 5, 5f, 67, 70, 72–76, 75t
in nontradable industries, 67–69, 69t
percent of workforce in, 172–76, 176f
worker characteristics, 70–76, 71t–75t, 78, 79f
tradable services. *See also* service trade
employment share, 66–67, 67t
examples of, 43, 45, 46b–48b
geographic concentration
across US regions, 172–78
locational Gini classes, 54, 55t–58t

244 GLOBAL TRADE IN SERVICES: FEAR, FACTS, AND OFFSHORING

Other Publications from the Peterson Institute for International Economics

Completing the Uruguay Round: A Results-Oriented Approach to the GATT Trade Negotiations*   Jeffrey J. Schott, ed.
September 1990   ISBN 0-88132-130-3
Economic Sanctions Reconsidered (2 volumes)
Economic Sanctions Reconsidered: Supplemental Case Histories
Gary Clyde Hufbauer, Jeffrey J. Schott, and Kimberly Ann Elliott
1985, 2d ed. Dec. 1990   ISBN cloth 0-88132-115-X
                          ISBN paper 0-88132-105-2
Economic Sanctions Reconsidered: History and Current Policy   Gary Clyde Hufbauer, Jeffrey J. Schott, and Kimberly Ann Elliott
December 1990   ISBN cloth 0-88132-140-0
                        ISBN paper 0-88132-136-2
Pacific Basin Developing Countries: Prospects for the Future*   Marcus Noland
January 1991   ISBN cloth 0-88132-141-9
                        ISBN paper 0-88132-081-1
Currency Convertibility in Eastern Europe*
John Williamson, ed.
October 1991   ISBN 0-88132-128-1
International Adjustment and Financing: The Lessons of 1985-1991*   C. Fred Bergsten, ed.
January 1992   ISBN 0-88132-112-5
North American Free Trade: Issues and Recommendations*   Gary Clyde Hufbauer and Jeffrey J. Schott
April 1992   ISBN 0-88132-120-6
Narrowing the U.S. Current Account Deficit*
Alan J. Lenz
June 1992   ISBN 0-88132-103-6
The Economics of Global Warming
William R. Cline
June 1992   ISBN 0-88132-132-X
US Taxation of International Income: Blueprint for Reform   Gary Clyde Hufbauer, assisted by Joanna M. van Rooij
October 1992   ISBN 0-88132-134-6
Who's Bashing Whom? Trade Conflict in High-Technology Industries   Laura D'Andrea Tyson
November 1992   ISBN 0-88132-106-0
Korea in the World Economy*   Il SaKong
January 1993   ISBN 0-88132-183-4
Pacific Dynamism and the International Economic System*   C. Fred Bergsten and Marcus Noland, eds.
May 1993   ISBN 0-88132-196-6
Economic Consequences of Soviet Disintegration*   John Williamson, ed.
May 1993   ISBN 0-88132-190-7
Reconcilable Differences? United States-Japan Economic Conflict*   C. Fred Bergsten and Marcus Noland
June 1993   ISBN 0-88132-129-X
Does Foreign Exchange Intervention Work?
Kathryn M. Dominguez and Jeffrey A. Frankel
September 1993   ISBN 0-88132-104-4
Sizing Up U.S. Export Disincentives*
J. David Richardson
September 1993   ISBN 0-88132-107-9

NAFTA: An Assessment
Gary Clyde Hufbauer and Jeffrey J. Schott, rev. ed.
October 1993   ISBN 0-88132-199-0
Adjusting to Volatile Energy Prices
Philip K. Verleger, Jr.
November 1993   ISBN 0-88132-069-2
The Political Economy of Policy Reform
John Williamson, ed.
January 1994   ISBN 0-88132-195-8
Measuring the Costs of Protection in the United States   Gary Clyde Hufbauer and Kimberly Ann Elliott
January 1994   ISBN 0-88132-108-7
The Dynamics of Korean Economic Development*   Cho Soon
March 1994   ISBN 0-88132-162-1
Reviving the European Union*
C. Randall Henning, Eduard Hochreiter, and Gary Clyde Hufbauer, eds.
April 1994   ISBN 0-88132-208-3
China in the World Economy
Nicholas R. Lardy
April 1994   ISBN 0-88132-200-8
Greening the GATT: Trade, Environment, and the Future   Daniel C. Esty
July 1994   ISBN 0-88132-205-9
Western Hemisphere Economic Integration*
Gary Clyde Hufbauer and Jeffrey J. Schott
July 1994   ISBN 0-88132-159-1
Currencies and Politics in the United States, Germany, and Japan   C. Randall Henning
September 1994   ISBN 0-88132-127-3
Estimating Equilibrium Exchange Rates
John Williamson, ed.
September 1994   ISBN 0-88132-076-5
Managing the World Economy: Fifty Years after Bretton Woods   Peter B. Kenen, ed.
September 1994   ISBN 0-88132-212-1
Reciprocity and Retaliation in U.S. Trade Policy   Thomas O. Bayard and Kimberly Ann Elliott
September 1994   ISBN 0-88132-084-6
The Uruguay Round: An Assessment*
Jeffrey J. Schott, assisted by Johanna Buurman
November 1994   ISBN 0-88132-206-7
Measuring the Costs of Protection in Japan*
Yoko Sazanami, Shujiro Urata, and Hiroki Kawai
January 1995   ISBN 0-88132-211-3
Foreign Direct Investment in the United States, 3d ed.   Edward M. Graham and Paul R. Krugman
January 1995   ISBN 0-88132-204-0
The Political Economy of Korea-United States Cooperation*   C. Fred Bergsten and Il SaKong, eds.
February 1995   ISBN 0-88132-213-X
International Debt Reexamined*
William R. Cline
February 1995   ISBN 0-88132-083-8
American Trade Politics, 3d ed.   I. M. Destler
April 1995   ISBN 0-88132-215-6
Managing Official Export Credits: The Quest for a Global Regime*   John E. Ray
July 1995   ISBN 0-88132-207-5

Asia Pacific Fusion: Japan's Role in APEC*
Yoichi Funabashi
October 1995   ISBN 0-88132-224-5
Korea-United States Cooperation in the New
World Order*   C. Fred Bergsten and
Il SaKong, eds.
February 1996   ISBN 0-88132-226-1
Why Exports Really Matter!*
                         ISBN 0-88132-221-0
Why Exports Matter More!* ISBN 0-88132-229-6
J. David Richardson and Karin Rindal
July 1995; February 1996
Global Corporations and National
Governments   Edward M. Graham
May 1996   ISBN 0-88132-111-7
Global Economic Leadership and the Group of
Seven   C. Fred Bergsten and
C. Randall Henning
May 1996   ISBN 0-88132-218-0
The Trading System after the Uruguay Round*
John Whalley and Colleen Hamilton
July 1996   ISBN 0-88132-131-1
Private Capital Flows to Emerging Markets
after the Mexican Crisis*   Guillermo A. Calvo,
Morris Goldstein, and Eduard Hochreiter
September 1996   ISBN 0-88132-232-6
The Crawling Band as an Exchange Rate
Regime: Lessons from Chile, Colombia, and
Israel   John Williamson
September 1996   ISBN 0-88132-231-8
Flying High: Liberalizing Civil Aviation in the
Asia Pacific*   Gary Clyde Hufbauer and
Christopher Findlay
November 1996   ISBN 0-88132-227-X
Measuring the Costs of Visible Protection
in Korea*   Namdoo Kim
November 1996   ISBN 0-88132-236-9
The World Trading System: Challenges Ahead
Jeffrey J. Schott
December 1996   ISBN 0-88132-235-0
Has Globalization Gone Too Far?   Dani Rodrik
March 1997   ISBN paper 0-88132-241-5
Korea-United States Economic Relationship*
C. Fred Bergsten and Il SaKong, eds.
March 1997   ISBN 0-88132-240-7
Summitry in the Americas: A Progress Report
Richard E. Feinberg
April 1997   ISBN 0-88132-242-3
Corruption and the Global Economy
Kimberly Ann Elliott
June 1997   ISBN 0-88132-233-4
Regional Trading Blocs in the World Economic
System   Jeffrey A. Frankel
October 1997   ISBN 0-88132-202-4
Sustaining the Asia Pacific Miracle:
Environmental Protection and Economic
Integration   Andre Dua and Daniel C. Esty
October 1997   ISBN 0-88132-250-4
Trade and Income Distribution
William R. Cline
November 1997   ISBN 0-88132-216-4
Global Competition Policy
Edward M. Graham and J. David Richardson
December 1997   ISBN 0-88132-166-4

Unfinished Business: Telecommunications
after the Uruguay Round
Gary Clyde Hufbauer and Erika Wada
December 1997   ISBN 0-88132-257-1
Financial Services Liberalization in the WTO
Wendy Dobson and Pierre Jacquet
June 1998   ISBN 0-88132-254-7
Restoring Japan's Economic Growth
Adam S. Posen
September 1998   ISBN 0-88132-262-8
Measuring the Costs of Protection in China
Zhang Shuguang, Zhang Yansheng, and Wan
Zhongxin
November 1998   ISBN 0-88132-247-4
Foreign Direct Investment and Development:
The New Policy Agenda for Developing
Countries and Economies in Transition
Theodore H. Moran
December 1998   ISBN 0-88132-258-X
Behind the Open Door: Foreign Enterprises
in the Chinese Marketplace   Daniel H. Rosen
January 1999   ISBN 0-88132-263-6
Toward A New International Financial
Architecture: A Practical Post-Asia Agenda
Barry Eichengreen
February 1999   ISBN 0-88132-270-9
Is the U.S. Trade Deficit Sustainable?
Catherine L. Mann
September 1999   ISBN 0-88132-265-2
Safeguarding Prosperity in a Global Financial
System: The Future International Financial
Architecture, Independent Task Force Report
Sponsored by the Council on Foreign Relations
Morris Goldstein, Project Director
October 1999   ISBN 0-88132-287-3
Avoiding the Apocalypse: The Future of the
Two Koreas   Marcus Noland
June 2000   ISBN 0-88132-278-4
Assessing Financial Vulnerability: An Early
Warning System for Emerging Markets
Morris Goldstein, Graciela Kaminsky, and
Carmen Reinhart
June 2000   ISBN 0-88132-237-7
Global Electronic Commerce: A Policy Primer
Catherine L. Mann, Sue E. Eckert, and Sarah
Cleeland Knight
July 2000   ISBN 0-88132-274-1
The WTO after Seattle   Jeffrey J. Schott, ed.
July 2000   ISBN 0-88132-290-3
Intellectual Property Rights in the Global
Economy   Keith E. Maskus
August 2000   ISBN 0-88132-282-2
The Political Economy of the Asian Financial
Crisis   Stephan Haggard
August 2000   ISBN 0-88132-283-0
Transforming Foreign Aid: United States
Assistance in the 21st Century   Carol Lancaster
August 2000   ISBN 0-88132-291-1
Fighting the Wrong Enemy: Antiglobal
Activists and Multinational Enterprises
Edward M. Graham
September 2000   ISBN 0-88132-272-5

WORKS IN PROGRESS